HarLan ELLISON

HaRLan ELLISON:
THe EDGe OF FOReveR

Ellen Weil

Gary K. Wolfe

THE OHIO STATE UNIVERSITY PRESS

Columbus

Library of Congress Cataloguing-in-Publication Data

Weil, Ellen.
Harlan Ellison: the edge of forever / Ellen Weil and Gary K. Wolfe.
p. cm.
Includes bibliographical references and index.
ISBN 0-8142-0892-4 (cloth: alk. paper)—ISBN 0-8142-5089-0 (pbk. : alk. paper)
1. Ellison, Harlan—Criticism and interpretation. 2. Science fiction,
American—History and criticism. I. Wolfe, Gary K., 1946– II. Title.
PS3555.L62 Z95 2002
813'.54—dc21

Cover design by Dan O'Dair
Text design by Jennifer Shoffey Carr
Type set in Adobe Granjon
Printed by Thomson-Shore

The paper used in this publication meets the mimimum requirement of the
American National Standard for Information Sciences—Permanence of
Paper for Printed Library Materials. ANSI Z39.48-1992

9 8 7 6 5 4 3 2 1

For

Susan

—know your moment—

and For

Alex, Jordan, Katie, Maggie, Ben, Jack, Shae,
Megan, Emily, Ryan, and Danny

Remember Grammy

contents

Introduction

The Golden Cage

> He had become a *personality,* something they had filtered out of the system many decades before. But there it was, and there *he* was, a very definitely imposing personality. In certain circles—middle-class circles—it was thought disgusting. Vulgar ostentation. Anarchistic. Shameful. In others, there was only sniggering: those strata where thought is subjugated to form and ritual, niceties, proprieties. But down below, ah, down below. . . .
>
> —"'Repent, Harlequin!' Said the Ticktockman"
> (*Galaxy Science Fiction,* 1965)

HARLAN ELLISON'S CHARACTERIZATION of Harlequin, the rebellious joker in a future society ruled by the clock, inevitably reads like a self-portrait to anyone who has met Ellison or seen him perform at his frequent lectures and readings, or who simply knows his reputation. In the various literary and media worlds he has inhabited—science fiction, television, film, comic books, radio, journalism, politics, theater, criticism—Ellison has always left behind a string of anecdotes and semi-apocryphal stories that threaten to overwhelm his own considerable achievements in many of these same fields. People who have never read Ellison have opinions about his writing; people who have never met Ellison hold passionate views about his personality. He is a central figure in the oral folklore of science fiction fan conventions, even though he attends but a fraction of the conventions he once did. In Hollywood, he gained a reputation as a mercurial and litigious screenwriter, prone to walk away even from lucrative TV contracts when he feels his integrity is compromised and dangerously successful in pursuing plagiarism cases. Academics know he will bring out a crowd when he speaks on campus, but are often nervous about what he might say. Television talk shows know him as a reliably opinionated and controversial guest, making him a regular on Tom Snyder's *Tomorrow* program in the 1990s and later on Bill Maher's *Politically Incorrect.* He shows up, thinly disguised, as a murder victim in Sharyn McCrumb's comic mystery novel *Bimbos of the Death Sun* (1987), and in Jane Yolen's 1992 Holocaust novel *Briar Rose,* one character speculates on another's mysterious past by wondering if she was "Harlan Ellison's secret muse" (Yolen 48). Even so unlikely a venue as Jon Winokur's *Curmudgeon's Garden of Love* (1989), a gift-book compilation of surly anecdotes and quotations, devotes an entire chapter to Ellison, longer than chapters on H. L. Mencken, Lewis Grizzard, George Bernard Shaw, and other well-known "curmudgeons." In all these communities and venues, eccentricity has become commonplace, even prized—but Ellison still manages to arouse passions. In a culture that views the protest movement as history, Ellison still protests, still gets outraged, still gets even—often at such high volume that, for a good many readers, the assertive personal voice threatens to drown out the subtler tonalities of his best fiction. But no discussion of Ellison's art can entirely avoid mention of his personality; as Stephen King has written, "The man and his work have become so entwined that it is impossible to pull them completely apart" (*Danse Macabre* 348).

Like the Harlequin, Ellison sometimes uses oddball tactics to shake up the system. The Harlequin ruins his mechanized utopia's timetable by unleashing millions of jellybeans into the motorized walkways that deliver people to work. Ellison has been reputed to mail dozens of bricks—individually—to a recalcitrant publisher. Like the Harlequin, Ellison is chronically (and famously) late when given deadlines, and he even cites this as the genesis of the story. The Harlequin survives by doing the unexpected, such as showing up early when everyone knows he will be late. Ellison's own career has been characterized by similar unexpected turns. For example, "'Repent, Harlequin!'" quickly established Ellison as a writer of manic satire, winning both of science fiction's top awards (the Hugo and the Nebula) in 1966—but his very next major story was the much darker and more violent "I Have No Mouth, and I Must Scream."

In the end of "'Repent, Harlequin!'" the Harlequin is captured, brainwashed, and returned to society as an uncomplaining drudge, like Winston Smith in George Orwell's *1984.* The only hope for lasting change is offered in a hint that the dreaded Ticktockman, the dictatorial timekeeper, has begun to lose his own grip on punctuality in the wake of his encounter with Harlequin. Here whatever parallels there are between Ellison and the Harlequin end. Whatever one thinks of his writing—and many critics find it wildly uneven—no one has ever accused him of being an uncomplaining drudge, and his writing never slips into a comfortable niche defined by past successes. But in another sense, Ellison *has* been caught. He may be part Harlequin, but he's also in part the Joe Bob Hick-ey of his later story "Silent in Gehenna" (1971). Hickey is a 1960s activist who finds himself transported to an alien world, where he is imprisoned in a golden cage above a public thoroughfare. In the street below, he witness-es small blue creatures enslaved and mistreated by bulb-shaped golden beings. Hickey screams his outrage at the injustices he sees. Hearing him, the golden creatures wail and flagellate themselves—but then carry on with their slavery and torture. "He finally realizes what happens to all of us who for some bizarre reason appoint ourselves the conscience of the uni-verse," Ellison later explained in discussing this story, "that he is a figure-head, that he is a token, that they come before him and beat their breasts and say yes, isn't it terrible, isn't what he says *true,* yes, this is awful—and they move on with their lives. And it is the worst hell he can possibly be in, because he realizes at last that he is a fool and a clown" (keynote address, 1988).

The theme of the frustrated do-gooder, the self-appointed Quixote who either can't find enough wrongs to right or can't right the wrongs he finds, permeates Ellison's work in all the various media he has worked in. When Ellison was given the chance, in 1970, to write a film script without con-straints, the plot he came up with (in what is now known only as "Harlan Ellison's Movie") involved a wealthy idealist who creates various schemes to solve social problems and increase public awareness, only to find each of his projects exacerbating the problems they were intended to resolve. Even Batman gets his comeuppance: Invited to script a 1986 issue of *Detective Comics,* Ellison concocted a story in which the caped crusader repeatedly arrives moments too late—to find a shopkeeper holding a gun on a bur-glar, an old lady beating up on a would-be mugger, a potential suicide already being rescued by the cops ("Night of Thanks but No Thanks"). The frustrated superhero is impatiently told to dial 911 in the first two instances, and by the end of the night is reduced to stopping a tough-look-ing hood for littering the sidewalk, only to find that the "hood" is an envi-ronmentally concerned citizen thankful for being reminded of his carelessness.

It's doubtful that Ellison views himself as either a fool or a superhero, but it seems evident that he fears the kind of entrapment that is the fate of Joe Bob Hickey and feels some of the frustration of his version of Batman. Entrapment is one of the most frequently recurring themes in his fiction, his journalism, his autobiographical writings, his public remarks—entrap-ment not only of himself but of other writers who work in popular genres and commercial markets. Joe Bob Hickey's golden cage is a nightmare image of the popular writer's dilemma: being given a public forum but not taken seriously, gaining attention but not respect, being made part of the system by the very act of trying to change it. Always the performer, Ellison once gained notoriety for his occasional practice of writing stories in public settings—in the window of a bookstore, for example, or on a television program. Fellow writer Michael Moorcock, somewhat appalled at this, even suggested that if Ellison "could produce his stories in front of about 2,000 people at Circus Circus, Las Vegas I think he would probably be in his element" (xi). Moorcock is right in arguing that Ellison has long sought to erase the barrier between writing and performance—his eventful public lectures and readings, frequent and voluminous personal introductions to stories in his books, occasional asides to the reader even within stories, and his mail-order business in recordings of himself are all evidence of this—but the image of Ellison at Circus Circus gets chillingly close to Joe Bob Hickey's golden cage. "When you look at what we do," Ellison once said of writers in the popular fiction markets, "understand that we are trapped in this place. Once in a while a Bradbury can escape; once in a while a Vonnegut can escape, but not even a Heinlein, not even an Asimov, not even a Clarke—for all the money they get—manages to escape. . . . We are condemned to a very strange Gulag" (keynote address, 1988).

Not surprisingly, the authors Ellison mentions as sharing his particular "Gulag" are all writers associated with science fiction, the genre in which Ellison achieved his greatest fame and with which he remains most closely associated in the public mind. But this "Gulag," this golden cage, was the product of a cultural trend far more broad-based and powerful than the constraints imposed on writers within the relatively insular field of science fiction. At the risk of oversimplification, this trend can be stated as a simple principle of American popular culture, one which most writers who work in popular genres or for film and television already know: *Genres create markets, then markets re-create genres.* Mysteries, westerns, spy stories, science fiction, horror, romance, crime stories—all have different patterns of origin, all existed in one form or another before anyone was aware that a genre was evolving, but each at one time or another gained enough cohesiveness to provide attractive market segments to purveyors of popular entertainment. Once these market segments were established, they increasingly took control of the genres that defined them, in many cases redefining those genres to conform to the dictates of the newly established market. This principle applies as much to science fiction magazines as to television sitcoms. Once the writers had developed the form, the audience—as defined and arbitrated by producers and editors—took over, and the form began to dictate to the writers, rather than vice versa. One of the first modern writers to fall victim to this situation was Arthur Conan Doyle, who came to feel nearly enslaved by the very pattern of Sherlock Holmes stories that he had created. Another was L. Frank Baum, who could never escape the demand for sequels to his most famous book, *The Wonderful Wizard of Oz* (1900).

By the time Ellison wrote "'Repent, Harlequin!' Said the Ticktockman," he was already an internationally known author who had been publishing prolifically in several markets for nearly a decade. In addition to magazine stories and articles, he had produced four books dealing with juvenile street life, one of the first novels about rock 'n' roll, a collection of mainstream stories drawn from his many contributions to men's magazines and crime magazines, and a science fiction book for the Ace Double series of paperbacks—which consisted of a story collection bound back-to-back with a short novel. For the most part, these early works were part of the huge mass of popular "throwaway" fiction that had inundated American culture since the rise of the pulp magazines in the 1930s and that survives in the mass-market paperback industry. Like much of this fiction, Ellison's first stories were characteristically workmanlike, often produced at a rapid pace, sometimes inspired, and sometimes simply terrible. Like many professional magazine writers (professional in that their income was directly related to their day-to-day production), Ellison at the time referred to these stories as "sales," because a sale meant rent money and recognition for further sales, while a story was just a story. "Story," after all, is an essentially literary or cultural concept, just as "genre" is an essentially literary concept for the kinds of popular stories that get published. It seems highly unlikely that Ellison and his fellow writers thought much about genre while they were looking to place stories in the venues available to them, but they thought a lot about markets. In a rough sense, "market" was to "genre" what "sale" was to "story." "We all have to work in the marketplace," Ellison still complained years later. "We despise it for the most part because it is a restriction . . . and because the marketplace is a savage creature, and bends us to its will. Whether we like it or not, the most independent of us, the most with-clout of us, we are all bent by the marketplace" (keynote address, 1988).

Like many successful writers today, Ellison can command respectable fees for his writings and public appearances, and enjoys residual incomes from royalties, rights, and reprint fees. When he began writing, however, the marketplace of which he speaks was a far more "savage" beast than it is even today—and it helped to generate a mode of writing which, for lack of a standard term, we might call "market fiction" or "street fiction." Other terms have been suggested; in his useful 1990 study *An Aesthetics of Junk Fiction,* Thomas J. Roberts suggests several—vernacular fiction, genre fiction, paperback fiction, even "junk" fiction (4–5). But none of these quite suggest the fiercely competitive environment in which Ellison and his fellow writers worked in the 1950s. In the first place, most of what Roberts and other scholars of popular literature discuss are novels—books consisting of a single narrative, in which the product sold, no matter what constraints may be imposed by publishers or readers, essentially *is* the text. Novels at least produce royalties (although publishers have easily found ways of circumventing that, with flat-fee payment schedules for series books and work-for-hire contracts for adaptations and tie-ins), and sometimes novels stand a chance of being reprinted. In the truest IRS sense of the word, they are "properties," and properties by definition represent potential future income.

The commercial short story or magazine article is another matter. For many of the writers working in these fields from the 1930s through the 1950s, the idea of the story as an income-producing property with possible reprints in anthologies or collections was a distant dream. Here the product is not the individual text but rather a periodical publication that must be produced, marketed, and read on a regular (usually monthly or bimonthly) basis. The author's contribution—the story or article—must accommodate the needs of that preexisting product in terms of length, style, and subject matter. A digest-sized crime magazine such as *Trapped,* in which Ellison appeared with some regularity between 1956 and 1959, would appear every other month whether or not Ellison got his stories in; the product depended not on any one author's talent or productivity but on the editor's ability to find enough usable material. (According to the oral tradition that makes up a good deal of science fiction history, one well-known editor of this period was famous for buying stories he had not even read because they were exactly the right length to fill "holes" in the current issue of his magazine.) In some cases, fiction was decidedly marginal to the publication's overall appearance and success; men's magazines such as *Gent* or *Rogue* were far more identifiable by their photo layouts, cartoons, and lifestyle features than by their fiction. That any author could achieve name recognition in such an unpromising and unliterary environment must be counted as something of an achievement.

The American popular short story then—the field in which Ellison has staked out his primary reputation—comes to us with a variety of extraliterary baggage that makes the tawdriest paperback novel look respectable by comparison. Not only were authors forced to work under ridiculous deadlines, to pitch story ideas to skeptical editors like auditioning vaudevillians, to write stories to match the size of a "hole" in the next issue or to make sense out of a prepurchased cover illustration—but they also had to adapt their style to the "personality" of the magazine and to work in whatever popular genre the magazine featured. Stories were selected for publication not because they were superior but because they were acceptable, and it was not unusual for an author to have three or four stories in the same issue of the same magazine, under various pseudonyms. "Those were the days," Ellison recalled in 1983, "when you had to have four stories in an issue; otherwise you couldn't survive, because we were being paid a penny a word" ("Loving Reminiscences"). And indeed, the March 1957 issue of *Amazing* featured three stories by Ellison, one of them written to match a hopelessly ridiculous cover illustration of a giant insect about to assault a sunbather. Readership preference surveys often consisted of no more than letters-to-the-editor columns or, more often, of an opinionated editor's mental picture of the typical reader. To a large extent, these factors were what initially led to Ellison's reputation as a science fiction writer, a reputation he has been trying vainly to escape for more than three decades.

By far the most important of these factors—in Ellison's case, at least— was the segmentation of the fiction magazine market according to genre, a process that had begun decades earlier with the pulp magazines and that continues to this day, at considerably higher stakes, with the paperback book market and increasingly with the hardcover market (not to mention such ancillary markets as media tie-in books, games, and CD-ROMs). Genre writers often speak of a "ghetto," by which they mean the effects of this kind of segmentation on an author's readership, reputation, and ability to sell his or her work. As early as 1953 Anthony Boucher (William Anthony Parker White), himself a veteran pulp author who became one of the most influential critics and editors in the science fiction and mystery fields (the mystery writers' annual "Bouchercon" is named for him), tried to analyze how such ghettoes arose. He identified four major factors: the tendency of readers to buy books and magazines by category; the tendency of publishers and booksellers to try to gain more predictable sales by segmenting target audiences according to these categories; the tendency of authors to try to achieve a more predictable income by specializing in one or more of these categories; and the more pervasive tendency of the literary culture at large to distinguish between "serious" or "mainstream" literature and popular or "genre" literature (Boucher 25). This last distinction is crucial, because it suggests that genre fiction—or ghetto fiction—differs from the mainstream not only in its means of production and marketing but also in the way it is read. Readers come to market fiction with specific and often quite narrow biases, expecting authors to follow certain rules established by the traditions of the form—whether these rules be the rather rigid formulas of the classical detective story, the mix of irony and violence in the tough crime story, or the parameters that make a story acceptable as science fiction rather than fantasy. The ghetto audience is thus a prepared audience, and this gives the writer the advantage of being able to write in a kind of narrative shorthand that implicitly refers to the common assumptions of the genre—while at the same time imposing constraints on the ability of the author to achieve a distinctive voice or vision.

Boucher's essay was written at a time that can arguably be regarded as one of those watershed periods in the history of American popular writing, comparable to the rise of the dime novel or the invention of the paperback: the demise of the pulp magazines, which in their heyday had seen a balkanization of popular fiction unlike anything before or since. In the mid-1930s, at their peak, some two hundred pulp magazines reached a combined audience of over ten million readers each month (Nye 215), and the categories of formula fiction that they published grew ever more specialized: love stories, western stories, western love stories, science fiction, mystery, horror, jungle adventure, war stories, aviation stories, aviation war stories, World War I aviation war stories, sports stories, superhero stories, "Oriental menace" stories. Each category had its own magazines, its own readers, and its own set of reader expectations. Frank Gruber, one of the most prolific and successful of the pulp writers, described it like this: "Everything was grist, every avenue of publication was explored. Every type of writing that offered a buck was attempted. Nothing was too low, nothing too cheap. I wrote Sunday School stories, I wrote spicy sex stories, I tried detective stories, sport stories, love stories. I wrote short-shorts and I even wrote a novel" (7).

Historians of popular culture often point to the garish cover illustrations of the pulps as one reason the fiction inside could so easily be dismissed as subliterary. Certainly these violent, colorful covers—designed to compete with increasing hysteria against other hysterical pulp covers—did not encourage readers to expect thought-provoking fiction, despite the efforts of some idealistic editors to establish standards of competence among their contributors. Nor did the cheap, short-lived acidic pulp paper on which the magazines were printed and which gave them their nickname. Nor did the endless ads for trusses and bodybuilding regimens that paraded through the back pages of every issue, competing for attention with the fiction. It's easy to imagine that authors writing for such magazines, like today's TV soap-opera writers, did not expect their work to last much beyond its initial exposure to the audience, which in their case meant the few weeks the issue remained on the newsstands. Few suspected their work might ever be reprinted or collected in book form, let alone make its way into "historical" anthologies and later be studied by academic critics and scholars. At best, they may have had ambitions similar to those described by Thomas Roberts:

> They want readers to use that modern honorific: professional. That is, they would like their readers to think of them as having rare natural gifts; as having developed those gifts through discipline; as having a clear-eyed recognition of the differences between the glamour and the realities of writing; and, especially, as having the capacity for writing, for rent money or by invitation, the kinds of stories that will make the very editors who commissioned them and established the parameters sit up in surprise at the depth and power of their storytelling. (203)

Just as there was much in the physical appearance of the magazines that argued for their summary dismissal from the precincts of mainstream culture, so was there much in the fiction itself that was hopelessly formulaic and unchallenging. A talented writer with a distinctive voice might publish stories of lasting excellence, only to watch them disappear into the mass of verbiage to be rediscovered years later, if at all. (At least one publishing house, Arkham House, was founded expressly to "rescue" the work of a single writer—H. P. Lovecraft—from the anonymity and ephemerality of the pulps, and other early "specialty houses," such as Fantasy Press, performed similar rescues on other popular pulp writers, a process that continues today through such independent publishers as Haffner or the New England Science Fiction Association.) Occasionally, a writer would escape by writing successful novels—Dashiell Hammett is an example—but often they would escape only to find that the ghettoes spawned by the pulps had taken on a life of their own and now dominated much commercial book publishing as well. The genres established with the help of the pulps had become eerily like the golden cage of Ellison's story—offering writers security and sustenance while keeping them isolated from and ignored by the culture at large.

Plagued by paper shortages during the war and rising competition from paperbacks, movies, and eventually television, pulp magazines began to die off in large numbers during the 1940s, but the patterns they helped form were by then firmly established in the minds of publishers, distributors, and readers. By 1940, Robert de Graff of Pocket Books had discovered that sales of Agatha Christie mysteries improved if more than one were displayed together (Bonn 40), and mysteries thus quickly emerged as an identifiable "genre" in paperback book displays. Science fiction would not enjoy this distinction for another decade; Donald A. Wollheim's pioneering *Pocket Book of Science Fiction* (1943), the first anthology to use the term *science fiction,* appeared as Pocket Book #214, not by way of introducing a series of science fiction texts but rather as part of a list of "one-shot" publications targeted to specific audiences; these volumes, which characteristically followed the proprietary title formula "The Pocket Book of ———," began with broadly generic topics as *The Pocket Book of Verse* (#62) or *The Pocket Book of Short Stories* (#91), but soon began to include such extraliterary oddities as *The Pocket Book of Boners* (#110)—mostly a collection of humorous schoolboy mistakes—*The Pocket Book of Vegetable Gardening* (#148), *The Pocket Book of Crossword Puzzles* (#210), and *The Pocket Book of Home Canning* (#217). Not until the advent of Ballantine Books in 1952 would science fiction become a substantial segment of any paperback publisher's program.

Paperbacks were not the only venue to inherit the fictional ghettoes of the pulps, however, and it is misleading to assume that the end of the pulp era meant the end of mass-produced short fiction. If anything, the digest-sized fiction magazines that appeared in remarkable numbers during the 1950s—replacing the pulps in many instances, continuing pulp titles under new formats in others—created whole new markets for a younger generation of writers, including Ellison. Between 1950 and 1960, more than 150 new fiction magazines were started in the mystery, crime, science fiction, fantasy, and horror fields alone. Less garish in appearance because of their smaller size, these magazines nevertheless continued most of the patterns of pulp writing and publishing. Today, such magazines are more widely forgotten—and more widely ignored by scholars and historians—than even the pulps, which at least have attained a patina of nostalgia and collectibility. But these are the magazines that Ellison and many other young writers hoped desperately to break into during the 1950s, and their appetite for instant, sensational fiction was easily comparable to that of the earlier pulps. The pay was comparable, too; at rates ranging from a half-cent to two cents per word, the sheer volume of writing required to stay alive as a professional writer was not significantly different from what it had been in the 1930s. Ellison's longtime friend Robert Silverberg, who began publishing only slightly earlier than Ellison, calculated that in order to earn a living after graduating from college, he would have to *publish*— not just write—50,000 words per month in order to generate a then-respectable income, at a penny a word, of $500 per month. On occasion, authors would boast of completing 50,000 words in a single week, or of selling over a million words in a year—nearly all of it in the form of short fiction and articles!

Obviously, under such circumstances, care and craftsmanship were often not even realistic options, and in retrospect it is surprising how much first-rate work managed to find its way into the pages of such magazines. Still, with the work of almost any author trained in such a marketplace, it is possible to detect a vestigial need to please some phantom editors—those nearly forgotten heroes and villains who shaped the very personalities of the magazines they edited and thus helped shape the entire course of American popular short fiction in this century. Survivors of the digest era, like survivors of the pulps, still share common understandings about story structure, about narrative conflict, about opening "hooks," and we can never fully appreciate their fiction unless we are aware of this heritage. For the digest writers, though, one important escape route existed that for the most part was not available to their earlier pulp counterparts: the paperback book. Pulp mystery writers could hope to sell a novel to the Crime Club, and pulp western writers could aspire to the success of a Zane Grey, but in most other genres—and for most short fiction in general—there wasn't much realistic hope of surviving into book form. Lovecraft was saved by Arkham House only because of the determination and marketing savvy of its founders, August Derleth and Donald Wandrei. For digest writers grinding out tens of thousands of words per month, the paperback market—which looked tawdry enough on its own terms—began to seem a distinct step toward respectability. In fields such as science fiction, even hardbound publication—the definitive uptown move—was not entirely beyond the grasp of a talented author. Fueled by the mass of unreprinted materials from the pulps, big hardbound science fiction anthologies had begun to appear with some frequency in the late 1940s, and the anthology quickly became a staple of science fiction paperback publishing as well. For Ellison, this meant that his science fiction stories, at least, had a chance for a life beyond the magazines. By 1958, only three years after he began selling to the digests, Ellison saw his short fiction in paperback. It would be another ten years before his first hardcover collection appeared.

This, in broad outline at least, is the commercial literary context in which Ellison began his career. In the chapters that follow, we will find ourselves repeatedly returning to this context as we explore the various ways in which Ellison energetically and almost defiantly constructed a distinctive voice and persona in venues that seemed unpromising at best. To further contextualize Ellison's writing, our first chapter offers a sketch of his life and career, based largely on his own recollections and memoirs. The second chapter examines the often crude early fiction which enabled Ellison to gain his earliest reputation in the post-pulp digest-sized fiction magazines of the 1950s. Ellison's first professional sales began in 1956, mostly to digest magazines dealing in crime (*Trapped, Suspect, Manhunt*) or science fiction (*Infinity, If, Amazing*), but with a few to the men's magazines that seemed a little less constrained by fiction-market formulas (*Dude, Rogue, Gent*). In all, some twenty-nine stories and articles appeared that year. The following year, the number rose to an impressive eighty-four sales. (By contrast, Isaac Asimov, who would turn out to be one of the most prolific of all American writers, reported selling nine stories in his second year as a professional; and Frank Gruber, one of the legends of the pulp era, reported selling fifty-five in his first year after breaking the market.) By mid-1957, Ellison had established himself to the point that readers of such magazines as *Fantastic* were asking for more Ellison stories in the letter columns; in June 1957, a story note in *Fantastic Universe* described him as "without a doubt one of the most widely known and discussed writers in the field" and the author of "an astonishing number of stories" ("Commuter's Problem" 44).

But although the digest magazines gave Ellison his most consistent exposure, from the beginning he was exploring other avenues of writing, and the next few chapters examine some of these new venues, beginning with his "juvie" fiction and journalism, and his pioneering rock 'n' roll novel, in chapter 3. Seeing a name similar to his own on a 1950 novel of juvenile delinquency, Hal Ellson's *Tomboy,* Ellison decided he might gain wider recognition by writing a book about teenage gangs. In 1954, he took up with a Brooklyn gang called the Barons, and by his own account "ran" with them for ten weeks to gather material for his writing. This experience yielded Ellison's first paperback sales—a novel (*Web of the City,* published as *Rumble* in 1958), two collections of stories (*The Deadly Streets,* 1958, and *The Juvies,* 1961, both assembled largely from earlier sales to the digest-size crime magazines), and a memoir (*Memos from Purgatory,* 1961). But as a popular genre, the "gang novel" was already in decline when Ellison went to Brooklyn; its first best-seller, Irving Shulman's *The Amboy Dukes,* had appeared in 1949, Hal Ellson's three most successful novels had all appeared in the early 1950s, and the field had in all probability peaked with the huge success of Evan Hunter's *The Blackboard Jungle* (1954) and its 1955 film version. Ellison did get one of his first major Hollywood assignments out of it, though: in 1963, he adapted *Memo from Purgatory* as an hour-long television play for *The Alfred Hitchcock Hour,* with James Caan playing Ellison's version of himself and a very young Walter Koenig (later of *Star Trek* fame) as a gang leader.

At the same time Ellison was working on his teen gang books, he produced one work in a related, but even more short-lived, genre: the rock 'n' roll novel. *Spider Kiss,* retitled *Rockabilly* by its publisher and loosely based on the career of Jerry Lee Lewis, appeared from Gold Medal Books in 1961. (Fawcett's Gold Medal imprint had since 1950 been pioneering the paperback original—paperbacks that were not reprints of previously published hardcovers—and the line featured a number of names that would later be well known, including John D. MacDonald, Louis L'Amour, and even Howard Hunt.) But here again, the public fascination with rock 'n' roll exposés had already reached its peak; the two most popular films in this genre, *Jailhouse Rock* and *A Face in the Crowd* (with a screenplay by Budd Schulberg that was also published as a Bantam paperback book), had appeared in 1957.

A more important development at this same time was Ellison's discovery of a somewhat more "open" market for short fiction in the various "sophisticated" men's magazines that had developed in the shadow of *Playboy,* and this becomes the focus of our chapter 4. Printed on slick paper (as opposed to the more pulplike stock of the rough-and-tumble men's adventure magazines), magazines like *Rogue* and *Gent* followed *Playboy*'s lead in trying to become arbiters of a hip lifestyle as well as catalogs of sexy pictures. Ellison even edited *Rogue* for a while, and while he was there the magazine became more genuinely literary even than *Playboy,* and served as an odd kind of outpost for science fiction writers seeking to branch out— Alfred Bester, Robert Bloch, Mack Reynolds, and Frank Robinson (who also served as editor) were regular contributors. Unlike the digest magazines, the men's magazine market was not defined by the fiction alone, but by a mix of articles, cartoons, jokes, reviews, and—probably most important—photo layouts. Since no particular fiction genre had defined this market, the market placed considerably fewer generic restrictions on its contributors, and for writers like Ellison this meant a new dimension of creative freedom. More immediate social issues such as civil rights or "sick" humor could be addressed, and stories didn't have to be targeted to a particular science fiction or crime or western market.

Stories from the men's magazines formed the core of Ellison's 1961 collection *Gentleman Junkie and Other Stories of the Hung-Up Generation.* Published by Regency Books, a small paperback house in Evanston, Illinois, which Ellison himself had helped start, *Gentleman Junkie* gave him his first substantial recognition outside of genre fiction. Reviews of original paperbacks were rare in 1961—the *New York Times Book Review* would not institute regular coverage of paperbacks until 1974 and did not begin publishing paperback best-seller lists until 1976 (Davis 294)—but somehow a copy of *Gentleman Junkie* found its way into the hands of Dorothy Parker, then writing her "Constant Reader" column for *Esquire* magazine. Parker described Ellison as a "good, honest, clean writer, putting down what he has seen and known, with no sensationalism about it" (quoted in *Gentleman Junkie* 1). Ellison had his first taste of mainstream recognition.

But *Gentleman Junkie* would prove to have an even more dramatic impact on Ellison's career in another, unexpected way, and this becomes the focus of chapter 5. One of the stories in that collection, "Daniel White for the Greater Good," was optioned by Hollywood director James Goldstone about the same time that Alfred Hitchcock's company bought the rights to *Memo from Purgatory*. In 1962, Ellison moved to Hollywood to become a screenwriter, eventually finding work on such potboiler films as *The Oscar*. Most of his work came in television, however, where Ellison eventually won more Writers Guild of America Awards than anyone had before. But for a writer seeking to maintain creative control over his work, the "Golden Age" of TV writers—Paddy Chayefsky, Robert Alan Aurthur, Reginald Rose, Rod Serling—was already in decline. Serling's *The Twilight Zone* and Rose's *The Defenders,* both widely heralded at the time as series created and controlled by writers, had begun to suffer in the ratings and went off the air in 1964 and 1965, respectively. Ellison instead found himself doing scripts for series as diverse as *Cimarron Strip, The Man from U.N.C.L.E., Route 66, The Young Lawyers, Ripcord,* and even *The Flying Nun!* His most consistent success came on a series titled *Burke's Law* (1963–65), for which Ellison wrote seven episodes, one of which featured the last TV appearance of Buster Keaton. In 1964, frustrated at the compromises and changes wrought upon his scripts, Ellison first adopted the disdainful pseudonym "Cordwainer Bird" for the screen credit of an episode of *Voyage to the Bottom of the Sea*. "Cordwainer Bird," Ellison has let it be widely known, is his way of protesting productions that have mangled his scripts. (The name is an amalgam of "Cordwainer Smith," the science fiction pseudonym of political scientist Paul Linebarger and the traditional gesture of "flipping the bird.") Hollywood, it seemed, was becoming another sort of golden cage—paying far better than the digests or even the men's magazines, but even more circumscribed and formulaic.

Given the constraints of all these markets, it isn't surprising that Ellison should find science fiction liberating, both in the magazines and in the Hollywood studios. Chapter 6 examines that group of stories and anthologies of the 1960s that earned Ellison the international reputation by which he still remains most widely known—that of an iconoclastic and controversial science fiction writer. To be sure, the science fiction magazines had their own formulas and limitations, but in the 1960s this began to change. Frederik Pohl, a science fiction writer who had made his name as a satirist rather than as a "hardware" writer, assumed the editorship of *Galaxy Science Fiction* and *If* in 1961, and Cele Goldsmith, an editor with a distinct sense of literary values and a willingness to experiment, was at the helm of *Amazing Stories* and *Fantastic* from 1958 to 1965. Ellison, who had virtually given up on the science fiction magazines in the early 1960s, now returned with some remarkably original stories. "Paingod" appeared in

Fantastic in June 1964, "'Repent, Harlequin!' Said the Ticktockman" in *Galaxy* in December 1965, "I Have No Mouth, and I Must Scream" in *If* in March 1967. In 1966, he began winning the long string of Hugo and Nebula Awards that would eventually make him the most honored science fiction writer in the world—and that would inescapably identify him with science fiction for the rest of his career.

Hollywood, too, began honoring Ellison for his science fiction. An *Outer Limits* episode, "Demon with a Glass Hand," earned him a Writers Guild Award for the best script in a TV anthology series of the 1964–65 season, and another Writers Guild Award followed in the 1967–68 season for "The City on the Edge of Forever" on *Star Trek* (an episode which also earned a Hugo Award). (Another *Outer Limits* script, "Soldier," would eventually earn Ellison a stranger kind of recognition: a plagiarism settlement from the producers of the 1984 hit movie *The Terminator,* which bore striking resemblances to Ellison's original idea.) Eventually, Ellison was approached to create his own TV series, and the result was a 1973 syndicated debacle called *The Starlost,* which very nearly cured Ellison of ever wanting to write for television again. The series became something of a cause célèbre in the science fiction field, providing material not only for one of Ellison's funnier essays ("Somehow, I Don't Think We're in Kansas, Toto"), but even for a 1975 science fiction roman à clef by Ben Bova, unsubtly titled *The Starcrossed* and published with a clearly identifiable portrait of Ellison on the cover.

With all these honors accruing, Ellison was by the mid-1960s a leading figure—perhaps *the* leading figure—in science fiction. It was far from a new world for him: He had helped found a fan club, the Cleveland Science Fiction Society, in 1950, and was a familiar and controversial figure at science fiction conventions well before he ever broke into print. He had published a "fanzine"—an amateur publication featuring commentary on favorite writers and occasional stories and distributed through the mail to science fiction's network of loyal readers—and most of his literary friendships were with science fiction writers. He quickly became one of the most influential editors in the field with two huge anthologies of original stories, *Dangerous Visions* (1967) and *Again, Dangerous Visions* (1971), and sprinkled them liberally with chatty introductions demonstrating his intimate involvement with almost all aspects of the field. These books, too, won Hugo Awards. He became a superstar at science fiction conventions and perhaps the main single source of convention folklore; everyone claimed to have met him, and everyone had a story about some outrageous experience involving going to dinner with Ellison.

Between 1965 and 1967, Ellison published three collections of his own fantastic stories, and even though not all the stories were science fiction, they were labeled as such. His blurbs called him the "best-selling science fiction writer in the world" (*From the Land of Fear,* 1973), although he wasn't, and when the "New Wave" of stylistically experimental science fiction was imported from Britain, it was Ellison whom the *New Yorker* labeled "the chief prophet of the New Wave in America" ("Talk of the Town"). And the awards kept coming: Hugos for "I Have No Mouth, and I Must Scream," the *Star Trek* episode, and *Dangerous Visions* in 1968; a Hugo for "The Beast That Shouted Love at the Heart of the World" in 1969; a Nebula for "A Boy and His Dog" in 1970; a special Hugo for *Again, Dangerous Visions* in 1972; Hugo and Jupiter Awards for "Deathbird," a Writers Guild Award for the unproduced pilot of *The Starlost,* and an Edgar Award from the Mystery Writers of America for "The Whimper of Whipped Dogs" in 1974; a Hugo for "Adrift Just Of the Islets of Langerhans: Latitude 38°54'N, Longitude 77°00'13W" in 1975; a Hugo for the film version of the story "A Boy and His Dog" in 1976; Nebula and Hugo awards for "Jeffty Is Five" in 1977 and 1978; a Hugo for "Paladin of the Lost Hour" in 1986 and a Writers Guild Award for the *Twilight Zone* teleplay based on it in 1987; a World Fantasy Award for the collection *Angry Candy* in 1989, a Lifetime Achievement Award from the World Fantasy Convention in 1993, a Living Legend Award from the International Horror Guild in 1999.

Ironically, only a handful of Ellison's award-winning stories could be considered science fiction by any reasonable definition of the term; most are fantasies, and a few might be classed as a kind of vernacular magic realism. Equally ironic is the fact that by the time Ellison began to be lionized by the science fiction world, he had virtually abandoned the science fiction magazine market to which he had contributed so prolifically in the 1950s. In 1965, the year "'Repent, Harlequin!'" was published, only two Ellison stories appeared in science fiction magazines. The following year, only one appeared—out of eight published stories—and in 1967, it was only one in nine. Furthermore, Ellison's total output of fiction was beginning to decrease radically, as he devoted more and more time to each story and to his movie reviews, newspaper columns, and essays. In the 1980s, he was diagnosed with chronic fatigue syndrome, which further hampered his ability to work at the extraordinarily high levels of energy that had characterized him in earlier years, and in 1996 he underwent quadruple bypass surgery.

But if Ellison's productivity slowed from its earlier epic levels, the stories themselves continued to grow in depth and complexity, and his story collections began to assume an aesthetic shape of their own. Chapter 7 examines the fantasies of contemporary mythology that made up Ellison's most famous collection, *Deathbird Stories,* and chapters 8 and 9 explore the personal and autobiographical themes that have grown increasingly central in Ellison's later work. Finally, in chapter 10, we examine some of the structural and thematic experiments with genre materials characteristic of Ellison's more recent fiction. Today, Ellison's fiction rarely appears in science fiction magazines, and his books seldom carry the science fiction rubric. But they still are more likely than not to show up in the science fiction sections of bookstore, and the *New York Times* still refers to him as a "science fiction writer." After escaping the stigma of being a utility writer for the digests, after graduating from paperback originals to hardcovers—and eventually to expensive limited editions—after surviving Hollywood, Ellison still finds himself in a version of Joe Bob Hickey's golden cage, by virtue of his greatest successes.

There is no doubt that Ellison's fantastic fiction is worth examining: It forms a vivid and passionate panorama of some of the key cultural anxieties and contradictions of American life in the twentieth century, and much of it ranks with the finest short fiction we have. Looked at from outside the narrow perspective of popular genre writing, Ellison's career also reveals itself as a dense tapestry of the last half-century of American cultural life, touching upon social concerns from the "juvenile delinquency" scare of the 1950s to the civil rights movement and Vietnam, from fears of nuclear annihilation and urban violence to anxiety over technology and computers. His fiction is both of and about such cultural expressions as rock 'n' roll, television, movies, pulp fiction, men's magazines, stand-up comedy, and alternative journalism—that whole vast underground reservoir of American writing represented by the pulps and their descendants, by the paperback industry, by specialty presses and genre magazines, by Hollywood. Ellison's large and imposing body of writing—more than sixty books, some twelve hundred stories and articles, dozens of produced and unproduced scripts, endless notes and comments on his own work and that of others—is as maddeningly diffuse and uneven as the culture it reflects and mythifies.

Decades ago, when Ellison was still a teenager editing a science fiction fanzine, he briefly titled it "Ellison Wonderland"—a phrase he later used for the title of a book and eventually as the name of his house, a sprawling hillside structure in Sherman Oaks, California, that is as filled with the memorabilia of American popular culture as is his fiction. The phrase smacks of the kind of celebratory hubris that has led many to confuse Ellison the public figure with Ellison the artist or to view him as a bizarre kind of performance artist for whom fiction is but another public stage. Ellison has undoubtedly contributed to this view; he has indeed become a "personality," like the Harlequin, living in a wonderland of his own making—a kind of dreamscape of fear and joy that grows more familiar the more we look at it and that is largely of a piece with his fiction, criticism, and journalism. For all its self-promotional excesses and gaucherie, the psychic space occupied by Ellison wonderland is a corner of the contemporary cultural landscape that is unmistakably his own and one that provides a unique perspective not only on the genres in which he has worked but on the last half-century of American cultural life.

The present study does not attempt to be a definitive survey or account of Ellison's literally thousands of publications, but rather an attempt to locate this mercurial figure in the context of the various fields in which he has worked, from both literary and historical perspectives. Any understanding of Ellison's "juvenile delinquent" fiction is incomplete without some awareness of the popularity that this evanescent subgenre of urban realism enjoyed during the 1950s, just as an appreciation of his achievements in science fiction depends on awareness of the authors he grew up reading, the down-and-dirty magazine markets of the 1950s, and the ferment which (with Ellison's enthusiastic participation) radically altered the field in the 1960s and 1970s. At the same time, autobiographical material is so pervasive in Ellison's work that it cannot be ignored, although this study makes no pretensions toward being a literary biography. Our opening chapter, in fact, is titled "An Estimated Life" mainly because it is essentially a summary of Ellison's own construct of his life, since it is this view that permeates his work. The five chapters that follow trace important phases of Ellison's career: his prolific early days in the digest-sized crime and science fiction magazines of the 1950s, his detours into juvenile delinquent fiction and journalism and his one rock 'n' roll novel, his discovery of a more open voice in the men's magazines of the 1960s, his often contentious relationship with Hollywood, his role in the revolution in science fiction that is often associated with the term *New Wave*. The concluding chapters examine his mature work as a fantasist, exploring both the broad mythological themes of *Deathbird Stories* and the more personal myths of the writer's life, Ellison's Jewish heritage, his major concerns with the persistence of the past and personal responsibility, and his experimentation with various fragmented or alternative narrative modes. Throughout, we found ourselves returning to Ellison's most pervasive themes of entrapment and the crucial importance of action, almost any action, in a morally indifferent or even hostile universe.

Portions of this book, in quite different form, have appeared in the *Journal of the Fantastic in the Arts,* the *New York Review of Science Fiction, Foundation: The Review of Science Fiction,* and *Locus: The Newspaper of the Science Fiction Field.* Harlan Ellison has been generously cooperative throughout—even when he has disagreed with our assessments—and we have benefited as well from the insights and information of John Clute, Charles N. Brown, Robert Silverberg, Philip José Farmer, Frank M. Robinson, Tim Richmond, Charlene Wexler, Bill Senior, our students at Roosevelt University (which also provided a research leave permitting the completion of the book), and several members of the International Association for the Fantastic in the Arts, at whose annual conference some of these ideas were first presented.

Finally, a textural note: All the italics in material quoted from Ellison are Ellison's own, including in some cases entire lines or sentences. Ellison often uses italics for stylistic purposes, and we have chosen to retain these even in cases in which the full context of the italicized words may not be included in the quotation.

1 | AN ESTIMATED LIFE

And *because* I'm living the best possible kind of life I can lead, I have adventures. Now maybe my adventures aren't as wild as Cousteau's or Lawrence of Arabia's, or even Mailer's, but because I'm a good storyteller, I can see the plot-line in the daily occurrences of my life, and when I retell them, I try and put a punch line to them, to tie them up dramatically the way I would a story. Now I'll grant you that this kind of minor rearrangement of the time-sequences, emphases and insights is akin to lying, but that's what I get paid to do: lie professionally. And it sure beats the bejezus out of the dull random manner in which life feeds us our experiences. So, in a very special way, everything I ever relate about how I live my life is a lie. Or maybe "lie" is too harsh a word. "Fib" is closer, but I suspect Vonnegut's "foma"—harmless untruths—is the best. I never change the facts, just the way they are colored or arranged. I'll never tell you I won if I lost, I'll never tell you I was a good guy if I was a bad. But there's a bit of the imp in me, and if I add a flying fish or troll to an otherwise ordinary tale, it's only to make you a little sunnier and happier as you move toward the grave. How can you condemn a man for such a noble and humanitarian activity?

—THE HARLAN ELLISON HORNBOOK, May 11, 1973

We invent our lives (and other people's) as we live them; what we call "life" is itself a fiction. Therefore, we must constantly strive to produce only good art, absolutely entertaining fiction.

—LEVENDIS, in "The Man Who Rowed Christopher Columbus Ashore" (1993)

ONE OF HARLAN ELLISON'S most clearly autobiographical stories bears the telling title "All the Lies That Are My Life," a title which takes on a dimension of tricksterism when one reads the tale and discovers that we are never quite told what these lies are. As a consummate performer, an ingenious and elliptical manager of an intense public persona, Ellison is a master at what has been termed "autofiction," the incorporation of autobiographical material in fiction and of fictional techniques in memoirs to the extent that, at certain points, the line blurs entirely. Those who have read Ellison's voluminous story introductions and impassioned, confessional journalism are quickly made aware that his work cannot be separated from his life and that he reinvents his life constantly—or has it reinvented for him by the endless anecdotes that have made him the stuff of oral legend, especially in the fan communities of science fiction, fantasy, and comic books. Ellison has never quite denied his habit of self-invention, and in a 1983 interview he spoke of his admiration for those artists—Scott Fitzgerald, Hemingway, even Wilde—who shaped their own lives as reflections of the values expressed in their fictions, creating their own legends or becoming heroes in their own picaresque narratives. "I don't think any other writer pleads his own case so often or at such length," wrote Michael Moorcock, referring to the multiple introductions, prefaces, story notes, and afterwords that pepper Ellison's books and magazine appearances (Moorcock ix). Moorcock compares these pieces with the patter of a stand-up comedian between routines, suggesting that Ellison sees himself as a performer who has to constantly work his audience, setting them up for each new story, offering sidebits and one-liners to keep the pace moving. For Ellison, each new piece of fiction is a "jam" or improvisation; he seldom does rewrites, and he loves to read new stories aloud. But over the years, Ellison's nonfiction pieces have become more than connective tissue; often the line between Ellison's own voice and that of a fictional narrator becomes blurred. The story introductions, Ellison writes, "began as simply random notes on theme in my first collection. Then, as the years have passed, they have become more and more important, more integrated with what I've been trying to say in my fiction" (*I Have No Mouth* 123). They also have become invaluable sources not only for clues to how Ellison works and how he views his work but for what he regards as the significant experiences of his life that contribute to that work.

For the most part, then, the outline of Ellison's life presented here makes no attempt to be definitive. It is generally based on Ellison's own accounts in his essays, prefaces, interviews, and newspaper columns, and only on occasion does it draw upon other sources to address a contradiction or present an alternative view of a particular episode or anecdote. Most of the "Ellison stories" that circulate among fans are not so much the stuff of biography as of fannish legend—that peculiar mixture of oral history and semi-apocryphal tall tale that has long served to define the science fiction community as an extraliterary phenomenon, a self-described "subculture" which can award almost heroic status to its members based on little more than sheer obnoxiousness. Certainly, Ellison deserves a significant place in this tradition—he was by all accounts one of the most obnoxious teenagers ever to visit himself upon a convention—but what all that tells us about his life and career is unclear at best. The folk history of Harlan Ellison is best left to those who were there, or pretend to have been there, and who look to celebrate the myth more than the man.

PAINESVILLE, OHIO

Ellison's roots are solidly Midwestern. He was born in Cleveland, Ohio, in the afternoon of May 27, 1934. His father, Louis Laverne Ellison, was a dentist who in his youth had worked riverboats and minstrel shows, gaining enough recognition as a singer to get his photo on the sheet music of "My Yiddishe Momma," a song popularized by Al Jolson. He worked as a dentist in Cleveland during Prohibition, counting some local gangsters among his clientele. Later, after losing the dentistry practice, he worked in a jewelry store owned by his in-laws in Painesville, Ohio, the small town some thirty miles northeast of Cleveland where Harlan spent most of his childhood. Despite having successfully helped build up the business, he lost that job as well in 1947, in an unsavory family incident fictionalized in the 1979 story "In the Fourth Year of the War" (discussed in chapter 9). The following year he opened his own store, but died suddenly of a coronary thrombosis on May 1, 1949, only a few weeks before his son's fifteenth birthday.

Harlan's life in Painesville was by his own account singularly unrewarding. His sister Beverly, eight years older, provided little companionship and eventually married and moved away (she and Ellison remained alienated thereafter). Ellison had no friends, and acknowledges that he was smaller than most kids and insufferably arrogant—an irresistible target, in other words. Adding to this was a general climate of anti-Semitism that, according to Ellison, was moderated only slightly when additional Jewish families either moved in or openly acknowledged their Jewishness. A 1946 group photo of the sixth-grade class of Lathrop Grade School in Painesville (reprinted in *The Essential Ellison*) tends to support Ellison's version of himself as a kid: By far the shortest member of the class (girls included), the young Ellison stands out not only by virtue of his stature and his Captain Midnight Secret Decoder Badge but also because of his aggressive hands-on-hips stance and bandaged cheek. He appears to be the sort of defiant kid one would expect to run away with the circus—which is exactly what Ellison says he did, more or less. The following year, he spent three months with a traveling carnival until he was caught in Kansas City and returned to his parents (an adventure described in Ellison's 1982 essay

"Gopher in the Gilly: A Reminiscence of the Carnival," reprinted in *The Essential Ellison*).

"One Life Furnished in Early Poverty" and "Final Shtick"

In fiction based on this period of his life, Ellison has often made little or no attempt to disguise autobiographical details. In "Final Shtick" (1960) and "One Life, Furnished in Early Poverty" (1970), the name of Lathrop Grade School is unchanged, as are Ellison's boyhood address, 89 Harmon Drive, the Colony Lumber Company, where he played as a child, and even the name of his schoolyard nemesis, Jack Wheeldon. In "Final Shtick," Painesville rather unsubtly becomes Lainesville, and in "One Life," the narrator's name is Rosenthal, the family name of Ellison's mother. Although published ten years apart, these stories reveal a great deal not only about Ellison's attitudes toward his childhood but also about how fantasy becomes an increasingly important strategy in dealing with these attitudes. "Final Shtick," which appeared in *Rogue* magazine in 1960, reflects much of that period's fascination with what was then called "sick" comedy. Ellison had enlisted comedian Lenny Bruce to write a column for *Rogue* in 1959, and the narrator of "Final Shtick" is a version of Bruce superimposed on Ellison's own childhood memories (one of Bruce's columns even appeared in the same issue of *Rogue* as "Final Shtick"). Like Bruce, Ellison's Marty Field is a successful stand-up comic who has gained a reputation for "sick" humor and who has changed his name partly to disguise his Jewish background. (Marty Field was Morrie Feldman; Lenny Bruce was Leonard Schneider.) Field is returning to Lainesville to be honored as a successful native son, and the experience brings back a flood of bitter memories of anti-Semitism and disastrous schoolyard fights, of being betrayed by a girlfriend and of learning that a neighbor woman had killed his dog while he had been away at summer camp (an episode later recounted in purely autobiographical terms in Ellison's 1983 essay "Driving in the Spikes"). Field is not quite Ellison or Bruce, however, and to emphasize this distance Ellison introduces a subtheme of Field's guilt over disguising his Jewishness and his self-contempt at using his sick humor only as a "shtick," rather than as an honest attempt to grapple with social issues. Resolving to use the opportunity of the celebration to expose the hatred and anti-Semitism that plagued his childhood, Field instead delivers a vapid, sentimental thank-you to the assembled crowd. Recognizing his own insurmountable cowardice, he flees in tears after the ceremony.

In a sense, then, the story is about failure of resolve, a common theme in Ellison. Like Joe Bob Briggs in "Silent in Gehenna," Field comes to realize that his protests are empty and meaningless. But the most revealing passages in the story are ones like the following:

> You are the only Jew on your street, the only Jewish kid in your grade school. There are seven Jewish families in town. You go to Lathrop Grade School and you are a little kid. At recess time they get you out on the ball diamond, and one of them picks a fight with you. Usually it's Jack Wheeldon, whose head is square and whose hair is cut in a butch, and whose father is a somethingorother at the Diamond Alkali plant. . . .
>
> You stand there while Jack Wheeldon calls you a dirty kike, and your mother is a dirty kike and you pee your pants because all kikes do that, don't they, you frigging little kike? And when you swing, and hit him on the side of the head, the circle of kids magically grows about you, and while you're locked in an adolescent grapple with Jack Wheeldon (who is all the things in this life that you despise because they are bigger than you and slower-witted and frightening), someone kicks you from behind. Hard. At the base of your spine. With a Thom McAn shoe. And then you can't help it and you start to cry. (*Essential Ellison* 776–77)

Interestingly, this same episode, or one very much like it, is recounted in "One Life, Furnished in Early Poverty," which appeared a decade later. During that decade, Ellison had moved to Hollywood and firmly established his reputation as both a TV and short fiction writer, and the later story shows a considerably higher degree of self-assurance and a willingness to confront the same material more directly. For one thing the narrator of "One Life," Gus Rosenthal, is much closer to home. A successful screenwriter with failed marriages behind him, Rosenthal abruptly decides to return to his childhood home to dig up a metal toy soldier he had buried there as a child. The house and neighborhood are strangely unchanged, and Gus soon encounters the childhood version of himself, on the school playground, being attacked by a group of fellow students:

> Gus fell, rolled face-down in the dust of the playground, and tried to sit up. The boys pushed through between the swings, avoiding the one that clanged back and forth.

Gus managed to get up, and the boys formed a circle around him. Then Jack Wheeldon stepped out and faced him. I remembered Jack Wheeldon.

He was taller than Gus. They were all taller than Gus, but Wheeldon was beefier. I could see shadows surrounding him. Shadows of a boy who would grow into a man with a beer stomach and thick arms. But the eyes would always remain the same.

He shoved Gus in the face. Gus went back, dug in and charged him. Gus came at him low, head tucked under, fists tight at the ends of arms braced close to the body, extended forward. He hit him in the stomach and wrestled him around. They struggled together like inept club fighters, raising dust.

One of the boys in the circle took a step forward and hit Gus hard in the back of the head. Gus turned his face out of Wheeldon's stomach, and Wheeldon punched him in the mouth. Gus started to cry. (*Essential Ellison* 784)

Although anti-Semitic insults are omitted from this account of the fight, the young Gus later asks the narrator why his tormentors called him a "dirty Jewish elephant" (a slur which was also used by the young Morry Feldman's tormentors). The narrator finds himself in the odd position of having to explain anti-Semitic stereotypes to himself as a child. He befriends the boy, sharing his enthusiasms for science fiction, movies, and radio serials, but soon finds himself wasting away—presumably from the effects of the time displacement—and the boy becoming increasingly anti-social, dependent on no one but him. The elder Gus realizes that he must leave and that he must try to explain this to the child. In the story's final scene, the first-person narration—which had so far been confined to the point of view of the older Gus—suddenly begins to jump back and forth between the two Guses:

He was watching me. Staring up at me from the pond side. And I knew what instant it had been that had formed me. It hadn't been all the people who'd called me a wild kid, or a strange kid, or any of it. It wasn't being poor, or being lonely.

I watched him go away. He was my friend. But he didn't have no guts. He didn't. But I'd show him! I was gonna get out of here, go away, be a big person and do a lot of things, and some day I'd run into him someplace and see him and he'd come up and shake my hand and I'd spit on him. Then I'd beat him up. (*Essential Ellison* 792)

This split narrator—a device that Ellison could hardly have gotten away with in the markets available to him a decade earlier—dramatizes Ellison's almost obsessive need, in fiction as in life, to hold on to the innocent outlook of childhood without abandoning the informed adult viewpoint. This dual perspective, which informs much of his important later fiction (such as "Jeffty Is Five," discussed in chapter 9), is already a fully formed technique in "Final Shtick." By casting "One Life" as a time-travel fantasy, however, Ellison seeks to confront his childhood anxieties more directly—not from the perspective of the suppressed rage of an unhappy adult but as a distant place with its own integrity and validity. Ironically, by presenting Harlan the kid as a character in fantasy, Ellison can draw on his memories more directly and not as functions of a fictionalized adult's memory (as in "Final Shtick"). Despite its rather self-indulgent title, "One Life" is a far more mature story than "Final Shtick," and is one of Ellison's most effective metaphors for a childhood that turns in on itself. In it, to the extent that we can read it as autobiography, Ellison literally becomes his only childhood friend, and in an ironic, Möbius-like twist, he is abandoned even by his adult self when the latter must return to the present.

FORMATIVE READING

The story also goes a long way toward helping us understand the kind of writer Ellison eventually became. Graham Greene's famous observation that "it is only in childhood that books have any deep influence on our lives" (13) is as true of movies, radio shows, and pulp fiction as it is of the classics of childhood, and even Greene admits a particular fondness for such pulpish entertainments as Captain Gilson's *Pirate Aeroplane*. Popular writers often seek to lend themselves an aura of literary authenticity by citing Dickens or Shakespeare or Poe as their childhood favorites—not long ago, one well-known science fiction writer was overheard trying persuasively to convince dinner companions that his true literary ancestor was Balzac, despite an almost total lack of supporting evidence from his own novels—but more often than not it is the movies, radio dramas, and pulp stories that first gave them their ideas of plot, style, and pacing. Ellison has occasionally shared in this quest for legitimate ancestors: In the introduction to his 1960 science fiction collection *A Touch of Infinity,* he claimed that before he discovered science fiction his favorite authors were Conrad, St. Exupery, Hemingway, William March, and Immanuel Kant! But for the most part he has been unpretentious in this regard, even permitting the inclusion, in the omnibus collection *The Essential Ellison* (1987), of two stories written when he was fifteen and serialized in a children's column in the *Cleveland News*. Both are crudely illustrated by the author, and each features characters and situations lifted wholesale from the pulp magazines: "The Sword of Parmagon" is a swordplay adventure set in sixteenth-century England, and "The Gloconda" tells of an African safari to capture a legendary giant snake.

But Ellison was reading more than just comic books and Kant, and he was becoming aware of the possibility of writing as a profession—certainly of the potential of writing to change people's lives. He credits reading James Otis Kaler's *Toby Tyler, or Ten Weeks with a Circus* (1881) as influencing his decision to run off with the carnival, and claims to have read all or most of Poe by the time he was nine. Also when he was nine, he saw the Jacques Tourneur suspense film *The Leopard Man,* and he remembers reading in the credits (the first time he had noticed movie credits) that the film was based on a novel by Cornell Woolrich. Ellison sought out the Woolrich novel, *Black Alibi,* and encountered not only modern suspense fiction but one of the early masters of manipulating genre materials toward a highly individual vision. (Woolrich is today most widely remembered for the story "Rear Window" and his screenplay for the 1954 Alfred Hitchcock film adapted from it.) In 1949, he encountered the work of another such master, Fritz Leiber, when he picked up a paperback copy of *The Girl with the Hungry Eyes,* with its stunning title story, a modern version of the vampire legend. (Ellison later paid tribute to this story by writing his own version of it in 1956, "Nedra at f:5.6.") Shortly thereafter, he discovered science fiction when he came across a copy of *Startling Stories* in his uncle's dental office in Cleveland. This in turn led him to other pulp magazines and to a copy of August Derleth's 1949 anthology *The Other Side of the Moon,* which included stories by Theodore Sturgeon, A. E. Van Vogt, Murray Leinster, and other already famous names in science fiction. Ellison was particularly impressed by Ray Bradbury's "Pillar of Fire," another atypical use of genre materials in the way in which it touched upon contemporary social issues—in particular, censorship, which would later become a favorite target of Ellison himself (as well as the subject of Bradbury's most famous novel, *Fahrenheit 451* [1953]).

CLEVELAND AND FANDOM

By the time his father died in May 1949, Ellison was already a voracious reader, gravitating strongly toward science fiction, and an aspiring writer.

The death, however, left his family in strained circumstances, and soon Ellison's mother, Serita, moved the family to a resident hotel on East 105th Street in Cleveland, where Harlan eventually got a job working in a bookstore. The move may have meant harder times financially, but the urban environment gave Ellison his first real chance to explore the science fiction community that had been opened up to him by the pulp magazines. Almost from its beginning, American popular science fiction had worked at becoming a whole subculture. Friends and enemies could be made in the letter columns of the magazines or through the amateur fanzines that had proliferated since the 1930s; local clubs sponsored regional meetings and sent delegations to the "Worldcons," which had been held since 1939 (except during the war years). Through such conventions and meetings, writers became accessible to their fans in a way unique among popular genres. Most important, science fiction provided an extended community for exactly the kind of kid Ellison had been—a bright, voracious reader whose interests were shared by neither teachers, nor family, nor fellow students.

It didn't take long for Ellison to enter this world full tilt. While a student at East High School, he became a founding member of the Cleveland Science Fiction Society, which like most such ambitiously named clubs met at the homes of its members. In an autobiographical story called "GBK— A Many-Flavored Bird," Ellison's narrator would write of the importance of such a club to a depressed youngster:

> If anything had saved me from becoming a real flip, from wasting my life and what little talent I had, after my father died and my mother and I moved to Cleveland, it was the science-fiction people. . . . Not only were they good people, and kind people, but there was a swirl of wonder about them, an unpredictability of imagination that turned my world of mourning sadness and widow's tears into a golden time and space of hyperspatial rocket ships, alien life-forms and concepts of the universe that I'd never even suspected existed. (*Love Ain't Nothing but Sex Misspelled* 89–90)

When the club decided to put out a fanzine of its own, Ellison soon became the editor and principal writer, and by mid-1952 the *Bulletin of the Cleveland Science Fiction Society* became Ellison's own fanzine, retitled *Science Fantasy Bulletin* and later *Dimensions*. Ellison remained an active fanzine editor until late 1954, and during this period he met or corresponded with a number of writers, would-be writers, and editors. A number of writers were just entering the field in the early 1950s, some of them only slightly older than Ellison, many of them trying to find ways to extend the thematic and stylistic boundaries of the genre. Philip José Farmer, who became one of Ellison's early mentors, published his controversial story "The Lovers" in 1952, and about this same time Algis Budrys, Philip K. Dick, Frank Herbert, and Robert Sheckley published their first stories. Budrys in particular became a friend and role model to Ellison, only three years older but already publishing prolifically and to considerable acclaim. Budrys even visited Ellison briefly in Cleveland and invited him to New York to attend a meeting of the Hydra Club, where the young fan met Sheckley, Fletcher Pratt, Katherine MacLean, Philip Klass, Harry Harrison, Willy Ley, and H. L. Gold, all of whom were major players in the science fiction world of the time. (Gold was even the editor of *Galaxy* magazine, which is often credited as having played a crucial role in introducing satirical social themes into the genre.) "It was a stellar gathering," wrote Ellison years later, "and I confess to feeling that I had at last found my people. I was hooked; it was the life of a writer for me, just as soon as I could get through college and blah blah blah" ("Troubling Thoughts about Godhood, Part Two," *Hornbook* 108–9).

These contacts also gave Ellison the opportunity to begin attending science fiction conventions as something more than an anonymous fan. The most important such convention, at least in the Ellison legend, was the 1953 World Science Fiction Convention in Philadelphia. Science fiction conventions are inevitably bizarre events that have probably done more even than fanzines to establish the field's self-described status as a subculture. Successful writers and editors mix with readers and fans—some of whom have attained substantial reputations just by *being* fans—in a long weekend of panel discussions, debates, and parties that range from celebration of the literature to utopian schemes to speculations on scientific and pseudoscientific concepts. These fan gatherings have been described, not too kindly but not too inaccurately, as the original revenge of the nerds. Fans were (and are) characteristically bright, fanatical readers who sought to develop a social life based not on fashions, or sports, or schools, or jobs, but on habits of reading and sometimes arcane intellectual interests. As a kind of extended surrogate family, fandom inevitably gives rise to alliances and feuds, and such alliances and feuds are often blown up into something resembling epic battles in fandom's self-generated folklore.[1] If Ellison is sometimes guilty of the hyperbole and self-aggrandizement of which he is so often accused, it's important to remember that he came of age in a quasi-literary community that viewed the Second World War as an unwelcome hiatus in the schedule of Worldcons.[1]

With some 750 in attendance, the 1953 Philadelphia Worldcon was the second largest ever, exceeded only by the previous year's gathering in Chicago. (In subsequent years, Worldcons have often exceeded 5,000 members, occasionally going as high as 8,000 or more.) Ellison arrived having already generated something of a controversial reputation based on his opinionated fanzine, and on the last night of the convention he was accosted by an offended fan from New York, who had brought along two brawny companions to help him "get" Ellison. Ellison's angry confrontation with these bullies in the lobby of the Bellevue-Stratford Hotel, in which, according to Robert Silverberg, he "avoided mayhem through a display of sheer bravado" ("Jet-Propelled Birdbath" 24), firmly established his reputation as a charismatic and contentious—not to mention fearless—leader of the fan community.

The reputation for contentiousness was further promoted by a public encounter with Isaac Asimov, already a near-legendary figure in science fiction because of his series of robot and galactic empire stories, which had virtually defined the science fictional universe of the field's leading magazine, *Astounding,* during the 1940s. Though Asimov was at least as well known as Ellison for his habit of embellishing minor contretemps into colorful anecdotes, his version of this encounter provides some notion of how Ellison so quickly entered science fiction folklore:

[H]e had sharp features and the livest eyes I ever saw, filled with an explosive concentration of intelligence.

Those live eyes were now focused on me with something that I can only describe as worship.

He said, "Are you Isaac Asimov?" And in his voice was awe and wonder and amazement.

I was rather pleased, but I struggled hard to retain a modest demeanor. "Yes, I am," I said.

"You're not kidding? You're *really* Isaac Asimov?" The words have not yet been invented that would describe the ardor and reverence with which his tongue caressed the syllables of my name.

I felt as though the least I could do would be to rest my hand upon his head and bless him, but I controlled myself. "Yes, I am," I said, and by now my smile was a fatuous thing, nauseating to behold. "*Really,* I am."

"Well, I think you're . . . " he began, still in the same tone of voice, and for a split second he paused, while I listened and everyone within earshot held his breath. The youngster's face shifted in that split second into an expression of utter contempt and he finished the sentence with supreme indifference "—a *nothing!*"

The effect, for me, was that of tumbling over a cliff I had not known was there, and landing flat on my back. I could only blink foolishly while everyone present roared with laughter. (Asimov 690)

When Asimov repeated this tale in an introduction to Ellison's 1967 anthology, *Dangerous Visions,* Ellison countered in a footnote with his own, somewhat less dramatic version:

There is an unsavory tone inherent in the remark I am alleged to have made to Dr. Asimov, noted above. This tone of contempt was by no means present at the time, nor at any time before or since. . . . I didn't say, "—you're a—*nothing!*" I said, "You aren't so much." I grant you, the difference is a subtle one; I was being an adolescent snot; but after reading all those Galaxy-spanning novels about heroic men of heroic proportions, I had been expecting a living computer, mightily thewed, something of a Conan with the cunning of Lije Bailey [a character in Asimov's robot novels]. . . . I have never been disappointed by an Asimov story, and I have never been disappointed by Asimov the man. (*Dangerous Visions* xv)

Meeting Silverberg in person was another important event for Ellison at the Philadelphia convention. The two had known each other through mail and phone contacts, each had published a fanzine, and they shared a desperate desire to be a published science fiction writer. As they became friends, this desire took on a competitive edge. According to Silverberg, Ellison told the toastmaster of the convention that he and a friend, David Ish, had sold a story to the prestigious *Magazine of Fantasy and Science Fiction,* and the toastmaster duly announced this feat at the convention banquet, to the envy of Silverberg and other young writers. Later, it turned out, the story had only been submitted and, in fact, was eventually rejected by the magazine's editor, Anthony Boucher. Ellison would not see a professional publication until two and a half years later, and even then in a second-string science fiction magazine.[2]

UNIVERSITY

Hoping it would help to hone his writing skills, Ellison entered Ohio State University in September 1953—almost immediately after the Philadelphia Worldcon. The world of an early Eisenhower-era, football-oriented, fraternity-dominated midwestern state university is about as unlikely an environment for Ellison as one could imagine, and it didn't take him long to alienate a considerable percentage of the campus's 30,000-odd population. He pledged a Jewish fraternity, Zeta Beta Tau, but came to view it as an enclave of materialistic students with whom he shared few values or interests. More directly, he later described them as "a gathering of Jewish gentlemen dedicated to the principles of fire engine red Caddy convertibles, torment of pledge 'brothers' and the indiscriminate fucking of as many Tri-Delts as they could locate" ("College Days, Part One," *Hornbook* 209). Outraged by the demeaning tasks exacted from new pledges, Ellison soon left the fraternity—expelled, as he recounts it, for having thrown one of the other "actives" off a third-floor fire escape in angry retaliation for a hazing incident.

Ellison didn't fare much better with other aspects of college life. He recalls a number of incidents which must have put a strain on his relationship with the university—being arrested and jailed for shoplifting a 45 rpm record, punching a professor, driving a car up the main sidewalk of the campus and onto the base of a commemorative statue. He did succeed in becoming a writer for the college humor magazine, the *Sundial*—an unusual achievement for a freshman—and two of the pieces he wrote are included in *The Essential Ellison*. One is a parody of Marlon Brando's tough-guy biker image from *The Wild One,* the other a parody of a gung-ho soldier who might well be modeled on Audie Murphy. Neither is particularly distinguished nor particularly funny, but both reflect the macho-guy-gets-his-comeuppance theme that would come to dominate much of the fiction that Ellison would later publish in crime-story magazines such as *Trapped.*

But the most significant event of Ellison's brief tenure at Ohio State—and the one which he believes was the most important single factor (along with a reported grade point average of .086) in his expulsion in January 1955—was his enrollment in a creative writing class. Even today, university creative writing classes are not known for their encouragement of writers who want to sell to commercial genre markets, and in 1954 one can only imagine the reaction of a writing teacher to the kind of stories Ellison would soon begin selling. Ellison's notion that he could get away with submitting one science fiction story after another, despite discouraging and in his words "vicious" comments from the professor, can only be described as evidence of naivete—not only in terms of the rather stultifying dynamics traditionally associated with college creative writing classes but also in terms of the attitudes of "mainstream" academics in general toward any sort of genre fiction in the 1950s. Ellison recalls a climactic confrontation with the professor in which, after hearing a diatribe about his lack of talent and skill, he replied, "Why don't you go fuck yourself" ("College Days" 212). That, according to Ellison, was the last straw that led to his expulsion from the university. Years later, perhaps as a way of helping to save younger science fiction writers from a similar fate, Ellison became one of the first and most frequent guest teachers at the Clarion Science Fiction Writing Workshops organized at Clarion State College in Pennsylvania and later elsewhere.

NEW YORK, 1955

While Ellison was suffering in his creative writing class, however, he was getting solid criticism on his stories from his friends in the science fiction world, particularly Algis Budrys. "Every shitty story I wrote during that period—1954–55—was sent to AJ, and every one of them received his special attention. The help was invaluable" (*Partners in Wonder* 283). Ellison also kept in touch with other friends—visiting Silverberg at Columbia University in December 1953, corresponding with Lester and Evelyn del Rey and others—all the while reporting that he was just on the verge of making his first sale. Returning to Cleveland after his expulsion, he continued publishing his fanzine *Dimensions* for another three months, but by now he was convinced that in order to write, he had to live where the action was. By April 1955, he was in New York, with little money and nowhere to live. He stayed for a while with the del Reys in Red Bank, New Jersey, and later with Algis Budrys on West 23rd Street. Finally, he moved into his own room on 114th Street, in a building near Columbia University where Silverberg was already living, and began a determined program to get something sold. Silverberg writes:

> The summer of 1955 was a long, hot, brutal one for Harlan. He didn't sell a thing. There was the famous time when he reported that he had a crime story "90% sold" to *Manhunt*—for so an editor of that once-celebrated magazine had told him. But the editors of *Manhunt* were pseudonymous myths, the stories were bought en bloc from Scott Meredith, and Harlan's story was in the mailbox, rejected, the next day. . . .
>
> So it went for him, one imaginary sale after another in a hellish summer of frustration and failure. That I was now selling stories at a nice clip did not improve Harlan's frame of mind, for our friendship always had a component of rivalry in it. When Randy Garrett came to town and moved into our building, he began collaborating not with Harlan the would-be writer, but with Silverberg, the successful new pro. The summer became a daze for Harlan. ("Jet-Propelled Birdbath" 25)

Ellison did continue to be published in fanzines during 1955, and had even sold a story script to an EC horror comic (*Weird Science-Fantasy,* June 1954), but the continuing elusiveness of professional fiction sales led him to some pretty strange behavior. Because of the similarity of the name with his own, he picked up a copy of a novel by Hal Ellson, one of the first successful writers to make a career out of the teen gang novel. Ellison had been struck by the threatening attitude of a gang he had seen shortly after arriving in New York, and now he decided that gang life could be an important—and saleable—focus for his writing. Disguising himself as a seventeen-year-old named Phil "Cheech" Beldone, he took the subway to Stuyvesant Street in the Red Hook section of Brooklyn and began what he describes as a weeks-long odyssey as an undercover gang member, returning only occasionally to the 114th Street apartment to check his mail and try to sell stories. The ploy very nearly gave Ellison his first sale: a cheap expose magazine called *Lowdown* paid him twenty-five dollars for a story called "I Ran with a Kid Gang!" and even took his picture for added authenticity. When the article appeared in August 1955, however, "Not one word of what I had written was in the piece. They ran my picture, and the art director had airbrushed a scar on my left cheek. I was still an unpublished writer" (*Essential Ellison* 28). Eventually, the Red Hook experience would provide Ellison with enough material for no fewer than four books, but when Harlan attended that year's world science fiction convention in Cleveland, he was still an amateur.

When things finally began to change, they changed dramatically. In April 1955, while still living with the del Reys, Ellison had written a story called "Glowworm" and sent it out to the usual round of rejections. Later in the year, Ellison offered it to his friend Larry Shaw, who had begun editing a new science fiction magazine called *Infinity*. Shaw bought it, and it appeared in the February 1956 issue (which actually appeared on the stands two days after Christmas 1955). Within a matter of months, Ellison was averaging better than a sale a week, and stories were seeing print at nearly the same rate: seven stories were out by the end of July 1956, another seven in August and September, fifteen from October through December. The magazines included not only science fiction titles (*If, Fantastic Universe, Amazing*) but also crime and mystery digests (*Manhunt, Trapped, Guilty*) and men's magazines *(Mr., Dude, Gent)*. When Ellison returned to the Worldcon in 1956 in New York, it was not as an arrogant young fan but as an arrogant young writer.

He was also married. He had wed Charlotte Stein on February 19, 1956, a union that would last four years. Of all the friends, relatives, and lovers who parade in endless anecdotes throughout Ellison's voluminous writing about himself and his life, Charlotte Ellison is one of the most invisible. He refers to the marriage as "four years of hell as sustained as the whine of a generator" (*Gentleman Junkie* 14) and alludes to an episode in 1959 when "My first wife had run off again, for the millionth time, taking with her the furniture, all my clothes, and every cent in the bank account" (*Hornbook* 91), but he never offers a clear account of what led to the marriage in the first place.

MILFORD AND THE MILITARY

More important than his marriage to Charlotte, and more important even than his growing stream of magazine sales, was his informal induction into the community of science fiction professionals at the first Milford Science Fiction Writers Conference in Pennsylvania during the week following the 1956 Worldcon. Over the years, science fiction writers and fans had organized endless "cons" and even made sporadic attempts to live together in clumps of various sizes; the legendary Futurian group, which began in New York in 1938, had group apartments called "Prime Base" or

"Futurian Embassy," and during World War II a group of fans in Battle Creek, Michigan, set about establishing a bizarre fannish utopian commune called "Slan Shack" (after the despised supermen of A. E. Van Vogt's novel *Slan*). But the Milford conference was one of the first purely professional conferences that grown-up science fiction writers had tried to organize among themselves, and that was defined by the participants' identity as writers, not as fans.

By the mid-1950s, Milford, Pennsylvania, had already become the home of a growing community of science fiction writers. James Blish and his wife had bought a house there in April 1953, Judith Merril moved nearby with her two children, and Damon Knight and his wife came along in 1955. Frederik Pohl and Cyril Kornbluth became occasional visitors. Knight and Merril organized the workshop and timed it to closely follow the Worldcon, so that writers could attend with minimal extra expense. Some thirty writers eventually showed up, including experienced "names" like Theodore Sturgeon, Anthony Boucher, Lester del Rey, Frederik Pohl, Katherine Maclean, Cyril Kornbluth, James Blish, and L. Sprague de Camp, and a few younger writers such as Ellison and Silverberg. "We were by far the youngest and most brash of the writers present," recalls Silverberg ("Harlan" 68), but the fact they were present at all is some evidence of their acceptance into the community of writers, not just of fans. Still Ellison felt badly treated. "I could do nothing right," he wrote. "They made me feel like two and a half pounds of dog meat" ("A Time for Daring" 103). Ellison began to feel an outsider among the science fiction writers he had so long admired and to think of himself as a different kind of writer altogether, one not defined by genres or markets. He would not return to Milford for another ten years.

Following the Milford debacle, Ellison began work on his first novel, *Web of the City,* completing an outline and enough text to begin shopping it around to paperback houses. He thought he had the novel sold to editor Walter Fultz of Lion Books, a small paperback house in New York that had published an early novel of Algis Budrys's in 1954 as well as early titles by Jim Thompson. An undated letter from Fultz—probably sent in February 1957—suggested a few changes (such as the advice that paperback buyers often made purchase decisions on the basis of opening paragraphs, which therefore should include both lively action and dialogue), and promised a forthcoming contract. In March, Ellison was drafted, and struggled to complete the book under the awkward circumstances of basic training at Fort Benning, Georgia. He had no way of knowing that Lion Books was already in trouble because of its dependence on the American News Company, a monolithic newspaper and magazine distributor which had held a near-monopoly on paperback sales until it fell victim to a 1952 antitrust suit. Over the next few years, one paperback publisher after another deserted American News, until it got out of the paperback business altogether. Those few small paperback houses that still depended on it, such as Lion, were out of luck. In 1957, probably only a short time after Ellison turned his completed manuscript in, the New American Library bought the Lion name and an inventory of unpublished titles, but Ellison's *Web of the City* was not among them.

The army, not too surprisingly, turned out to be even less of a congenial match for Ellison's temperament than Ohio State had been. He recalls that he was sent to the ten-week course of rigorous Ranger training at Fort Benning rather than the usual six weeks of basic at Fort Dix because he had slugged an officer on his first day at Dix's reception center, and that on another occasion he narrowly escaped court-martial by phoning his friend and fellow writer Joe R. Hensley, then a practicing attorney in Indiana. He did manage to find an assignment that permitted him to continue writing, however. Stationed at Fort Knox, Kentucky, he became Troop Information NCO in the Public Information Office, writing articles ("Armor School Celebrates 17th Birthday," "Girls Attend French Legion of Honor School") and book reviews for the weekly post newspaper, *Inside the Turret*. These reviews provide one of the few objective sources for gauging Ellison's reading during this period in his life. Ellison published as many as ten reviews in a single issue, sometimes apparently drawing upon books he had read before entering the Army, sometimes reviewing contemporary novels and nonfiction, sometimes reviewing genre paperbacks. As an example of Ellison's eclecticism, his review column in the issue of November 29, 1957, covers such titles as Wright Morris's *Field of Vision,* Ayn Rand's *The Fountainhead,* Rex Stout's *Before Midnight,* Robert Sheckley's *Pilgrimage to Earth,* and William Irish's *The Phantom Lady* (Irish was a pseudonym of Cornell Woolrich). Other columns would find Ellison revisiting such classic authors as Twain, Chekhov, Wells, Dostoyevsky, and Sinclair Lewis; examining nonfiction science books such as Darwin's *The Voyage of the Beagle* and George Gamow's *The Creation of the Universe;* and covering pop culture autobiographies like Billie Holiday's *Lady Sings the Blues.*

Opening a box of review copies from Pyramid Books in July 1958, he was astonished to find his name on a novel called *Rumble*. Somehow, Pyramid had apparently bought the manuscript—or possibly even a production state—of *Web of the City* from the defunct Lion Books and provided it with a new title. Ellison's undoubted pride in seeing his first book in print must have been mixed with considerable chagrin at the retitling; nothing resembling a gang "rumble" occurs anywhere in the novel. His first-novelist's thrill of self-recognition was also his first direct experience with the sometimes seedy realities of the paperback world.

Web of the City was far from the first work of fiction to be based on Ellison's experiences with the Brooklyn street gang in 1955. Since mid-1956, his gang stories had been appearing regularly in *Guilty, Manhunt, Trapped, Hunted, Murder,* and *Sure-Fire,* and he had sold Ace books a collection of eleven of these stories. *The Deadly Streets* appeared shortly after *Rumble,* and a year later was picked up by a London publisher, giving Ellison his first taste of international success (or at least international exposure). As a book author, Ellison was gaining a reputation as an author of "JD" stories, but by the time these books appeared, he had almost abandoned writing such fiction altogether. The army had put something of a cramp in his productivity, and the wildly eclectic mix of markets that he had appeared in during the preceding two years—everything from *Famous Western* to *Dude* to *Good Humor*—began to give way to a strong focus on the science fiction magazines; between May and December 1958, for example, fourteen of Ellison's nineteen magazine stories were in science fiction publications. Science fiction had become a kind of home base. It had given Ellison his first professional sales, his earliest reputation, his most solid circle of friends and fellow writers.

EVANSTON, *Rogue*, AND REGENCY BOOKS

This began to change rapidly upon his discharge from the army on April Fool's Day, 1959. Although most of Ellison's publications during his army stint had appeared in the science fiction magazines, much of what he was actually writing was submitted to *Rogue* magazine, to which he had been a fairly regular contributor since 1956. Now the magazine's publisher, William Hamling, invited him to Evanston, Illinois, to work as an editor. Hamling had been a science fiction fan since the 1930s, and had been an editor since 1947, first of *Fantastic Adventures* and later of *Imagination,* which was published by Hamling's own Greenleaf Publishing Company in Evanston. *Imagination* died in October 1958, however, and *Rogue,* which Hamling had started in 1956 in the wake of *Playboy*'s growing success in the "upscale" men's magazine market, became a flagship publication of the company. Since Hamling had been so involved with the science fiction world, many of his editors and columnists came from that world. Frank Robinson and Mack Reynolds were on the editorial staff along with Ellison, and contributors included Robert Bloch, Alfred Bester, William F. Nolan, and Damon Knight.

Ellison didn't find working for Hamling very congenial, though. Already separated from his wife Charlotte, unhappy in Evanston, he was clearly at loose ends:

> I was in rotten shape. I didn't drink or do dope, but I started trying to wreck myself in as many other ways as I could find. Endless parties, unfulfilling sexual liaisons with as many women as I could physically handle every day, dumb friendships with leaners and moochers and phones and emotional vampires, middle-class materialism that manifested itself in buying sprees that clogged my Dempster Street apartment with more accoutrements and sculpture and housewares than the goddam Furniture Mart could hold.
>   And I wasn't writing. (*Gentleman Junkie* 14)

Despite his unhappiness, Ellison is credited by Robinson as having been the creative spark that, for a time, turned *Rogue* into a legitimate competitor with *Playboy,* at least in terms of the quality of its writing. But Robinson also recognized Ellison's frustration and growing self-destructiveness. Witnessing a particularly uncontrolled tantrum at one of Ellison's many parties, Robinson encouraged him to get out of Chicago and resume his full-time career as a writer. Taking Robinson's advice, Ellison quit his job at *Rogue* and began working on *Spider Kiss,* a rock 'n' roll novel that Fawcett Gold Medal eventually published under the title *Rockabilly.*

In late summer of 1960, now divorced, Ellison returned to New York and almost immediately got into trouble over a typewriter. Some five years earlier, he had borrowed a portable typewriter from fellow science fiction fan Ted White (later a novelist and editor of *Fantastic* and *Amazing*) and in turn loaned it to another fan named Ken Beale, who pawned it and lost the ticket. Now Ellison met Beale again, at a party, and began to threaten him if he didn't at least pay up. Beale told a friend about the threat, and the friend's mother apparently thought the reasonable solution was to get Ellison arrested. On September 11, the police arrived at his apartment on Christopher Street, having received an anonymous tip that the apartment included a secret cache of narcotics and weapons. Ellison invited them to conduct a search, during which they turned up a revolver, a couple of knives, and some brass knuckles. Some were props from Ellison's days as an imitation JD; others had been given to him or used in occasional lectures on juvenile delinquency. Nevertheless, he was arrested for violating New York's Sullivan Act forbidding illegal possession of guns, and spent the night in New York's famous municipal jail, the Tombs.

Bailed out the next day by his mother, who had been visiting for the weekend, Ellison found himself already something of a cause célèbre. The doorman of his apartment building had told the newspapers of his arrest, and the Associated Press had put it on the September 12 wire. Although all the charges were dismissed by a grand jury on October 31, Ellison's reputation as a tough guy was cemented, at least throughout the science fiction community. More important, however, was the literary mileage Ellison eventually got out of the experience. He had already been writing for the *Village Voice,* and now Ted White suggested he do an article based on his experiences. Bill Hamling saw the article and asked Ellison to expand it into a book for his newly formed Regency Books line of paperbacks back in Evanston. Ellison decided to combine his account with an expanded, nonfiction version of his earlier experiences as "Cheech" Beldone, and *Memos from Purgatory* appeared the following year.

Even more important, Hamling wanted Ellison to return to Evanston to edit the whole Regency line. In November, Ellison married Billie Joyce Sanders and needed the steady income to support her and her thirteen-year-old son. So in 1961 Ellison was back in Evanston, establishing a line of then-expensive fifty-cent paperbacks with the rather unsubtle slogan "Regency Books Mean Controversy." And, indeed, the Regency list was filled with hot topics: incest, homosexuality, miscegenation, religious cults, drugs, overpopulation, corrupt cops, corrupt missile contractors, corrupt TV quiz shows. Robert Silverberg contributed a pseudonymous biography of the Marquis de Sade and what amounted to a book-length *Rogue* article titled *How to Spend Money, or The Complete Guide to Savoir-Faire and Enjoying the Most Good Living for Your Dollar without Losing the Chance to Make Lots More.* But in general, the line was hardly more sensational than many competing paperback houses, and Ellison made a genuine effort to bring talented authors into print, including Philip José Farmer (with his first non–science fiction novel), Robert Sheckley, Robert Bloch, Donald Honig, Clarence Cooper, Thomas N. Scortia, Lester del Rey, Algis Budrys, and his own onetime inspiration, Hal Ellson. He published the first collection of stories by B. Traven, as well as his own *Gentleman Junkie and Other Stories from the Hung-Up Generation.*

But he was miserable. He had already decided to divorce his second wife, and he became involved in an extramarital affair. Hollywood had bought rights to *Memos from Purgatory* and one of the stories in *Gentleman Junkie,* Algis Budrys had arrived from New York prepared to take over the editorship at Regency, and California seemed to hold out the promise of a renewed career—possibly even in film and television. In an attempt to raise the money for the move to California, Ellison took his family to New York in the winter of 1961, hoping to sell a collection of science fiction stories to Fawcett Gold Medal, who had published *Rockabilly* earlier that year. Knox Burger, the editor at Fawcett who had bought *Rockabilly,* told Ellison of the January 1962 issue of *Esquire,* which contained Dorothy Parker's glowing review of *Gentleman Junkie.* Ellison was dumbfounded. "I was no longer all alone in my opinion of my worth," he wrote in the introduction to a later edition of *Gentleman Junkie.* "I was no longer a writer ambivalently torn between the reality of being a commercial hack and the secret hope that he was something greater, something that might produce work to be read after the writer had been put down the hole" (*Gentleman Junkie* 20). Some months or years later, Ellison sought out Parker in California, where she again spoke highly of his work.

HOLLYWOOD

Fawcett didn't buy Ellison's proposal for a story collection, but Gerald Gross of Paperback Library did, and in January 1962 Ellison drove with his family to Los Angeles, almost getting killed in an accident in Fort Worth, Texas. By now he was already living apart from Billie and her son, but he had agreed to move them to California before the divorce. They moved into an apartment, and Ellison took a room on Wilshire Boulevard. He started trying to sell scripts by attending the open "cattle calls" that gave freelance writers a chance to view pilot episodes of new series. *Ellison Wonderland* came out in June and kept him afloat until he finally began to get assignments in television. Not counting an adaptation of one of his stories by Larry Marcus for *Route 66,* Ellison's first TV work was an episode of the syndicated United Artists series *Ripcord* in 1963. But in 1963, alerted by his agent to a cattle call on a new series produced by Aaron Spelling for Four Star Productions, Ellison made contact with producer/actor Richard Newton, who liked his irreverent attitude, and eventually with Spelling, who liked his first script. By the 1963–64 TV season, Ellison had become a regular scriptwriter for *Burke's Law,* a mystery series with the unlikely premise of Gene Barry as a millionaire Los Angeles police chief. The following season saw him contributing episodes to *Voyage to the Bottom of the Sea* and *Outer Limits* (one of which, "Soldier," led to his later settlement over the similarly plotted movie *The Terminator*). His own adaptation of *Memo from Purgatory* appeared on the *Alfred Hitchcock Hour* in December 1964, and by 1965 he was at work on his only "major" motion picture, *The Oscar,* although what he actually wrote for this is hard to see on screen, given the subsequent rewrites and editing of the film. Nevertheless, he had become a Hollywood writer, attending Hollywood parties and meeting Hollywood stars. The most famous such meeting, later documented in an article by Gay Talese for *Esquire* magazine, was a brief confrontation with Frank Sinatra in a Beverly Hills club in late 1965. Talese described Ellison as "a little guy, very quick of movement, who had a sharp profile, pale blue eyes, light brown hair, and squared eyeglasses. He wore a pair of brown corduroy slacks, a green shaggy-dog Shetland sweater, a tan suede jacket, and Game Warden boots, for which he had recently paid $60" (105). He was, in other words, the epitome of the youthful Hollywood cool of that era, and Sinatra, just approaching fifty and feeling irritable because of a cold, first approached Ellison to ask about the boots. He then complained about Ellison's general mode of dress, and finally, upon hearing Ellison had written *The Oscar,* began berating it as "a piece of crap" (106). Despite pleas from both his own companions and Sinatra's, Ellison would not back down, and the tale of this brief scene soon circulated throughout the club. As Talese notes, Sinatra probably forgot about it at once and Ellison would probably remember it all his life, which he has, but what small significance attaches to this episode is not merely the aging Sinatra objecting to the style of a newer generation, but Ellison—hardly a major Hollywood figure—steadfastly refusing to be intimidated in a situation in which he was clearly not the aggressor. The incident would barely register in Sinatra lore—and would be unknown altogether except for

Talese's "new journalism" account, which in 1966 was as famous for its style as for its subject—but it became a key element of Ellison's own emerging Hollywood lore.

In early 1966, Ellison was married and divorced a third time (to Lory Patrick, and for less than seven weeks), and he moved into the rambling house in Sherman Oaks where he has lived ever since. Ellison's magazine publications tapered off considerably during this time, but he had found a particularly attractive market in *Knight,* an oversized men's magazine with an unusual emphasis of text over pictures. Ellison covered the March 1965 march on Montgomery, Alabama, for *Knight,* and subsequently published several other essays there, along with his stories. The experience in Montgomery produced one of his most effective pieces of reportage and probably gave him his most direct firsthand experience of the social underbelly of society since his night in the Tombs in New York. Ellison had already written a number of remarkable stories on civil rights themes; now he was attacking such themes head on, without the mediation of fiction. He also was developing a growing interest in criticism; as a result of a rather weird bet with Aaron Spelling concerning whether or not Ellison could get himself into a very elite nightclub, he met the editor of *Cinema* magazine (whose uncle ran the nightclub), and agreed to write film reviews in exchange for a pass to the club. The July/August 1965 issue of *Cinema* thus saw the beginning of an extended film criticism career.

But other events of 1965 would draw Ellison back toward the world of science fiction. He sold his collection *Paingod* to Pyramid Books for a $1,750 advance—small potatoes, by Hollywood standards, but money that he sorely needed at the time—and won his first Writers Guild Award for "Demon with a Glass Hand," a science fiction script for *The Outer Limits.* And he returned to Milford, determined to impress the crowd he felt had belittled him a decade earlier. In the intervening years, Milford had become the premier peer workshop for science fiction professionals. Submitted stories were read by all participants and discussed openly and mercilessly. Ellison recalls arriving without a story, but writing "'Repent, Harlequin!' Said the Ticktockman" in his hotel room and submitting it that night. Half the participants, he says, hated it—including Damon Knight and his wife, Kate Wilhelm—while others, including Keith Laumer and Frederik Pohl, thought it a masterpiece. Pohl bought the story for *Galaxy,* a leading science fiction magazine that Ellison had never before been able to crack, and it subsequently appeared in Terry Carr and

Donald Wollheim's *World's Best Science Fiction* annual and won both the Hugo Award (from the World Science Fiction Convention) and the Nebula Award (from the Science Fiction Writers of America, an organization which *Knight* had founded as an outgrowth of the first Milford conferences). That fall, in Las Vegas and Los Angeles, Ellison wrote "Pretty Maggie Moneyeyes." The following year he would write "I Have No Mouth, and I Must Scream," which would win another Hugo Award. These stories and others seemed to represent to Ellison a new, mature voice, a way of taking advantage of the imaginative liberation science fiction and fantasy offered without conforming to the constraints of 1950s formulas and expectations.

THE "NEW WAVE"

Ellison now began to suspect that the liberating voice he had found for himself might be present in other writers as well, if only they had the needed encouragement. While editing at Regency, he'd tried to get an anthologist to assemble a collection of new science fiction stories that would mean controversy in the way that Regency Books meant controversy, but the project fell through. Now, in October 1965, a conversation with Norman Spinrad—a writer famously as outspoken as Ellison—led to a discussion of the problems with science fiction anthologies, and Spinrad suggested Ellison do one himself, reflecting the "new thing" in science fiction (or speculative fiction, as Ellison was beginning to call it). Robert Silverberg, who had begun assembling the first of a long list of anthologies of his own, had already suggested the same thing. Ellison called an editor at Doubleday, Lawrence Ashmead, and began pitching the idea of a massive new anthology of groundbreaking stories that would revolutionize the field.

Later genre historians would reasonably question whether the field really needed revolutionizing. Editors such as Frederik Pohl and Cele Goldsmith were already willing to buy stories that were experimental by the traditional standards of the field (Pohl's purchase of "'Repent, Harlequin!'" was itself evidence of this), and Michael Moorcock in England had taken over a magazine called *New Worlds* with a manifesto lionizing William Burroughs as the new model for science fiction writers and with a stable of highly innovative writers that included Brian Aldiss and J. G. Ballard. The 1965 Nebula awards recognized not only Ellison but Aldiss and Roger Zelazny as well—both with stories that would have had a hard time getting published only a few years earlier. The field had seen innovative novels by Philip K. Dick, Thomas M. Disch, Samuel R. Delany, and others; and outside the field, novels such as Kurt Vonnegut's *Cat's Cradle* (1963) and Anthony Burgess's *A Clockwork Orange* (1962) had won praise despite their manifestly science fictional content. Even though Ellison's bombastic introduction actually included the line "The millennium is at hand," it seems that the real purpose of *Dangerous Visions* was not to introduce a radically new kind of fiction so much as to launch an all-out assault on the last remaining barriers that separated science fiction from the mainstream—and in the process, possibly to give birth to a new American literary environment, one that would be more congenial to the kinds of stories that Ellison had now discovered he could write.

It didn't work. *Dangerous Visions* and its sequel, *Again, Dangerous Visions,* sold enormously well, became textbooks for college courses on science fiction, and helped generate more debate over purely literary questions than the field had ever seen before. But it also had the perverse effect of cementing Ellison into the science fiction world more than ever. The year after the book appeared, Ellison's first original hardcover collection of his own stories, *Love Ain't Nothing but Sex Misspelled,* appeared from Trident without a science fiction story in sight. Although the book was well received and was easily Ellison's best collection of his stories so far, its impact paled in comparison to the unprecedented clutch of awards heaped upon him at that year's World Science Fiction Convention in Oakland, California: Hugo for short story ("I Have No Mouth"), Hugo for dramatic presentation ("City on the Edge of Forever," an episode of *Star Trek*), special award for *Dangerous Visions*.

AFTER THE 1960s

Ellison continued to work occasionally in films and television (including a remarkably short-lived career of less than half a day at the Disney studio), but more and more of his time was being devoted to his lively and opinionated reviewing, for which he was developing an audience quite apart from his science fiction readers. His *Cinema* reviews ended in fall 1968, but he continued to review films for various other publications, and in October he began a weekly column of television commentary for the *Los Angeles Free Press* (later collected in *The Glass Teat* and *The Other Glass Teat*). He made brief forays into rock journalism, touring briefly with the Rolling

Stones in 1967 and Three Dog Night in 1970, and even began to write comic book scripts again in 1970 (*The Incredible Hulk, The Avengers*), for the first time in more than a quarter-century. In 1971, he quit TV writing (his last script was a *Young Lawyers* episode that aired March 10), but worked for a few weeks at the end of the year and the beginning of 1972 as a story editor for a misconceived ABC series about an investigator of occult phenomena, called *The Sixth Sense*.

Meanwhile, he continued to write—and win awards—for the particular style of impassioned, visionary fantasy that he had begun to make clearly his own. *Alone against Tomorrow,* a retrospective collection published in 1971, seemed almost designed as a farewell to the science fiction field, which he felt was a less and less appropriate venue for his work. He did write one genuine science fiction classic during this period, the novella "A Boy and His Dog," but most of his fiction was science fiction only by virtue of where it got published; the vast majority of his stories in the early 1970s appeared in the science fiction magazines and original anthologies that he had virtually abandoned back in the mid-1960s. Perhaps the *Dangerous Visions* anthologies, or the sea change of which they were a part, had had some effect on the publishing world after all. But whether that effect was to breach the boundaries of the ghetto or simply to enlarge their dimensions was a question that Ellison and other writers would grapple with for years to come.

For a writer trying to escape both television and science fiction, Ellison undertook about the most unlikely project he could have contrived in 1973: He became deeply involved in the development of an original, syndicated science fiction TV series. Titled *The Starlost,* the series was to be coproduced by Fox and the BBC, and Ellison was to provide the "bible" (describing the setting, situation, and parameters for scripts), prospectus, and a pilot script. Disaster followed upon disaster. The BBC wasn't interested in the series after all, and it was sold to a Canadian production company. A program outline and bible were circulated based on garbled versions of what Ellison had described in his initial interviews. The Writers Guild went on a strike which Ellison insisted on honoring until the Canadian Writers Guild approved the project, and they only approved it if Canadian writers—inexperienced in series TV—were hired. Production compromises made hash of the show's original premise and setting. Special effects designer Doug Trumbull and science adviser Ben Bova left in frustration. Ellison's own pilot script was never produced. And Ellison had his now-famous sarcastic pseudonym, "Cordwainer Bird," inserted in place of his own name on the credits. The final product was genuinely painful to watch, and Ellison's only real consolation was winning another Writers Guild Award for the original, unproduced script for the pilot episode.

Ellison's fiction, meanwhile, was growing consistently more ambitious and complex, as though he were trying to locate the mythic core of the pop culture materials and social issues that had for so long undergirded his fiction and journalism. "The Whimper of Whipped Dogs," based on the famous Kitty Genovese murder of 1964, won him his first Edgar Award from the Mystery Writers of America in 1974, and more science fiction Hugos came for "The Deathbird" and "Adrift Just off the Islets of Langerhans: Latitude 38° 54'N, Longitude 77 00'13"W." These and other stories were collected in his most thematically consistent book, *Deathbird Stories,* in 1975.

In June 1976, Ellison was married a fourth time, to Lori Horowitz. In August, his mother, who had been living in Miami, suffered a stroke and heart attack, and she died October 8. In what amounted to a final confrontation with his family, Ellison delivered a moving, highly personal eulogy at her funeral. Scarcely more than a month later, his new wife left him, and they were divorced the following March.

By now, Ellison's love-hate relationship with the science fiction world was becoming widely known, as was his habit of combining increasingly serious-minded fiction with unrestrained showmanship. 1977 saw Ellison honored with a special issue of *The Magazine of Fantasy and Science Fiction* and recognized with the first academic chapbook on his work, George Slusser's *Unrepentant Harlequin* (followed less than a year later by a second book, Andrew Porter's more fan-oriented *Book of Ellison*). That April, he resigned from the Science Fiction Writers of America as the culmination of a series of disagreements and frustrations that had begun with a debate over the method of determining the Nebula Award for dramatic presentations. But it was during this same period that Ellison's reputation as a kind of literary performance artist reached its peak: Writing a story a day for a full week in the window of a bookstore in Los Angeles, writing other stories in bookstore windows in London and Boston, writing a story specifically for a radio reading, writing while sitting under a plastic tent in the lobby of the Hyatt Hotel in Phoenix while the Worldcon bustled around him, living out of a camper at that same convention as a protest to Arizona's having failed to ratify the Equal Rights Amendment.

Nor was Ellison's tempestuous affair with the TV world quite finished. As if he hadn't learned enough from his experience with *The Starlost,* he and Ben Bova had filed suit accusing ABC television of plagiarizing the premise of the series *Future Cop* (which ran between March and August 1977) from a 1970 story titled "Brillo," which the two authors had worked to develop into a TV movie for ABC in 1973. In April 1980, they won a settlement of $337,000. Nevertheless, Ellison plunged back into the world of network TV only four years later, when he took the position of creative consultant on CBS's revived version of *The Twilight Zone*. Ellison sold stories to the series, wrote scripts, and even did a little directing, and the program gave wide exposure to adaptations of some of his best stories, including "One Life, Furnished in Early Poverty," "Shatterday," and "Paladin of the Lost Hour" (for which he received his fourth Writers Guild Award). But less than a year later, in November 1985, he resigned in a flurry of publicity over the network's censorship of a script he had adapted from a Donald Westlake story, "Nackles," and turned into a strong antiracist polemic set during the Christmas season. The network's Standards and Practices Department apparently felt the holidays were no time to confront ugly social problems.

So Ellison gave up on television again. And tried again: by early 1987 he was busily working on a pilot for a series being developed by famed low-budget movie producer Roger Corman, to be titled *Cutter's World*. Again it went nowhere. This time Corman finally gave up trying to deal with the exigencies demanded by the medium. With a growing body of unproduced media work in his files, Ellison took the unusual step of publishing the scripts themselves: "Nackles" appeared in the February 1987 issue of *The Twilight Zone* magazine, and in November of that year a script based on Isaac Asimov's *I, Robot,* which Ellison had developed in the late 1970s, began appearing as a serial in *Isaac Asimov's Science Fiction Magazine.* An original screenplay which Ellison had written for producer Marvin Schwartz in 1972 and 1973 (and which had already been serialized in his "Harlan Ellison's Hornbook" column for the *Los Angeles Free Press*) was reprinted in a limited edition of *The Harlan Ellison Hornbook* in 1990. Ellison may now hold some sort of record for the number of commercially published yet unproduced screenplays.

MARRIAGE

On September 7, 1986, Ellison married Susan Toth, whom he had met the year before in Scotland, and for the first time the marriage took. Admiring but not sycophantic, opinionated but not overbearing, Susan seemed to bring to Ellison's domestic life a stability and focus he had perhaps never known before. No longer the enfant terrible of almost every venue he has worked in, Ellison began to appear less and less frequently at science fiction conventions (although he and Susan were guests of honor at the World Fantasy Convention in Tucson in 1991) and to spend more time in Ellison Wonderland, which was for once becoming more a home and less a hostel for homeless or visiting writers. With his once-astonishing productivity hampered by what was eventually diagnosed as chronic fatigue syndrome, he turned the focus of his fiction more inward, to the search for meaning in childhood ("Jeffty Is Five," "Adrift Just off the Islets of Langerhans"), to the search for his father ("The Avenger of Death"), to the search for love ("Grail"), to the deaths of his friends ("The Function of Dream Sleep"). He has also begun to experiment more openly with devices of magic realism, dream logic, and multiple points of view, in stories like "The Man Who Rowed Christopher Columbus Ashore." And in recent years he has started to focus on putting his past work in some kind of order, with huge volumes of criticism (*Harlan Ellison's Watching*) and commentary (*The Harlan Ellison Hornbook*, *An Edge in My Voice*), a giant omnibus overview of his career (*The Essential Ellison*), and an extensive program of hardcover reprints of his works—with corrected texts and some uncollected material—from White Wolf Publishing (*Edgeworks*). There is perhaps a note of anxiety in these large projects, a hunger for literary immortality or at least survival, summarized by the usually expansive Ellison in the one-line afterword to *The Essential Ellison*: "For a brief time I was here; and for a brief time I mattered" (1015).

2 | BREAKING INTO THE GHETTO

Ellison and the Fiction Markets of the 1950s

Just as dawn oozed up over the outline of the tatters that had been New York, he finished his work on the ship.

—"Glowworm"

NOT EVEN ELLISON'S most ardent admirers could get very far trying to defend the style—or even the syntax—of his first professional publication. The story was rejected by all of the major science fiction magazines of the time and by most of the minor ones as well. Ellison himself is fond of quoting the assessment of science fiction writer and critic James Blish that it was "the single worst story ever published in the field of science fiction" (quoted in *Essential Ellison* 29). If that were actually the case, the story would at least be a benchmark, but Blish is being far too generous to the competition. Yet, for all its appalling turns of phrase and inadvertent hilarities ("Now no one was left. No man. Just Seligman. And he glowed."), the story is in many ways pure Ellison. It not only anticipates the themes of alienation, betrayal, and entrapment that would come to be the hallmarks of his fiction; it also reveals a good deal about the popular fiction materials he inherited and how he was already trying to transform them into something more clearly his own.

"Glowworm" is almost a catalog of science fiction themes of the postwar era, and these themes in turn are almost a catalog of popular fears and anxieties during that same period. Its title character is Seligman, a soldier who has been biologically altered to be virtually invulnerable. Designed to be the perfect warrior, Seligman never gets a chance to test his new powers; instead, he finds himself alone on Earth after a nuclear war has killed everyone else—except those who had earlier escaped to distant planets. He decides that he should become a messenger for his dead world, seeking out those who had left earlier to tell them what became of Earth. After canni-balizing ruined spaceships to build one of his own, he blasts off (from Newark) and quickly discovers that his amateur welding won't hold the ship together. The walls of the spaceship promptly blow out, and Seligman discovers he no longer even needs air or heat. Even if he completes his journey in the fragmented spacecraft, he has become so alien that he can never be part of any human community.

Obviously, the plot of this piece isn't much more overwhelming than its style. But look at where it leads. First, there is the postnuclear wasteland, which had become a staple setting for science fiction tales in the years fol-lowing Hiroshima and which Ellison would revisit in some of his most powerful later stories (such as "A Boy and His Dog"). A prominent feature of this landscape is the industrial ruin of the Newark Spaceport—an image of an abandoned future that would haunt science fiction writers and illustrators up to and including J. G. Ballard, who was perhaps the first writer to exploit this image for its purely metaphoric power. Second, the idea of a biologically reconstructed supersoldier of tomorrow not only invokes the Frankenstein myth and echoes fears of rumored Nazi experi-ments during World War II (the story refers to "the myopic little men with their foreign accents and their clippings of skin from his buttocks and shoulders"), but also partakes of science fiction's long fascination with the superman theme. A similar "designer warrior" later became the central figure in Ellison's story "Soldier" (1957), which he adapted for television on *The Outer Limits* and which eventually provided the evidence that won him a settlement from the producers of *The Terminator* (1984), Holly-wood's own special effects–drenched version of the myth—videotapes of which now credit "the works of Harlan Ellison." (The film, by the way, also prominently features the blasted industrial landscapes we mentioned earlier.) Third, the last-man-on-Earth theme is another of the genre's most enduring fantasies, dating back at least to Mary Shelley's *Last Man* (1826); Ellison's added fillip that the last man discovers he is both grotesque and unable to die anticipates one of his best-known stories, "I Have No Mouth, and I Must Scream," which also takes place after a nuclear war has killed off the population. Fourth, the colonization of space was perhaps the cen-tral dogma of science fiction since the 1930s, and the idea that such colo-nization might provide an escape from a war-torn Earth—a combination of the nuclear war and space travel themes—was well on its way to becom-ing a consensus among science fiction writers; it remains very much alive today in such works as Joe Haldeman's *Worlds* trilogy and Octavia Butler's *Parable of the Sower* series. "Glowworm" may be no prize, but it fits easily into a number of dominant traditions and points up several important directions for Ellison's later fiction.

Equally prescient in terms of Ellison's later development is his central character, Seligman. Far from being one of the competent mechanic-heroes that were so prevalent in much of the science fiction of the time, Seligman is a victim rather than a master of science and engineering. Like Frankenstein's monster, he is a creation of experimental science who only gradually discovers his powers and who finds himself both hideous and alone. He is alienated, confused, and bitter at what has happened to him and what has happened to the world, and he can't even weld together a decent spaceship. His technological solution to his dilemma doesn't work, and he realizes that even if it had, it would not end his isolation. In short, the story is about a bleak character, in a bleak setting, whose attempts to do something about it only result in an even more bleak situation. "You can't win," Ellison said in a much later interview, referring not to this story but to a philosophical thread that runs through his more mature fiction. "You can't break even, and you can't get out of the fucking game" (Wolfe 1987).

THE COMPETENT MAN

Two years before "Glowworm" appeared, *Astounding Science Fiction* had generated quite a bit of controversy by publishing a story by Tom Godwin that has since come to be regarded as a kind of benchmark in science fiction's coming of age. "The Cold Equations" described the dilemma of a spaceship pilot, on a mission to deliver serum to a plague-stricken planet, who discovers a young girl stowaway whose extra weight will prevent the spaceship from reaching its destination. The pilot is competent and compassionate, but the "cold equations" of weight-to-fuel ratios dictate that the girl must be ejected. The story was supposed to be revolutionary because of its uncompromising illustration of the manner in which the universe is indifferent to human needs but rigorously adherent to principles of mathematics. (Its author, Godwin, had provided a traditionally contrived happy ending in the story's first draft, but editor John W. Campbell Jr. supposedly insisted on the present ending.) The heroic competence of the story's pilot-hero is never questioned, however; he tries every ingenious idea in the book, only to come up against the contrivances of Godwin's plotting at every turn. The girl dies because she fails to know enough about science to understand the risks involved in stowing away. It's tough, but it's her own fault. She simply lacks the competence to live in a technological environment in which survival is governed by the laws of physics. Despite its sentimentality, the story's dominant tone is one of stoic acceptance of the universal laws implied by the title.

Godwin's girl stowaway is literally a throwaway character, in more senses than one. The hero of the story is the problem, and in this case the problem wins. Ellison's first contribution to science fiction lies in bringing the plight of that girl, or characters like her, into the foreground—in populating his stories with losers, victims, innocents, even klutzes who can't weld their spaceships together properly. From the beginning, he showed very little interest in the heroic space captains, but the unforgiving universe is very much a part of his fiction. If Godwin's message was, in part, that the universe is uncaring and we have to be very careful in dealing with it, Ellison's revision of this message is that we characteristically aren't that careful, that we may not be as much a match for the universe as we think we are, that we are more likely to be imperfect—like the girl—than universally competent. In the words of science fiction writer Norman Spinrad, "It was Ellison, writing SF and contemporary 'gang' or 'street' fiction simultaneously, who did the most to bring the sensibility, style, rhythm, and characters of the demimonde of the street into the clean white middle-class worlds of 1950s SF" (*Science Fiction in the Real World* 110). This "demimonde," as Spinrad calls it, would later serve as a major source of the mise-en-scène of the "cyberpunk" worlds of William Gibson and other authors of the 1980s.

No writer had done more to promote science fiction's myth of the competent man than Robert A. Heinlein, an author who is almost never cited among Ellison's precursors or influences. Heinlein's hard-edged stories all point in the direction of "The Cold Equations" by portraying a mechanistic universe in which the engineer, by virtue of training and skill, is the natural master. "Very early in life when I read Robert Heinlein I got the thread that runs through his stories—the notion of the competent man," Ellison once told an interviewer. "I've always held that as my ideal. I've tried to be a very competent man" (Platt 166). But Ellison is missing the point. Heinlein's imaginary worlds, like those of Isaac Asimov and other writers of science fiction's "golden age" of the 1940s, seem deliberately constructed to reward the kinds of competence that science fiction readers thought they already possessed—technical facility, arcane knowledge, an understanding of scientific principles, above all problem-solving skill—and that too often go unrewarded in the messy worlds of schools, jobs, and social relationships. Classic science fiction often portrays a kind of techno-geek utopia, and Ellison was never able to fully buy into this world. From the very beginning, his fiction brought to the surface the underlying fears and anxieties of the readers' real world—loneliness, alienation, insecurity—and suggested that all the technological fixes of science fiction couldn't eliminate them.

"Invulnerable," a much more controlled story than "Glowworm," which appeared in *Super-Science Fiction* in April 1957, returns to the themes of invulnerability and immortality but with a much clearer focus on social relations. (Stephen King once described the story as "Superman and Krypto the Wonder Dog for thinking adults" [*Stalking* 8].) The narrator, Eric Limmler, has lived indestructibly for three hundred years, assuming identity after identity, avoiding emotional relationships, and hiding out from governments that would seek to exploit him. Alienated and lonely, he is able to take advantage of none of the benefits of his condition and sees himself as a freak and a pariah. When Limmler is persuaded by an attentive woman to participate in the first moon landing (in 1983), the mission appears successful until all the crew members except Limmler unaccountably drop dead after returning. Realizing that his invulnerability will now be regarded as a necessary prerequisite to space exploration, Limmler again sees the specter of exploitation and once again disappears into anonymity. A virtual superman, he is trapped rather than liberated by his invulnerability, and he notes with bitterness, in the story's closing line, that he is only invulnerable "from the outside." Like Selig, Limmler learns that spaceflight, far from liberating, is merely another trap. This theme occurred with regularity in Ellison's work of this period. Another story from *Super-Science Fiction,* "Psycho at Mid-Point" (December 1956), describes a crewman who goes mad during an extended spaceflight and murders his fellow crew members.

One suspects, though, that readers responded to these early stories more because of their passion than their ideological content; in a field dominated by the relatively cool, transparent style of stories like "The Cold Equations," Ellison's prose seemed angry, aggressive, and magnetic. To some extent, this freedom to write bitter, angry stories may have been encouraged (or perhaps merely tolerated) by the much-maligned editor of *Super-Science*

Fiction, W. W. Scott, who bought ten of Ellison's stories for that magazine during its eighteen-issue run from 1956 to 1959. (Robert Silverberg sold no less than thirty-six stories to the same magazine—averaging two per issue—bringing his and Ellison's combined total to well over a third of the 120 stories published during the magazine's life!) Scott knew and cared little about science fiction and probably was more comfortable with the two crime magazines he edited, *Trapped Detective Story Magazine* and *Guilty Detective Story Magazine,* which appeared in alternating months between 1956 and 1962. These magazines provided a market for much of Ellison's crime and JD fiction—nine of the stories in Ellison's 1958 story collection *The Deadly Streets* first appeared in them—and Scott apparently made little distinction between the tough, melodramatic tone of those stories and the similar tone of Ellison's science fiction. More important, it is likely that Scott was aware only in a very limited sense that there *were* any traditions of style or content in science fiction. He seemed to increasingly confuse print science fiction with movie science fiction, and by the end of *Super-Science Fiction*'s run, the magazine had settled upon the marketing device of a series of particularly cheesy "special monster issues" targeted more toward a teenage horror market than to the traditional science fiction reader. In short, Scott had found in Ellison a useful and prolific contributor who could do both crime and science fiction, and he didn't seem much interested in holding Ellison to anything resembling traditional standards of science fiction narratives, let alone the developing intellectual traditions of the genre.

THE KYBEN STORIES

But other editors did have clearer notions of what science fiction was supposed to be, and while this didn't really dampen Ellison's passion, it did help to move him in the direction of the more traditional tropes of the time. Ellison's second published story, "Life Hutch" (*If,* April 1956), for example, was his version of the ingenious-spaceman-solving-a-puzzle tale. Like "Glowworm," "Life Hutch" is a one-character story describing the plight of a wounded spaceman who finds refuge in a "life hutch," a kind of automated rescue station on a remote asteroid, only to be trapped by a faulty service robot that attempts to destroy anything that moves. After three days of terrified immobility, the spaceman realizes that by shining his flashlight beam on the electronic computer console that conceals the remote-controlled robot's brain, he can trick the robot into destroying its own command center. "Life Hutch" is a neat little science fiction puzzle story that could almost have been written by Isaac Asimov. The entrapment here is, as in much science fiction of the period, less an existential condition than a problem to test the protagonist's ingenuity. We expect the problem to be solved, and it is, because that is the formula inherited from stories in the Campbell tradition. Like too many puzzle stories, the plot of "Life Hutch" is more than a bit contrived—it wouldn't work unless the robot were conveniently a remote unit and unless the "brain" happened to be in the same room. But it nevertheless stumbles upon an interesting conundrum that would later occupy philosophers of mind such as Daniel Dennett and David Hawley Sanford, namely, is the "robot" located in the brain or in its remote-controlled body? Ellison's first computer story, like most of his later ones, show almost no real understanding of how computers work (though computers in general were still rare in science fiction in 1956), but suggests an intuitive knowledge of the issues that their presence raises—and perhaps more important, introduces a theme of entrapment that would later become almost endemic to Ellison's fiction, although increasingly less amenable to such easy fixes.

More significant in terms of Ellison's attempts to conform to science fiction conventions is the fact that "Life Hutch" is the first of what would come to be a series of "Kyben war" stories, about an ongoing intergalactic war between humans and a dimly understood race of aliens called the "Kyben." Ellison's only series of linked stories, the Kyben sequence is of interest more for what it reveals about Ellison's attempts to write "normal" science fiction than for consistency, or even coherence, of theme. The stories, Ellison later wrote, "are not, in truth, linked by anything except the background of The War." "It was convenient, when I first became a professional writer, to use such a device. But it was never intended as anything more potent than a framework. An Orient Express, on which Agatha Christie could locate a murder. An intergalactic Ship of Fools against which I could examine the human stories (and alien stories) that interested me" (*Night and the Enemy,* endpaper). But the stories interested Ellison enough that, long after the initial sequence was published in 1956 and 1957, he returned to this background in 1974 (with an undistinguished story called "Sleeping Dogs") and again in 1987, when he provided an overall framework for the series in a "graphic novel" adaptation of several of the stories entitled *Night and the Enemy.* The most recent Kyben story, "The Few, the Proud," appeared in his 1997 collection *Slippage.*

For a writer working in a highly competitive market, the series story has always been a means of developing reader loyalty, continuing sales, and a kind of brand-name identity. For the writer of science fiction short stories, it has been a kind of godsend, obviating the work of establishing a background milieu for each new tale, thus freeing up precious wordage for development of plot, character, or theme. Ellison was well aware of the reputations that authors such as Isaac Asimov and Ray Bradbury had developed through series of linked stories, and the idea of an ongoing galactic war with an alien race must have seemed particularly well suited for Ellison's emerging characteristic themes of violence and betrayal. It was also a theme particularly appropriate for a 1950s audience already steeped in cold war propaganda about a mysterious and powerful enemy with brutal imperialistic goals. But for some reason—most likely Ellison's own profound lack of interest in the idea of a continuing series—the Kyben stories never came together as anything more than a group of essentially unrelated stories with little in common other than the use of the name Kyben and the occasional description of the aliens as golden-skinned and tentacle-fingered. Only two stories actually devoted much attention to the war itself, and one of these, "Trojan Hearse" (*Infinity,* August 1956), is little more than a trick-ending short-short story. "Run for the Stars" (*Science Fiction Adventures,* June 1957) is thus the only real Kyben story to imply a larger scenario of ongoing galactic war. One of the longest stories Ellison had published, "Run for the Stars" has also proved to be one of Ellison's favorites from among his early stories. It was the lead story in his first science fiction collection, *A Touch of Infinity* (1960), was reprinted again in his 1969 collection *The Beast That Shouted Love at the Heart of the World,* was the lead story again in *Night and the Enemy,* and was reprinted as part of a Tor SF Double in 1991.

Like many of these early stories, "Run for the Stars"—described by Russell Letson when it was reissued in 1991 as "a violent, head-bashing, alien-zapping tale cast in an overwrought, neo-tough guy mode" (50)—is remarkable only when viewed in the context of the science fiction of the time. Again, the competent hero is replaced by a coward and a victim, and in fact none of the story's characters are in the least sympathetic. In the sixteenth year of the war with the Kyben, Benno Tallent, a dope addict and petty criminal on an outpost planet called Deald's World, is busy looting a food store when he is captured by retreating Earth forces, who decide to use him as a human time bomb to delay the Kyben conquest of the planet, thus giving them time to warn the Earth. They surgically implant a "sun bomb" in his abdomen and warn the advancing Kyben of his presence on the planet, hoping that the delay caused by the Kyben searching for him will give them the time they need. But Tallent proves more resourceful than they had expected. He survives several battles with the Kyben, losing a hand in the process, and then captures a Kyben doctor and forces him to remove the bomb and graft it onto his stump, where he can detonate it at will. He then takes over the Kyben fleet to create a renegade army of his own, with Earth as its first target.

The idea of a dope addict and looter as hero was unusual enough in the pages of *Science Fiction Adventures,* but the revenge motif—which would quickly become an Ellison trademark—effectively turned what might have been a conventional alien war story on its head. Tallent is dehumanized—literally turned into a bomb—not by a cruel enemy but by the even more cruel military establishment of his own people. His need for revenge motivates him not only to overcome his addiction to "dream-dust" but to become a skilled guerrilla fighter and finally a godlike leader with absolute power of life and death over his followers. Far from becoming the unlikely hero who saves Earth from its enemies, he becomes Earth's worst enemy himself. We never learn what becomes of Tallent's plans for revenge, but we get a bracing lesson in the power of the victim who becomes the victimizer.

The effects of victimization are also the theme of another Kyben story, "The Untouchable Adolescents" (*Super Science Fiction,* February 1957), but here the motivating response is not revenge but distrust. The adolescents of the title are an immature race of telepaths whose planet is about to be nearly destroyed by a series of volcanic eruptions. Scientists on board an orbiting Earth ship have discovered this and try to warn the inhabitants, who have become fearful of outsiders because of an earlier invasion by the Kyben. They reject offers of help and are unable to reestablish contact with the Earthmen when the destruction begins. Again, the topic is the effects of betrayal on the betrayed; again, the expected science fiction set-up of a world-saving scenario is reversed as the would-be rescuers are unable to win the trust of the natives and later unable to hear their telepathic cries for help.

But by far the most interesting of the Kyben stories takes place on the planet Kyba itself and has very little to do with the war against Earth. "The Crackpots" (*If,* June 1956) depicts a society of lunatics, descendants of those "unfit" individuals left behind eleven centuries earlier when the Kyben abandoned their home planet to set about conquering the galaxy. The main character, Themis, is a "Watcher," a low-level bureaucrat assigned to monitor and report on the odd behavior of Kyba's inhabitants, who regard the "normal" Kyben as "Stuffed-Shirts." Themis witnesses a series of bizarre and apparently pointless acts: A beggar demands a handout, then refuses the coin Themis offers and demands a lesser coin in Themis's pocket. An old woman rips out a sewer pipe that seems to have clear water running in one direction and sewage in the other. Another woman paints over the numbers written on the wall of a phone booth, only to write new numbers over the fresh paint. Invited by a young woman to a mysterious place called the Cave, Themis there meets the leaders of this lunatic society and learns that, in fact, the crackpots represent the intellectual and creative elite of Kyben society, that they had, in fact, expelled the bureaucrats rather than been abandoned centuries earlier, and that all the apparent random acts are coded messages of new discoveries and inventions, deliberately staged so that Watchers will report on them and analysts later interpret them. The story clearly looks forward to Ellison's more famous "'Repent, Harlequin!' Said the Ticktockman" (1965) in its view of social outsiders and oddballs as the creative force in an otherwise regimented conformist society—a view that must have set well with the young science fiction fans who read it at the time.

ELLISON WONDERLAND

By the end of the 1950s, Ellison had published enough stories in science fiction magazines alone to populate a number of short story collections, and his first science fiction book, a paperback Ace Double (two short books bound back-to-back, a popular marketing gimmick for Ace's westerns, crime stories, and science fiction), appeared in 1960, including his short novel *The Man with Nine Lives* and six stories under the title *A Touch of Infinity*. Pre-1960 stories also made up a substantial portion of his next two science fiction collections, *Ellison Wonderland* (1962; reprinted several times as *Earthman, Go Home*) and *Paingod and Other Delusions* (1965). Of these collections, *Ellison Wonderland* provides what is perhaps the most representative selection of Ellison's early science fiction, including sixteen stories, thirteen of which originally appeared between 1956 and 1958.[1] Looking at these stories together provides a much different perspective than looking at the Kyben war stories. Whereas the latter may have represented Ellison's halfhearted attempt to create a kind of space adventure franchise like many other SF writers, these other stories, like those discussed earlier, reveal a consistent pattern of difference, an implied reaction to and critique of the dominant science-fictional worldview of the time, as represented in stories like Godwin's "The Cold Equations."

Aliens, for example, almost never appear simply as monsters or adversaries, and often are portrayed as morally or technologically superior, bringing with them object lessons about human hubris. "The Sky Is Burning" (1958) begins with the spectacular flaming mass suicide of members of a vastly superior alien race who have traveled to our solar system, like lemmings, merely to burn up in the atmosphere of Earth and the other inner planets. When one of the aliens is asked why Earth's solar system was chosen, his simple response is that this is the dead-end of the universe—a response that is taken by the narrator and others to mean that humanity would never truly be welcome in such an advanced galactic society, and thus has no real future beyond Earth. The idea of the Unwanted thus expands to include the entire human race. "Mealtime" (1958)[2] and "Hadj" (1956) are on one level little more than comeuppance jokes: in the former, a crew and its spacecraft are swallowed whole by a strange planet that is one huge organism—and then vomited up, presumably as indigestible; in the latter, a wealthy industrialist is selected to return to the home planet of visiting superior aliens in hopes of gaining great technological secrets, but upon arriving is told to go to the servants' entrance.

"Commuter's Problem" (1957) begins as a version of the familiar science fiction trope that might be termed the "strange neighbors" tale, earlier examples of which include Henry Kuttner and C. L. Moore's classic "Vintage Season" (1946) and—perhaps more to the immediate point—Jack Finney's "Such Interesting Neighbors" (1951), both of which involve time travelers. Ellison's story takes off in a slightly different direction: A disillusioned suburban commuter named John Weiler—Ellison's version of the Organization Man—discovers a bizarre plant in the backyard of his strangely reclusive neighbor's house, then has his concerns somewhat alleviated by the neighbor's rather sketchy explanation of where he and his wife came from and why they keep to themselves. But Weiler later finds himself absent-mindedly following the neighbor onto his commuter train—which arrives not in the city but on a distant planet called Drexwill, for whose residents Earth is merely a distant suburb used to alleviate urban overcrowding. Bored and stressed by his unrewarding job, Weiler pleads to stay among the aliens and vows to find a useful role for himself. The notion that a self-described "man in the grey flannel suit" could grow so alienated from his job and family that he chooses to move to an alien planet that he discovers by random chance serves as a fairly bitter indictment of 1950s conformity and anticipates a much better known feminist treatment of a similar theme, James Tiptree Jr.'s "The Women Men Don't See" (1973), in which two women rendered invisible in male-dominated society are willing to cast their fate with a spaceship full of mysterious aliens rather than return to their unrewarding lives. But Ellison adds a final ironic twist, as we learn that the narrator is telling this story in order to be approved for a charge account on the new planet—a clear implication that he has traded one treadmill for another.

"The Wind beyond the Mountains" (1956; originally published as "Savage Wind") is an even more direct critique of the expansionist ethos that had become a virtual consensus among science fiction readers and writers of the 1940s and 1950s. Ellison begins the story from the viewpoint of an alien creature named Wummel, as he watches a spaceship descend into his peaceful forest environment. We are given enough glimpses of Wummel's society—references to the Book of the Ancestors, to telepathic communication, to a leader called The One—to understand that it is an ancient and stable culture which has long ago decided to forgo space travel because "home shall be where the heart is" (134). The viewpoint shifts to the crew of the spaceship, who are from Earth's "Mapping Command" and are under considerable pressure to make a significant discovery in order to prevent their appropriations from being cut. They eventually capture Wummel, whose telepathy enables him to understand that he will be the prize which saves the Command and enables humans to continue their restless exploring until they find "the last planet ever" (141). But Wummel dies when separated from his home planet. "We broke its heart," says the Captain (141), who during the last moments of Wummel's life connects with the alien's thoughts and experiences an epiphany: "Don't you see?" he angrily says to another crew member who is bemoaning the failure of the mission. "The Command, the mercantile guilds, Earth, the searching, the always hungering for more more more more" (141). Humanity has lost its roots, its sense of home, he suggests, and in the final moments, "It just pitied us."

The rather lame moral that seems to be at the center of this oddly moving tale—"Home is where the heart is"—disguises its highly critical view of what had become one of the central myths of science fiction: the notion of ever-expanding human hegemony, driven by the promise of accumulating capital and organized in quasi-military bureaucracies. In this mythos (which also provided the central premise of the *Star Trek* television series a decade later), aliens have no role other than as adversaries or potential resources (in the form of trade partners, military allies, or raw goods—one crew member looks at Wummel and wonders if he is edible). In the context of science fiction in 1956, Ellison has not only taken the unusual step of showing us ourselves from an alien point of view, but of suggesting that the whole myth of space exploration may be dehumanizing and deracinating. Humans are to be pitied for having, through their own ambitions, condemned themselves to an eternity without rest.

The stories in *Ellison Wonderland* are unusual not only for their critique of the accepted myths of science fiction but for their often unsympathetic mix of characters. We are told of one of the spacemen who gets eaten and regurgitated in "Mealtime," for example, that "He hated Negroes and Jews, Catholics and Orientals. He was uncomfortable in the presence of poor people, sick people, crippled people or hungry people" (95). Wilson Herber, the wealthy industrialist and statesman in "Hadj," keeps his managers bound to him by means of blackmail. The main characters in "Battlefield" (1958; originally published as "His First Day at War")—high-tech soldiers who commute into outer space daily to conduct an ongoing war—see nothing inconsistent about spending a pleasant Sunday afternoon with a friend and his family, then killing that same friend the following Monday because he is on the opposing side. Such characters commit the cardinal Ellison sin of lacking all conviction. Even wrongheaded passions, Ellison sometimes implies, are better than no passions at all.

Nowhere is this idea clearer than in "The Silver Corridor" (1956), a tale of a high-tech duel to the death between two intellectual adversaries that eerily anticipates the virtual reality scenarios and role-playing games of four decades later. Like Ellison's later, more famous story, "I Have No Mouth, and I Must Scream," "The Silver Corridor" concerns characters trapped in a computerized environment that transforms their fantasies into an illusory reality. Marmorth and Krane are fierce political enemies who agree to enter the Silver Corridor, a legalized dueling environment managed by a shadowy corporation, in order to fight it out over the unlikely issue of which of their rather vaguely defined "theorems" of government will be presented to a governing Council; Marmorth believes that Krane's theorem is a twisted corruption of his own, while Krane believes he has corrected seriously faulty assumptions in Marmorth's. The "duelsmaster" explains that the corridor creates illusions drawn from the minds and convictions of the opponents, that these illusions are substantial enough to result in real death or disfigurement, and that in every such duel so far, there has been only one survivor. As the two men battle their way through a series of environments that reads like a catalog of pulp science fiction clichés—a galactic throne room, a starship, the chamber of a giant spider—all the while shouting egregiously melodramatic dialogue at one another—they end up inside an active volcano, confronting a lizard-headed woman right out of a pulp Virgil Finlay illustration, who informs them that each is so completely trapped by his own ego that neither can win. "You are both egomaniacs," she chastises. "You could not possibly be convinced of the other's viewpoint. Not in a hundred million years. Any message dies between you. You are both too tightly ensnared in yourselves!" (61). The problem is solved—we think—as each is shamed into acknowledging the lizard-woman's point. But then, "the instant each considered the other's viewpoint—the illusion barriers shattered, of course, and the red-hot lava poured in on them, engulfing both men completely in a blistering inferno" (61).

This ending may not work, but what ending would in a story like this? Ellison describes it merely as "an adventure" (43), and for all its energy and inventiveness, it fits quite well into the pages of *Infinity*. The conflict is viewed unambiguously, and the combatants are hardly interesting at all (in one chess-playing sequence, the characters literally become black and white). The intensity of imagery and feeling, the relation of character to landscape that would later seem so compelling in "I Have No Mouth, and I Must Scream," are evident here only if one deliberately looks past the story that is for the story that might have been. The very conventions and exigencies of the form seem to work against the kind of moral complexity that Ellison is striving to achieve. As a result, the tale seems either morally confused or nihilistically cynical: two arrogant and unsympathetic figures finally learn the importance of compromise, the value of dialogue, and are instantly destroyed for it. If what they finally learn is the truth, asks critic George Edgar Slusser, "Is not this 'truth' monstrous in form because it is the ultimate lie, a cruel joke played on us by our universe?" (Slusser 33). Slusser ingeniously argues that the real point of the story is that duelling is folly and that the antagonists' fatal mistake was entering the Silver Corridor in the first place, thus permitting the interpretation that "the universe does allow for rational solutions, after all" (33). A less patient reader might argue that the ending is simply a facile irony, an expedient means of getting out of a story that has little to offer beyond its central conceit. But it is equally possible to view the tale as another of Ellison's implied critiques of a dominant science fiction ethos of his time: the notion that reason and dialogue will make you free. The story is so stripped of setting and background that it seems little more than a fable. We never learn why a society which so highly values political theory would legalize capital duels, or why the mysterious Council would be expected to accept a theory of government determined in such an arbitrary manner—or why it would sit still to listen to either of these maniacs in the first place. Each is a far cry from the hyperrationality of Hari Seldon, the "psychohistorian" whose socioeconomic formulas so accurately predict much of the future in Isaac Asimov's *Foundation* stories and who by the mid-1950s was easily the genre's archetypal political theorist. Each, in fact, is a fanatic, and Ellison suggests that fanatics are so thoroughly trapped by their illusions that recognition of the truth can only destroy them—that truth and reason, in fact, are value-free commodities when divorced from human character and action.

Most of the pre-1960 stories collected in *Ellison Wonderland* make for decidedly awkward reading today. Even those driven by compelling conceits, such as "The Wind beyond the Mountains," are marred by poor execution and gain interest largely because of the ways in which they reveal Ellison's emerging preoccupations and, perhaps more important, his efforts to subvert the accepted wisdom of pop science fiction from within its own parameters. A handful of stories in the collection, however, are not science fiction but fantasy, and it is interesting to note that these tales tend to be more relaxed and congenial in style than the more frenetic SF tales, even when their subject matter is thoroughly trivial. "Gnomebody" concerns a high school misfit who only wants to be the fastest runner in school and has his wish granted by a tree-spirit—who turns him into a centaur. "Rain, Rain, Go Away" is even sillier, with its premise of a meek drudge who comes to realize that he has always managed to stop rain by singing the old children's song "come again another day," but that "another day" has finally arrived, bringing with it a lifetime of delayed rainstorms. As with the science fiction stories, what lends these tales their greatest interest is their focus on the meek, almost invisible figures who seem to occupy the interstices of the world, the descendants of Melville's Bartleby who would come to play an increasingly important role in Ellison's fiction.

"Are You Listening?"

The best story in *Ellison Wonderland* (removed from later editions of the book, but included in other collections) focuses entirely on such a character and upon his growing invisibility, and is written with an understated confidence that is much more characteristic of the Ellison of the 1980s than of the 1950s. "Are You Listening" (1956; retitled "The Forces That Crush" for the collection but with the original title restored in later reprints) returns to the theme of entrapment which we have seen in stories such as "Commuter's Problem," "Life Hutch," and "The Silver Corridor," but the vision of entrapment here does not yield to ingenious science fictional solutions, and the tale itself is stripped of science fiction paraphernalia. Albert Winsocki, the narrator, awakes one morning to discover that he has literally ceased to be noticed by other people, or for that matter even by his wife's cat. His wife shouts for him to come down to breakfast, unaware that he is standing beside her; he is unable to hail a taxi and goes unnoticed when he fails to pay his fare on the bus; even his attempts at sexual harassment or physical violence go unnoticed by his victims. Eventually he comes across two other people who can see him but who are themselves in the same predicament. One of them, a former art history professor, explains:

> "There are forces in the world today, Mr. Winsocki, that are invisibly working to make us all carbon copies of one another. . . . You walk down the street and never see anyone's face, really. You sit faceless in a movie, or hidden from sight in a dreary living room watching television. When you pay bills, or car fare or talk to people, they see the job they're doing, but never you.
>
> "With some of us, this is carried even further. We are so unnoticeable about it—wallflowers, you might say—all through our lives, that when these forces that crush us into one mold work enough to get us where they want us, we just—poof!—disappear to all those around us. Do you understand?" (154)

This passage may be Ellison's first clear statement of what would become one of the most significant recurring themes in his fiction as well as his essays, journalism, and personal philosophy, and the story may be one of the most direct metaphorical expressions of this theme. It was originally reprinted under the title "The Forces That Crush," and that phrase, or some variation of it, later became a leitmotif of Ellison's prose: a washed-up actor in the 1968 story "The Resurgence of Miss Ankle-Strap Wedgie" is described as "a man familiar to the point of incest with the forces that crush and maim" (*Love Ain't Nothing* 159); the introduction to Ellison's 1971 retrospective collection *Alone against Tomorrow* speaks of the role of the artist in an alienating society that always "finds the strength to keep rolling, grinding, crushing" (2). The anonymous drudge, beaten into near invisibility by these forces of conformity and alienation, is the antinomy and foil to Ellison's passionate, anarchic Harlequin figures, and we will see this opposition played out in various ways throughout Ellison's later fiction, from "'Repent, Harlequin!' Said the Ticktockman" (1965) to "A Boy and His Dog" (1969) to "Shatterday" (1975) to "Jane Doe #112" (1990), where such figures are described as "shadows of lives unlived" (*Slippage* 231). The figure of Albert Winsocki—ironically given a name taken from a popular football cheerleading song—is the most haunting figure from this early period in Ellison's career, and he is the first fully realized expression of a defining Ellison archetype.

3 | SKETCHES OF THE DAMNED

JD and Rock Fiction

THE 1950s WAS A TIME famously marked by profound contradictions in American popular culture—the decade of Mamie Eisenhower, Mamie Van Doren, and Auntie Mame. It began with the publication of David Reisman's famous study of conformity and "other-directed" behavior, *The Lonely Crowd,* followed six years later by William H. Whyte's investigative critique of corporate "belongingness," *The Organization Man.* Popular fiction and film gave rise to a new genre of corporate melodramas such as Sloan Wilson's *Man in the Gray Flannel Suit* (1955; film, 1956), Cameron Hawley's *Executive Suite* (1953; film, 1954), and Rod Serling's *Patterns* (teleplay, 1955; film, 1956). On television, the innocent comedy and variety shows during the first half of the decade, led by *I Love Lucy,* were undercut by the working-class anger of *The Honeymooners,* while popular music featured the witless ballads of Patti Page on the one hand and the unruly rise of rock 'n' roll and rhythm and blues on the other. Norman Vincent Peale's *Power of Positive Thinking* (1952) remained an enormous best-seller for much of the decade, but Alfred Kinsey's dense reports on the sexuality of men and women (published in 1948 and 1953, respectively) remained among the most persistently discussed books. In literature, the decade saw the twilight of the careers of Hemingway and Faulkner and the growing reputations of Saul Bellow, Norman Mailer, J. D. Salinger, Bernard Malamud, John Barth, and many others. But the most visible and controversial literary and cultural movement of the decade set itself firmly in opposition to the middle-class values of corporate suburban America; the Beat

Movement, which had been coalescing since before the end of World War II, suddenly erupted into public awareness in 1956 with the publication of Jack Kerouac's *On the Road* and Allen Ginsberg's *Howl and Other Poems*. And along with the corporate novels mentioned above, the fiction best-seller lists were dominated by writers like Frank Yerby, Taylor Caldwell, Erle Stanley Gardner, Grace Metalious, and Mickey Spillane—who at one point could claim that seven of the ten best-selling novels in American history were Mike Hammer mysteries (Nye 54)!

Spillane's crude, simplistic epics of sex and violence, beginning with *I, the Jury* in 1947 (which was originally intended as a comic book), seemed drastically at odds with a society that spent its Wednesday nights watching *Father Knows Best*. But, in fact, they merely represented the popular exploitation of a much darker vision of America that evolved in the pages of paperback novels, digest-sized crime magazines, and *film noir* movies pioneered by émigré European directors. While mainstream best-seller readers were being shocked at the scandals of small-town life in novels like Grace Metalious's *Peyton Place,* paperback readers were growing accustomed to the sociopathic protagonists and drifters of Jim Thompson (who published five novels in 1954 alone), Charles Willeford, Gil Brewer, Wade Miller, the early John D. MacDonald, and even William Burroughs, whose first book, *Junkie,* appeared as half of an Ace Double paperback in 1953. While *Saturday Evening Post* readers were enjoying the whimsical adventures of a tractor salesman, readers of *Manhunt* were discovering the bleak crime stories—often not mysteries at all—of authors ranging from Nelson Algren and James M. Cain to Donald Hamilton and Richard S. Prather. And in the minor magazines that aspired to *Manhunt's* success, the fiction was still tougher, cruder, and seedier. Sometimes retroactively labeled *noir* fiction, these crime stories and novels collectively came to represent an alternative vision of an America steeped in violence and betrayal, an America somewhere on the other side of even the hard-boiled novels of Chandler and Hammett.

This subterranean literature also developed its own genres, some of which were inherited from the pulp magazines (science fiction, westerns, hard-boiled crime stories), some of which emerged in the wake of a single best-selling author who established a viable market. Such "instant genres" included the rural "white trash" novels in the wake of Erskine Caldwell's enormous best-seller, *God's Little Acre* (1933), the blustery, violent historical novels that followed the success of Edison Marshall and Henry Treece, and later the parade of sexy espionage novels and films that followed the success of Ian Fleming's James Bond series and its endorsement by John F. Kennedy. But of all these genres, the one which may have most clearly reflected the paradoxes of the time—and which is virtually forgotten today—is what came to be known as "JD" or "juvie" fiction, sensational and quasi-documentary portraits of juvenile delinquents and their urban gangs, which had increasingly become a focus of concern for journalists and policymakers during and after the war years.

The theme of youth gone wrong had long been a favorite one in American literature, and it gained particular attention during the Depression with the publication of James T. Farrell's *Studs Lonigan* trilogy (1932–35) and Nelson Algren's *Somebody in Boots* (1935), followed by *Never Come Morning* (1941). But the novel which most clearly established the market for paperback JD fiction was Irving Shulman's *The Amboy Dukes,* a tale of a loosely organized gang in the Brownsville section of Brooklyn, whose criminal activities are vaguely ascribed to Depression-related poverty and lack of parental supervision while adults worked in defense plants during the war. Published in 1947, *The Amboy Dukes* sold nearly four million copies over the next several years and was the basis for the 1949 film *City across the River,* notable now chiefly for the appearance of a very young Tony Curtis. Also published in 1949 was *Duke,* a story of a Harlem gang leader, which was the first of Hal Ellson's weakly plotted but sociologically astute series of novels that would gain him a reputation as the leading paperback JD novelist throughout most of the 1950s. Popular Library reprinted *Duke* in 1950, 1956, and 1959, and the novel eventually sold well over a million and a half copies. Ellson's second novel, *Tomboy,* about a girl gang member, appeared in 1950, followed by *The Golden Spike* in 1952 and fifteen more novels by the early 1960s. It was Ellson whose similar name seen on a paperback helped inspire Harlan Ellison to explore the booming field of JD fiction and journalism.

By 1952, juvenile delinquency had become enough of a national issue to prompt congressional hearings. The notorious Gathings committee, famous for its attack on the colorfully violent horror comics then being published by William M. Gaines (later founder of *Mad* magazine), also heard testimony to the effect that *The Amboy Dukes* may have contributed to the delinquency problem by glamorizing gang violence. (This eagerness to hang the messenger was nothing new; Algren's *Never Come Morning,* which portrayed the street life of Chicago's Polish slums, was even decried as anti-Polish Nazi propaganda during World War II!) Prompted in part by the publicity attendant on the Gathings committee hearings, popular magazines began to devote more and more space to "the problem"; the *Reader's Guide to Periodical Literature* recorded an average of eighteen articles per year on the subject from 1950 to 1952, but seventy-two articles per year from 1953 to 1955. The genre's next major best-seller, Evan Hunter's *Blackboard Jungle,* appeared in 1954 and was filmed in 1955—the year that also saw James Dean in *Rebel without a Cause,* which remains the iconic film of youthful disillusion during this period. Prompted by the success of these and other films (such as Marlon Brando's 1954 *The Wild One*), Hollywood adopted the JD genre as a staple of low-budget films, often with paperback tie-ins, with titles like *Juvenile Jungle* (1958) and *Cry Baby Killer* (1957, produced by Roger Corman and starring a very young Jack Nicholson). By 1957, the fascination with youth gangs had percolated all the way up to Broadway, with the Leonard Bernstein/Stephen Sondheim musical *West Side Story.*

The juvenile delinquent had by now become not just a social problem but a minor American myth. As Geoffrey O'Brien writes,

> "These kids" had taken on a life of their own. The writers were not shaping them; they were being shaped by them. The kids had entered another realm, were now mythological creatures exercising a power that no sociological analysis could cope with. . . .
>
> Those actual gray lives had been magically transformed into glamorous pulsating ritual presences, presences that seemed effortlessly to capture the stray energies of the society. They radiated sex, fear, and power, amid trancelike patterns of rhythm and group formation. (132–33)

In other words, the figure of the juvenile delinquent had become enough of a hard-boiled icon that the editors of crime magazines saw no problem in including JD fiction in their pages, along with the usual tales of small-time hoods, gangsters, tough cops, and tougher private eyes.

Only months after Ellison's first science fiction stories appeared, he was already in the pages of *Guilty* with a story called "I Never Squealed!" (later reprinted under the much more delightful title "Johnny Slice's Stoolie"). Like most of Ellison's gang fiction (later collected in *The Deadly Streets* [1958] and *The Juvies* [1961]), this brief account of a gang member falsely accused of ratting to the cops is less important for its plot and structure than for the violent, half-mythical street world it implies. Far more than his Kyben war science fiction stories, Ellison's gang stories constitute a nearly coherent series, portraying a consistent, if lurid, vision of the Brooklyn neighborhood where he had lived briefly in 1954. Characters with names like Johnny Slice or Sharkmouth or Vode and gangs with names like the Jolly Stompers or the Strikers reappear from story to story, talking like B-movie versions of Budd Schulberg punks: "It wasn't me was a stoolie. . . . I was a good member. I never ratted. . . . That Dumb Chollie, boy, did he screw himself up" ("Johnny Slice's Stoolie," *Deadly Streets* 88). Girls are called debs or drags; cops are bulls or harness boys. Everyone wears black leather jackets and "stomping boots" and carries a switchblade, except when they are attending one of the anomalously middle-class dances sponsored by the gangs, when they switch to sports jackets and narrow ties. Gang headquarters occupy the back rooms of pool halls or bowling alleys, where the inevitably overweight proprietor has been terrorized into giving up the space for free. Family life is universally a mess, with helpless but worried old-world mothers and fathers who, if they haven't deserted the family altogether, are apt to be weaklings, alcoholics, or drug addicts.

The weak or absent father had been a likely suspect in both fictional and sociological analyses of juvenile delinquency for decades. The unemployment and poverty of the Depression had been followed by the war, which drew many fathers away from their families, and the postwar years had seen a return to problems of unemployment or underemployment in the inner cities, not to mention shifting demographics. Ellison seemed to focus on this figure with particular consistency. "Home was nothing," thinks Petey in "Kid Killer" (1957). "Just an old, yielding man, a tired man, who was too weak even to slap his son when he'd done something wrong" (*Deadly Streets* 112). Chickie, the female narrator of "Made in Heaven" (1956), describes her father "layin' on the couch, all dirty T-shirt and scrubby beard and sweat-stink. I couldn't see how my old lady could take him" (*Deadly Streets* 179). The narrator of "The Dead Shot" (1957) recalls how his father "got his in a bar about three years ago, and they smashed open his skull with a chair leg," but adds, "I don't miss him, honest" (*Deadly Streets* 165). In *Web of the City,* Rusty Santoro's father is a vagrant wino and dope addict who is never home and who even fails to come to Rusty's aid when he sees him being beaten by gang members. Virtually the only strong father figure to appear in these stories is a police captain in "Look Me in the Eye, Boy!" (1957) whose son is involved in gang violence and who refuses to intervene on his behalf. One can't help but wonder if Ellison's loss of his own father at the age of fifteen didn't preoccupy him during this period; certainly the theme of the search for a father would reemerge as a central concern in his later fiction.

Web of the City (first published as *Rumble* by Pyramid Books in 1958) was Ellison's first novel, written during April and May 1957 while he was still in the army, and it would prove to be his most ambitious fictional treatment of the JD theme. In the story of Rusty Santoro, a third-generation Puerto Rican who is attempting to disentangle himself from his gang, Ellison is reaching for a dimension of tragedy that his short stories on the topic would not permit, while at the same time maintaining the rhythm of swift, punchy action that the post-pulp market demanded. Set during a two-week period in the summer of 1957 in Brooklyn, the novel opens with Rusty receiving a brutal beating at the hands of the Cougars, a gang that the had led until his abrupt resignation two months earlier. The theme of the dysfunctional family is introduced almost immediately: After police disperse the gang members, Rusty crawls into an alley to nurse his wounds and discovers his alcoholic father, who has lain there in a stupor as the fight took place. Rusty's only trusted authority figure is a concerned woodworking teacher named Carl Pancoast, into whose custody he had been released after being caught trying to break into a liquor store. Pancoast believes Rusty has enough talent to become an industrial designer, promises to help him if he will quit the gang, and even rescues him from an assault at school the next morning when the gang's new leader, Candle, attempts to knife him in class. Even Rusty's girlfriend, Louise, is torn between her loyalty to him and her fear of separating from the gang, especially after she sees him attacked again in the local ice cream shop after school and challenged to a duel by Candle.

In the novel's first two brief chapters, then, Rusty is nearly stomped to death, assaulted with a switchblade, and slugged in the ice cream shop—all the while brooding over his fate in a series of self-pitying asides that vitiate the impact of the violence by very nearly turning it into parody. "You can't get free," he thinks after his first beating. "Once stained, always stained. The seeds of dirt are sown deeply. And are harvested forever" (8). After the incident in the ice cream parlor, he muses, "Why was his past always calling? Always making grabs on him? The blood was flowing so thick, so red, and it smothered him. He felt as though he was drowning. . . . Wouldn't he ever be free?" (27). Later in the novel, these melodramatic interpolations grow increasingly ridiculous. After a violent argument with his sister, Rusty entertains the rather unlikely thought that "perhaps dinner would kill the animosity, the fury, the hatred boiling in the house. But he knew it wouldn't" (65). Whenever Rusty faces a difficult or threatening task, his thought is "It was gonna be tough as banana peels" (50). And in what is perhaps the book's most surrealistic mixing of metaphors, "The blood that filled the manholes to the tops came from sick minds and fast action" (143–44). Intrusive, breathless narration mars the entire novel and makes it difficult for the contemporary reader to view it as much more than the journeyman work of an impassioned writer trying to learn his craft. Even by the standards of the JD fiction of the time, the style is overblown; Hal Ellson's style, by contrast, is characterized by short declarative sentences with a minimum of affect (although Ellson, too, was prone to preface his novels with high-minded commentary on the kids as victims of a failing society).

These stylistic problems are doubly unfortunate because *Web of the City* is not really badly plotted, and it is far better structured than Ellison's other longer works of this period. (His science fiction "novel" *The Man with Nine Lives,* published only two years later, is by contrast a crude "fix-up" based on two earlier published short stories.) As Rusty prepares for his fight with Candle, he argues with his mother, goes to a dance where he gets into another fight and briefly gets high on marijuana, and has another argument at home, this time with his younger sister, Dolores, whom he had gotten involved with the Cougars' girls' auxiliary and whom he now wants to extricate from the gang. Rusty's guilt-ridden protectiveness toward his sister becomes his central motivation in the novel, and Ellison makes it seem believable in this early scene.

The centerpiece of the novel's fourth chapter is a detailed account of the ritualized knife fight between Rusty and Candle, who must fight separated only by the length of a handkerchief, which each combatant holds by a corner between his teeth. Rusty gains the advantage by forcing Candle to release the handkerchief, but refuses to go in for the kill, thus satisfying his need to maintain honor without committing further violence. Dolores congratulates Rusty, but this leads to another confrontation over her involvement with the gang, and she storms out to attend a dance at the gang's headquarters behind a bowling alley. Rusty, however, knows that a rival gang plans to raid the dance, and sets out to find her. She has already left when he arrives, but Rusty is caught in the rumble and packed off in a paddy wagon when the police break it up. After spending the night in jail, Rusty is released into Pancoast's custody again, only to learn that during the night Dolores has been raped, stabbed to death, and left in an alley under a pile of garbage.

The second half of the novel becomes a kind of detective story as Rusty, accused by his mother of being responsible for Dolores's death, vows to find and kill the murderer, even though he knows this will return him to the cycle of violence. He talks briefly with Pancoast, who warns, "Be good, son. They'll find the bastard" (110). He later catches sight of his father slouched drunkenly in a doorway, and finally walks all the way downtown to "the cesspool of Forty-second Street between Seventh and Eighth Avenues" (111), where he rebuffs an advance from a fat homosexual, then goes to an arcade, where he imagines all the targets in a shooting gallery to be figures from his past. At a Jayne Mansfield movie, he picks up a girl with whom he spends a desultory night of sex in a cheap hotel, returning home the next day to find his mother collapsed from grief and in the care of neighbor ladies. He begins his investigation by invading a meeting of the Cougars, where he is nearly killed before a huge, slow-witted gang member called the Beast rescues him and tells him that Dolores left the party with a man in a camel's hair coat. Knowing this could not be a Cougar, Rusty enters the turf of the rival Cherokee gang and learns that drugs are somehow involved in Dolores's murder. Back home, he meets a teacher from school who asks him to give up his investigation.

This central section is one of the novel's strongest, in its kaleidoscopic portrayal of a tougher, more desperate, but far less introspective Holden Caulfield moving randomly through a seedy vision of New York City in the mid-1950s. But the sense of Rusty's alienation is mitigated by his essentially middle-class sensibility, which on occasion gives the novel an almost comic sense of dislocation; for example, after being beaten up three times, participating in a rumble, spending one night in an alley and another in jail and a third in a seedy hotel, learning of his sister's murder, witnessing his mother's collapse, being threatened with murder, and beating up a rival gang's functionary—all in one weekend—"Rusty realized he had missed the entire day of school" (154).

Rusty receives additional warnings from the owner of the ice cream shop and from his father, who almost never speaks to him. Realizing that the only possible connection between the rival gangs, the teacher, and his father is their dependence on drugs, he abducts the pusher for the Cougars, Boy-O, and through beatings and withholding drugs forces him to reveal his supplier, a wealthy drug dealer living on Central Park West. The dealer is indeed the man in the camel's hair coat, but he denies being involved in Dolores's murder and instead describes an independent drug dealer working out of Rusty's neighborhood who is the more likely suspect. Rusty recognizes this as the Beast, who had only feigned slow-wittedness and who had rescued Rusty from the Cougars in the hope that he would successfully find and kill his competitor in the drug trade. With a false fire alarm, Rusty flushes the Beast into the street and lures him to the roof of his building, where a violent, eye-gouging struggle leads to the Beast's death. Some days later, Rusty decides to leave his neighborhood and the city behind, knowing that he will not really escape. "He had come from these streets, and he would someday go back to these streets, for he was umbilically joined to them and the rottenness they spawned" (214–15).

Ellison clearly does not hold out much hope for Rusty, whose vague and inarticulate yearning for "decency" seems to produce little in the way of concrete plans. But in his odd mixture of innocence, idealism, and violence, Rusty Santoro is Ellison's first successfully sustained character and his first successful portrayal of the trapped idealist, just a bit given to whining, who would come to occupy so many of his later stories—and later self-portraits. Other characters tend to be archetypes of the JD genre, straight from central casting: the useless, abusive father; the powerless but well-meaning mother; the girlfriend who is "weak and watery and scared and only doing her best by living the rules as they'd been put to her" (60); the pathological bully gang leader Candle; the caring teacher who finally simply doesn't understand; the animal-like Beast; the courtly but vicious drug kingpin Morlan. The city, which Ellison seems to hope will take on a life of its own as the real protagonist of the novel, only really comes alive in the brief central section after Rusty has learned of Dolores's murder. It wouldn't be until 1973, with "The Whimper of Whipped Dogs," that Ellison would be able to fully capture the violent urban environment of New York as a kind of consuming myth, but by then he had learned how to meld his journalistic eye for detail with his dark fantasy vision—which in 1958 was not yet fully formed.

If Ellison's characters often talk in a kind of Hollywood version of street language, Ellison himself sometimes lapses into a homiletic Pat O'Brien mode when writing about them: "All they need is a chance—a square chance," he wrote in the 1958 introduction to *The Deadly Streets*. "Nobody's asking for charity; dammit, all they need are a few breaks, and they'll come through" (20). Unfortunately, this tone pervades Ellison's nonfiction treatment of gang life in *Memos from Purgatory* (1961), his account of his own experiences as an undercover gang member in Brooklyn in the summer of 1954. "It sounds trite," Ellison acknowledges in the 1975 prologue to *Memos,* "—Father Flanagan and all that—but these were kids who merely needed a break, a chance, an escape. . . . They were the children of the gutters, born into a life with no doors, no windows. . . . They were the lost, not the guilty" (23). As if this were not enough, *Memo* is also the first of Ellison's books to introduce the annoying habit of instructing the reader on how to read: "Every time you read the word 'I' there must be the identification of yourself as narrator, walking through the stinking streets of Brooklyn, or clattering down the corridors of a gray, thankless prison" (25). If Ellison's model for his JD fiction was Hal Ellson and other paperback writers, his model here—and for much of his nonfiction—might as well be Walt Whitman. "What I assume you shall assume," he seems to be telling us. Or, in another passage from Whitman which was a favorite of Nelson Algren's (and was used as the epigraph for *Never Come Morning*):

> I feel I am of them
> I belong to those convicts and prostitutes myself
> And henceforth I will not deny them
> For how can I deny myself?

This kind of proclamation of selfhood is everywhere in evidence in *Memos from Purgatory,* and it comes to dominate the second half of the book to an almost embarrassing extent. *Memos* is divided into two parts, the first being an account of Ellison's several weeks as a member of a gang he calls "The Barons" disguised as Phil "Cheech" Beldone, the second an extended account of a night he spent in jail seven years later, when he met one of his former gang colleagues and learned something of the fates of the various other Barons. Lacking the discipline imposed by the demands of character development and plotting, the book nevertheless bears striking similarities to *Web of the City,* most notably in a knife fight sequence that at times is borrowed almost word for word from the earlier novel. As in *Web of the City,* the gang member who picks a fight is named Candle, only now it is

Ellison himself who is challenged. Here is how part of the knife fight is described in *Web of the City:*

> The ground was worn into a rough circle as they went tail-around-head past each other. The gang fanned out and watched, making certain an idle sweep of the blades could not touch them. The two boys bent forward from the shoulders, putting their bellies as far back as possible, for that was the direction in which trouble lay.
>
> Feet widely spread, they stopped every few seconds, swinging, making certain they did not throw themselves off-balance.
>
> Grunts and explosions of sweat marked their circular passage and soon Rusty felt his arms getting weak. (56)

Here is the parallel passage from *Memos from Purgatory:*

> Pretty quick the ground was worn into a dark brown rough circle as we went tail-around-head past each other. The Barons and their Debs fanned out, watching, making sure that a wild swing could not touch them. We bent forward from the shoulders, putting our bellies as far back as possible.
>
> We stopped every half-circle, our feet wide apart, swinging for an opening, fencing for a thrust, making certain we didn't throw ourselves off-balance.
>
> I could hear Candle grunting, and my own explosions of sweat only made me more aware of how tired my arm was getting already—and nothing had happened. (77)

Did Ellison really participate in such a knife fight and then describe this experience as fiction, only to return to the same description when he had the opportunity to present it as nonfiction? Or was the knife fight largely fictional to begin with and only appropriated to lend color to a supposedly journalistic report? In a sense, the question is irrelevant, since *Memo from Purgatory* is only the first of endless examples of Ellison's concatenation of invention and memoir.

Other aspects of *Memo from Purgatory,* however, reveal an acutely self-conscious and remarkably innocent twenty-one-year-old midwesterner taken aback by the most commonplace and unstartling aspects of street life. When the youthful Ellison locates the Barons' hangout and first enters

Ben's Malt Shop, he comments on "the girls sitting on the stools, and the couples in the back dancing—despite the absence of a cabaret license that permitted dancing!" (33). A gang member named Fat Barky is described as "a bully, a loafer, a sadist, and—there were those who had reason to suggest—a pervert" (66). Ellison later rather primly states that "not everything I did while as a member of the Barons was legal; I make no apologies for this. It can be chalked up to 'method acting' or protective coloration or milking my material for everything in it—whichever seems to exonerate me most fully" (89). In perspective, the book is full of shocking revelations which don't quite shock, of startling observations which never seemed likely to startle, often cast in the most tendentious rhetoric. When Ellison sees members of the Barons teaching younger children how to fight, he comments, "Thus does the evil perpetuate itself" (95). References to the Holocaust abound: A young gang member is described as "grinning like Eichmann" (51), another comments on "how cool the Nazis had been in gassing anyone who got in their way" (65), the crowd watching the knife fight reminds him of "Dachau and Auschwitz and the Colosseum and every temple of horrors from the first cave to Torquemada's Inquisition Chambers" (72), the judge who peremptorily hears Ellison's case after his arrest is grandiosely compared to Eichmann and Hitler (166).

If Ellison's attempts to lend sociological and historical import to the activities of a rather unexceptional gang sometimes get out of hand (after all, there is little in the book that was not already widely documented in the earlier JD fiction and films of the 1950s, which were already well in decline by the time *Memo from Purgatory* appeared), Ellison's account of his own night in jail is positively Thoreauvian. Ellison tells us that in the years following his days with the Barons, he often lectured on the topic of juvenile delinquency, using some of the weapons he had obtained as props. His lectures, as he reports them, offered few new insights and firmly reinforced the "family values" approach to juvenile crime. "As long as there is a solid family unit that will recognize the kid as an integral part, that will respect his intelligence, his honesty, his status," he reports himself as saying in one lecture, "there's a chance" (117). "Stop the rumble by forming more youth groups," he says in another (118), taking to task police, parents, and teachers in succession. But it isn't just gang life that dehumanizes, Ellison soon learns. It's the whole structure of the criminal justice system, which he finally experiences firsthand in 1960 and which he indignantly reports on at length in the second half of the book.

After threatening an acquaintance who owed him money, Ellison found himself denounced to the police as possessing weapons and drugs in his apartment. In September 1960, the police arrested him under New York's Sullivan Act for illegal possession of a gun—one of his lecture props left over from the days with the Barons. Ellison ended up spending only a night in jail, but as he reports it, it might as well have been the Bastille—"a treadmill horror underneath the city of New York" (127), where he spent a "24-hour period that filled me with such hopeless desperation that at times I thought I would crack" (123). On several occasions, Ellison mentions his fear that he might go mad from the horror, but what he describes seems to be little more than an average night in a crowded city jail. Nevertheless, everything takes on an epic quality. The smell is not just bad, it is "a stink that must offend God, for Man cannot take it for too long, and its persistence in reality *should* offend God. (But after a few hours in the System, one begins to suspect there is no God)" (156). When the lawyers show up, the inmates approach them "like animals, fighting for a piece of meat" (159). And the hastily scribbled defenses the overworked public defenders prepare seem woefully inadequate to the cosmic horror of the situation: "How terrible it was, to know you were going up against the System, the Machine, the Beast, with nothing standing between you but a paper lance" (160).

Ellison's bail is raised by his mother and a small group of friends, he is released, and the charges are later dropped, but not before a chance meeting with Pooch, one of the Barons whom Ellison had known years earlier, gives him a chance to learn the fate of some of his fellow gang members. His rival, Candle, after having a tragic love affair with a Puerto Rican girl who died in a botched abortion, has taken a job as a store clerk in a different neighborhood. Filene, who had been Ellison's "Deb" while he was in the gang, had moved to Idaho and gotten married. Another gang member became a pool hustler and was later killed in an auto accident. Only Pooch, the leader, had tried to remain with the Barons long after his contemporaries moved on, and he had become a petty criminal. While Ellison's brief talk with Pooch provides the only substantive link with the earlier section of the book, it seems little more than a footnote to Ellison's description of his own agonies as a prisoner, and ironically this undercuts the melodramatic rhetoric of the rest of this section. What is one to make of these descriptions of aimless and often violent lives, when it is clear that Ellison's real concern is with his own suffering during a single night in jail?

If *Memo from Purgatory* seems seriously overblown as reportage, it still provides valuable hints regarding the tone and imagery of what would later become some of Ellison's most powerful fiction. It reveals, more than any other Ellison work, the naive innocence that underlies the streetwise tone that eventually came to be the Ellison trademark. And its exaggerated metaphors, which often seem so inappropriate for what is apparently intended to be documentary reportage, often stray toward the kinds of fantastic imagery that would seem so powerful in his works of science fiction and fantasy. For example, Ellison's 1967 story "I Have No Mouth, and I Must Scream," about a group of people trapped inside a vengeful computer and endlessly tortured, clearly contains echoes of the experiences cataloged in *Memo*. When Ellison describes one of the Barons as "literally, voiceless in the world" (93), he even anticipates the title image of that later story. Later, machine and computer imagery dominates his description of the Tombs, New York City's jail. It is "a treadmill of horror underneath the city of New York" (127), where he felt like "one of a great string of bodies run through a computing system that would break me down into component parts and file me away like a piece of fruit in the proper bin" (128). The goal of the Tombs "is to turn you from a human being into a number, a piece of flesh that will obey, a body that will be *where* they want it, *when* they want it. The total dehumanization of a man" (168). He comments on how there is no sense of time in the Tombs and how he feared he would be there "forever and forever" (188)—which is exactly what happens to the narrator of "I Have No Mouth." The whole justice system is repeatedly referred to as a "machine." None of this imagery is especially surprising nor even especially original in terms of the literature of incarceration, but when Ellison would later develop such imagery on its own imaginative terms, divorced from his own rather unremarkable autobiographical experiences, it would provide the most natural and powerful voice for his emerging talent as a writer.

By the time of Ellison's arrest in 1960, he had already begun to shift the focus of his mainstream fiction from JD stories and crime stories to the rapidly emerging hipster culture of the early 1960s, with its iconoclastic new stand-up comics, cool jazz, trendy nightclubs, European movies, and self-conscious clothing styles. He had written and worked as an editor for *Rogue* magazine, and had begun writing the first of a number of stories that would begin to mark his maturity as a writer of well-crafted, nonformulaic short stories. *Spider Kiss,* which initially appeared under the title

Rockabilly in the same year as *Memo from Purgatory,* was his longest work of fiction to date and seems in many ways to represent his transition from JD and crime literature toward this new less formulaic approach. Developed from a short story called "Rock and Roll and Murder," which Ellison had sold to W. W. Scott's *Trapped Detective Story Magazine* in 1958, the novel has been widely viewed as a roman à clef based on the career of Elvis Presley. Rock critic Greil Marcus wrote, "The most interesting novels about Elvis were published before his death and remain little known," saying that *Spider Kiss* was "the first . . . and it's still the best, even if Ellison, as he says, modeled the main character after 'the killer, Jerry Lee Lewis'" (277).

Like *Web of the City, Spider Kiss* focuses on an inarticulate young protagonist, Luther Sellers, and is frequently marred by clichés and breathless rhetoric. Like the stories that would follow, it shows a firmer grasp of character, a fascination with the world of show biz, and a mordant sense of the corruptibility of the innocent (though one of the novel's strengths lies in the ambivalence it shows about whether Sellers was ever really that innocent to begin with). Its topic, rock 'n' roll (or more specifically the early offshoot called rockabilly), also suggests this transition: a kind of music and culture associated with adolescents such as those in Ellison's JD fiction, but controlled by agents, managers, and promoters. The novel also provided Ellison with an opportunity to open his settings up from the claustrophobic urban atmosphere that had so dominated not only his JD fiction but most of his crime and science fiction as well, and to explore a broader spectrum of American culture. Most important, *Spider Kiss* represented Ellison the pop culture critic—a role that would increasingly come to characterize his nonfiction during the 1960s, as well as a good deal of his fiction. Unlike *Web of the City* and the earlier crime and science fiction stories, *Spider Kiss* did not have a clear formula to draw on, and thus represented one of Ellison's earliest attempts to confront an American cultural institution on its own terms, unmediated by a tradition of commercial writing. To be sure, the novel reflects some of the conventions of earlier Hollywood novels by Nathanael West, Budd Schulberg, and others, but there was never really an identifiable trend of what might be called "rock 'n' roll" stories in either the paperback or magazine markets. There were plenty of exposé biographies, chiefly of Elvis Presley, and plenty of rock 'n' roll movies, but only a few of these, such as Elia Kazan's *A Face in the Crowd* (1957; with a screenplay by Budd Schulberg), tried to make serious comments about the cynicism and exploitation of the media industries or what Pauline Kael called "the fascist potential in American mass culture" (177). (Even the Kazan movie was only marginally about rock 'n' roll, since its protagonist, Lonesome Rhodes, was technically a country singer and the film's real focus is on the power of television.) There had also been numerous attempts to establish a link between juvenile crime and rock music, and such a link seemed implicitly to be made in films such as *The Blackboard Jungle* (1955), which used Bill Haley's "Rock around the Clock" as a theme even though the kids portrayed in the film were clearly from a pre-rock era. While these links never quite took hold, the notion that the music business was at least a haven of corruption gained enormous prominence through the payola scandal the year before *Spider Kiss* appeared, which even led to House hearings in February 1960 and remained in the news, off and on, for the next two years.

For all these reasons, it isn't surprising that show business corruption should be the next social issue Ellison would tackle after moving on from the JD scene. Much of what is implicit in rock 'n' roll culture—sex, class, race, greed, power, ambition—is also what was coming to fascinate Ellison as a focus for fiction, and the idea of fiction as a kind of moral action must have been reinforced by his relative success with the JD stories. Like those stories, the novel is weakened by heavy-handedness, clichés, and sententiousness: The narrator repeatedly refers to New York as "Jungle York"; the aspiring singer mourns "I can make it, all I need is the chance" (65); the narrator says of a hooker that "her face and her body were her dues, and she paid them regularly" (79); a cabaret performer is "no longer a spring chicken" (102); a magazine refers to the new singer as "the hottest thing since sliced bread" (76). On a few occasions when Ellison finds the complexity of his material leading him toward a more sophisticated style, he catches himself and almost apologizes to the reader. Shelley Morgenstern, the public relations flack who is really the novel's central character, at one point finds his mind drifting to random events in his past, and suddenly Ellison interrupts with this remarkable passage:

> He caught himself. Stream of consciousness is all right if your name is James Joyce, but if it's Sheldon Morgenstern, keep them thoughts on Car-lene (whom you are keeping, but whom you have not seen since Louisville), on the Mercedes-Benz (which you are paying on, but haven't driven since before Louisville), on the kid in there who is climbing into his continental

suit, this very moment (a kid who has taken up your time completely, since Louisville). Thoughts. The bane of the working classes. (66–67)

Later, when faced with a difficult choice of metaphors, Ellison resorts to a bizarre technique of giving readers a multiple choice. A girl's green eyes are described as

> Choose one:
>> an unset emerald, slightly flawed
>> green slime on a condemned pond
>> a snake's skin
>> dollar bills old, wrinkled being sent back to the mint to be burned
>> the color on the base of old toy soldiers. (81)

When a fan gets a chance to meet her pop idol, the reader is asked:

> What would be *your* reaction, coming face to face with:
>> (If you are a dancer) Eglevsky . . .
>> (If you are a writer) Shakespeare . . .
>> (If you are a lover) (male) Cleopatra . . .
>>> (female) Don Juan . . .
>> (If you are a philosopher) Solomon . . .
>> (If you are a physician) Hippocrates . . .
>> (If you are a religious man) God . . . ? (120)

The effect is nothing short of egregious, like a streetcorner huckster showing off his box of metaphors, or a hungry young writer so desperate to assert his personal voice that that voice burns straight through his own narrator to speak eagerly to the reader. As clumsy and immature as these stylistic tricks may seem, they are nevertheless evidence of Ellison straining to push his writing beyond the quick-sketch style of the digest magazines and into an area more commensurate with his growing interest in addressing more substantive issues.

Further evidence of this is Ellison's overall narrative strategy in the novel. Rather than focus exclusively on Stag Preston, the young singer from Kentucky who becomes a pop sensation, Ellison gives the point of view to Shelley Morgenstern, a PR man who works as an assistant to Colonel Jack Freeport, a successful promoter who seems to be loosely based on Colonel Tom Parker (although little of the rest of the novel suggests parallels with Elvis Presley's career). Shelley is a stereotype in his own right—a version of the once-idealistic promoter disillusioned by his own corruptibility—but his cynical perspective gives Ellison a chance not only to display his growing fund of insider's knowledge about show biz but to call attention to a number of the social and moral issues that were coming to preoccupy his fiction during this period. The novel opens in traditional Hollywood fashion with Shelley musing on his own lost innocence as he watches Stag at the height of his popularity and later procures a young fan for Stag's enjoyment. This quickly leads to a flashback narrative as Shelley recalls how, on a trip to Louisville with Colonel Freeport, he discovered a young singer named Luther Sellers in the back room of a poker parlor, introduced him to the Colonel, and met the stepparent who had been managing his small-town career. Though concerned about the boy's coldness toward the people who had raised him and his apparent willingness to be exploited, Shelley participates enthusiastically in this exploitation, since he owns 30 percent of the contract. Luther is given a new name, Stag Preston, a new image (resembling that of Bobby Rydell more than Presley or Jerry Lee Lewis), and a detailed schedule of concerts and record demos. Preston becomes a sensation, and the novel quickly expands beyond an exploration of the rock culture to become an all-purpose indictment of various aspects of show business. By a third of the way into the novel, Stag has ceased to be a rock 'n' roll singer in any significant sense of the term. Pop songs are written for him by Sammy Fain and Ross Bagdasarian; he records a popular movie theme; he is compared to Johnny Mathis; he appears on Ed Sullivan; he signs a movie deal. But Morgenstern finds Preston increasingly difficult to control. The singer tries to rape a secretary, becomes violently drunk at nightclubs, impregnates a young black girl, spends himself into debt, and finally causes the death of a one of the fans Shelley has invited to his hotel room. With Stag fast becoming a liability and a publicity risk, Colonel Freeport sells off his interest in the contract and urges Shelley to do the same. Under his new managers, Stag fades quickly and seems to disappear completely after being attacked and knifed in the throat by hired thugs. Shelley chances upon him years later in a strip joint in New Orleans. His singing is as compelling as ever, and he begs Shelley for help, but Shelley has finally learned his own lesson.

Part of Shelley's lesson has to do with the limits of tolerance. Early in the novel, when Shelley and the Colonel meet with Stag's stepparents, a chance anti-Semitic remark causes him to react with anger and briefly to lose sympathy for them despite Stag's own apparent lack of loyalty. Later, Stag's own anti-Semitism comes to the surface, directed at Shelley, and Shelley realizes that Stag's brand of intolerance is even more offensive than that of his stepparents, who were more ignorant than hateful. When Stag gets a young girl pregnant, Shelley is again taken aback by the racist attitudes of both Stag and the Colonel. And Stag's universal contempt for women recurs throughout the novel, although Shelley's (and the narrator's) own attitude doesn't seem that much more enlightened. Shelley is not unaware of the compromises he has made to live and work in a world based on image and conformity, but his experiences with Stag and the Colonel seem to bring his own guilt to the surface. Through the sensibility of Shelley, Ellison is able to introduce the themes of racism and intolerance that would come to characterize some of his best fiction of this period.

Also through Shelley's sensibility, Ellison began to develop a kind of ongoing critique of hipsterism that would become the other major pole in the "adult" fiction he was writing for the men's magazine market. In retrospect, hipsterism seems a kind of pale middle-class response to the rebellion embodied in artifacts of 1950s culture from James Dean to Presley to the Beat poets and writers. But for Ellison—and for many of his readers at the time—the distinction between "hipsterism" and being truly "hip" was a crucial one:

> There is a great deal of difference between a truly "hip" person (that indefinable *awareness* of what's right, what is current, lasting; beyond sophistication, beyond class, it is the essence of being "with it") and a hipster.
>
> A hipster is a pseudo. The good-looking girl from Fond du Lac, Wisconsin, who feels stifled (for the wrong reasons) in Fond du Lac, Wisconsin, and immigrates to Chicago. Look for the girl two months later in the bars on Chicago's Rush Street. Look for her just off Times Square; on L.A.'s Strip. You know her. The sleek, well-fed, looks-to-be-good-in-the-hay chick who crosses her legs too high. The chick who gets her meals bought, who has to worry about paying only for her extensive clothing needs and the rent. . . . See, then, a cultural phenomenon. A leech personality, singularly devoid of purpose or substantiality. The shadow-people. (112–13)

Hipsterism, for Ellison, gradually becomes the embodiment of the trendy upscale conformity of the late 1950s and early 1960s (even as he writes articles with titles like "Adam's Bachelor Test for Hipness" [*Adam,* March 1967])—a kind of middle-class cultural imperative that appropriates the language and style of the "true" nonconformist and thus renders him powerless. The process is at work in *Spider Kiss,* as Stag's raw rockabilly music is gradually moved further into the mainstream, first with backup singers, later with full orchestras, and finally with Hollywood songwriters and movie deals. By the end of the novel, Ellison has moved well beyond his earlier championing of troubled youth, beyond rock 'n' roll, and almost beyond the sensational exposé style that had given such a naive and moralistic tone to his writing about juvenile delinquents. He was ready to take on not just the subcultures of petty crooks and JDs and show business, but the diseases that he perceived as plaguing the culture at large—and his relatively newfound market in the men's magazines gave him just the platform he needed.

4 | ROGUE/ KNIGHT

Adventures in the Skin Trade

VIEWED IN RETROSPECT, American men's magazines of the late 1950s and early 1960s present strangely contradictory notions of what American males must have thought of themselves. The titles of these magazines alone tell a story, if titles imply anything at all about targeted readership. Some readers, it seems, were *Rogues, Cads, Knaves, Dudes,* and (of course) *Playboys,* always prepared for a *Caper* or a *Fling.* Others saw themselves as *Knights* and *Gents* and *Cavaliers* who wanted to be addressed as *Sir* or *Mr.* Less ambitious, apparently, were the readers of the cheaper men's adventure magazines which—printed on pulpier paper and apparently unable even to afford faux-Anglophile words in their titles—appealed to *Real Men, True Men,* and *For Men Only.* These working-class magazines stressed adventure and sports stories, spiced up by a few cartoons and an occasional photo layout. Their slicker cousins, inheriting the tradition of *Playboy* (and before that, of *Esquire*), sought to appeal to a younger, more affluent market—a market that suspiciously resembled Ellison's scathing description of the pseudo-hipster in *Spider Kiss.* They characteristically featured a mix of lifestyle articles, personality profiles, current events reports, reviews (of stereo and photo equipment as well as books, movies, and records), opinion columns, food and drink features, and fiction, all separated by tasteful photo layouts of Hollywood starlets or strategically posed seminude models. Pubic hair had not yet been discovered, and a risqué cartoon was one in which an amazingly endowed blonde bombshell drew witless remarks from popeyed men in hats. Ellison's friend Robert

Silverberg, whose output in those days was said to exceed a million words a year, recalled some of his own pseudonymous contributions: "Horror Rides the Freeways," "I Was a Tangier Smuggler," "Hot Rod Challenge," and "Buried Billions Lie in Wait" ("Sounding Brass" 21). Ellison's included such memorable titles as "The American Male: His Systematic Castration," "The Fine Art of the 15-Cent Pickup," "How Girl Gangs Fight and Love," "The Shocking Orgies of Italian Nobility," and "The Vampire Cult Still Lives."

Here, for example, is the August 1960 issue of *Rogue,* the "special issue on bachelor bartending." The cover features a pert brunette sipping a Tom Collins through a long straw as she gazes suggestively at the reader. The contents page lists William Hamling as editor and publisher, his wife, Frances, as executive editor, Frank Robinson as managing editor, and Harlan Ellison as contributing editor. Facing this page is an installment of a column by comedian Lenny Bruce, and listed among the contents are another column by Alfred Bester; a profile of Dean Martin by William F. Nolan; an article on martinis by Robert Silverberg; another on saloons by Mack Reynolds (who also serves as travel editor and contributes another piece on Dublin); humor features by Robert Bloch and Karl Wagenheim; pictorials titled "Lovelies of Libation," "A Modern Mona Lisa," and "A Gambol with the Arty Set"; a feature on new talents (which turns out to be about Phyllis Diller and Tom Lehrer), three more articles on booze, one on men's fashion, and short stories by Harlan Ellison, Robert Walter, and Damon Knight. The Ellison story is his semiautobiographical account of a Lenny Bruce–style comedian returning to his hometown, "Final Shtick."

What is most interesting about this list is that an extraordinary number of the names mentioned—Hamling, Robinson, Ellison, Silverberg, Bester, Reynolds, Bloch, Knight—were already widely familiar names in the science fiction world. William Hamling, the publisher who started the magazine in 1955, had begun his career as an active participant in science fiction fandom in the 1930s, and later edited both mystery and science fiction digest magazines. Long before the collapse of most of these magazines in the late 1950s, Hamling had established his Greenleaf Publishing Company in Evanston, Illinois, and started *Rogue.* Ellison had appeared in its pages as early as 1956, as had other writers such as Bloch and Reynolds. Frank Robinson, who edited the magazine in the early 1960s (and later edited *Cavalier*), added regular features by his colleagues from the science fiction community. As these men's magazines grew in sophistication and began to inherit experienced writers and editors from the diminished short fiction magazine markets, they began to provide significant new opportunities for genre writers to reach a broader (and perhaps better educated) spectrum of readers. Distinguished science fantasy writer Gene Wolfe published his first professional story in *Sir* in 1970, and more than half the stories in Stephen King's first story collection, *Night Shift* (1978), had appeared earlier in *Cavalier.* Fiction may not have been the raison d'être of such publications, but for writers accustomed to writing to order—or to match a preprinted cover illustration—for low-paying digests, the men's magazines must have seemed a well-paying and editorially liberal market.

Ellison's association with *Rogue* from 1956 to 1962 (including his two years as editor in 1959 and 1960) gave him an opportunity to publish a more experimental brand of science fiction (such as "Eyes of Dust," December 1959) and to develop a series of thoughtful tales on contemporary issues ("Daniel White for the Greater Good," March 1961; "The Universe of Robert Blake," June 1962) and a number of character studies that would likely have found no market in the digests ("Mona at Her Windows," "GBK—A Many-Flavored Bird," both June 1962). In all, Ellison wrote more than twenty stories for *Rogue,* together with a considerable number of nonfiction pieces like those mentioned above. Later, after moving to California, he became a regular with *Knight,* in which he published some fifteen stories between 1963 and 1972, including "Pretty Maggie Moneyeyes" and an early version of his complex and ambitious myth-tale "Deathbird" (December 1972). With these two magazines as his major nongenre markets during the 1960s, Ellison was able to develop a freer voice, more attuned to character and less constrained by editorial demands for quick narrative hooks and snap endings. Explaining in 1967 why he had so often appeared in *Knight,* Ellison wrote: "*Knight* does not edit my stories but prints them untouched as I submit them; . . . they pay me much less than many other markets, but very much a top dollar as far as their own rates are concerned; they let me experiment. . . . It has been my contention for several years, that science fiction and the mainstream are no longer distinctly separate branches of the literary swim" (*I Have No Mouth* 53–54).

Ellison's move into the men's magazine fiction market was dramatic. In 1958, he published twenty-five stories in the digest magazines (nineteen of them in science fiction titles) and one story in *Rogue.* In 1959, his men's magazine stories outnumbered his digest stories by twelve to nine, and between 1960 and 1964, twenty-six Ellison stories appeared in the men's magazines, compared with only two in the science fiction digests and seven in the mystery digests. Not all of this was due to Ellison's growing desire for freedom from editorial control, of course. A good deal of it probably had to do with the general collapse in the science fiction magazine market in 1958, due largely to the court-ordered divestiture of the monopolistic American News Service. As writer Barry Malzberg describes it: "Twenty magazines perished in 1958, and the sales of the leaders were halved. These magazines could not reach the newsstands in sufficient numbers. The audience could not find them. But the audience had already diminished; it had never been large enough to support more than a few successful maga-zines, a few continuing book lines, and Sputnik in 1957 had made science fiction appear, to the fringe audience, bizarre, arcane, irrelevant" (30–31). In other words, the men's magazine market could not have come along at a better time for Ellison. Not only did they encourage him to develop mainstream, contemporary stories; they helped sustain what would other-wise have been a severely diminished market for his fantastic fiction. But this fantastic fiction was now being sold to an audience somewhat broader than the narrow genre audience of the digests, and this in turn demanded stories that could stand more completely on their own terms, apart from familiarity with genre conventions.

There seems little doubt that this newfound discipline, along with this newfound freedom, was one of the crucial turning points in Ellison's career and an important but little-known chapter in the history of Ameri-can science fiction. If the pulp magazines and their digest-sized descen-dants had served to "ghettoize" the genre's readers and writers, these more mainstream publications helped weaken the walls of that ghetto, helping SF writers connect with a broader audience and move more freely between fantastic and mimetic modes of fiction—perhaps even preparing, in some slight way, for the more radical blurring of genre/mainstream barriers in what became known as the New Wave movement of the 1960s. (Earlier, in the 1940s and 1950s, a few mainstream magazines such as *Collier's* and the *Saturday Evening Post* bought occasional science fiction stories by Robert A. Heinlein, Jack Finney, and others, but never constituted as significant a market as the men's magazines became, and never encouraged SF writers to attempt different kinds of writing.) When Ellison returned as a regular contributor to the slightly revived science fiction markets of the mid-1960s, he brought with him the stories that would make his "overnight" reputation as one of the boldest innovators in the genre: "'Repent, Harlequin!' Said the Ticktockman" (1965), "I Have No Mouth, and I Must Scream" (1967), "The Beast That Shouted Love at the Heart of the World" (1968), "A Boy and His Dog" (1969). By 1969, Ellison seemed again firmly ensconced in the genre magazines—now a much smaller field, with more rigorous standards—with eight stories appearing there as compared with only five in the men's magazines.

What had happened? Some clues may be found in one of the science fiction stories that Ellison published in *Knight* in 1964. "World of the Myth," which concerns a spaceship crew stranded on a planet where an army of telepathic ants causes them to confront their worst inner selves, provides no easy solutions and ends with the main character, Cornfield, "hoping there was a future, but doubting it; really doubting it" ("I Have No Mouth" 78). As in the earlier "Silver Corridor" and the later "I Have No Mouth, and I Must Scream," the story prominently features images drawn from the characters' unconscious minds and projected as real by the group-mind of the ants. (These ants aren't really ants, of course. They are *science fiction* ants, which in this case means that they are antlike aliens who have evolved a powerful collective intelligence with psychic powers.) At first these images depict simple emotions and figures of speech—a weeping woman manifests sorrow, a gibbering madman appears upon the use of the expression "you're crazy!" a horde of comic-book devils descend following the expletive "devils!" But soon the images are being drawn from deeper sources, and the antagonist Rennert commits suicide after being confronted with the ant-projected unadulterated image of himself as he really is. Cornfield's concluding expression of lost hope follows upon his realization that he, too, will probably succumb to the temptation to find out from the ants what he really is.

In terms of plot, this story seems to have little to do with either "The Silver Corridor" or "I Have No Mouth, and I Must Scream." But in terms of its handling of the fantastic, it provides a number of indicators as to how Ellison moved from writing one kind of story to writing another. In "The Silver Corridor," simplistic characters take a backseat to the spectacular "duelling machine" that is the center of the story—the silver corridor itself. The illusions in that story are clearly more derivative of standard science fiction tropes than of the characters' individual personalities. In "World of the Myth," the characters move closer to center stage, and the illusions become a function of their growing self-awareness. By the time we get to

"I Have No Mouth, and I Must Scream," the science fiction elements are still more streamlined and so highly abstracted that they give Ellison leave to write a story that is almost pure feeling. In these three stories alone, we see a consistent movement away from science fiction for its own sake and toward science fiction as an instrumentality of character and theme—specifically the themes of entrapment and self-confrontation that would emerge as Ellison's most characteristic. (The inability of the characters in "World of the Myth" to continue functioning in the face of revealed truths about themselves also anticipates "The Cheese Stands Alone" [1982], in which customers in a mysterious bookshop find themselves unable to go on after learning that the greatest moments of their lives have already passed.) Ellison, in other words, seems to have used his near-hiatus from the genre magazines to broaden his range of fictive expression and to discover his own most enduring themes.

A curious parallel occurred in the career of Ellison's longtime friend Robert Silverberg, whose own science fiction output declined during the same period—from an astonishing sixty-seven stories and novels in 1958 to only three in 1961. Like Ellison, Silverberg returned to science fiction in the mid-1960s to newfound acclaim as a "serious" writer. Silverberg has explained that he found the juvenile fiction and nonfiction markets more rewarding, and that the science fiction world simply could no longer absorb "all the wordage I was capable of turning out" (Clareson xvii)—especially, one suspects, with the market virtually decimated. Ellison's case was a bit different, however; his overall output did not simply shift to new markets during this period. It actually declined substantially. Some of this was certainly due to market conditions (most of the magazines that had bought his stories by the dozen only a couple of years earlier became fatalities of the 1958 distribution collapse), some may have been because of his work in Hollywood in the early 1960s, and some may have had to do with his breaking into the world of paperback books during this same general period. But such factors do not fully explain the change in the nature of his fiction that led him, almost suddenly, to become the most honored writer in science fiction by the late 1960s. The answer to that puzzle can only be found in the fiction itself, and in the maturation of Ellison's voice as a writer—a maturation already clearly in evidence in the men's magazine stories that eventually went to make up substantial portions of the collections *Gentleman Junkie and Other Stories of the Hung-Up Generation* (1961) and *Love Ain't Nothing but Sex Misspelled* (1968).

Some of these stories reflect the same concern with hipsterism and show business that is evident in *Spider Kiss*. "The Truth" (*Rogue,* September 1959) concerns a jazz musician who protects his own mediocre talent by refusing to hire a kid he knows is a better performer. "Have Coolth" (*Rogue,* June 1959) is set in the world of Greenwich Village jazz clubs, but reverts back to crime-magazine formula when the narrator is seduced into committing murder by "the most appealing witch I'd ever dug": "She jammed her hot body against me, so I used the knife" (*Gentleman Junkie* 215–16). "This is Jackie Spinning" (*Rogue,* August 1959) reflects the 1950s radio "payola" scandals by portraying—in a style meant to suggest live radio—a disc jockey who successfully resists pressure from racketeers, only to be killed by a girl in another pulp-surprise ending. While such stories demonstrate Ellison's reaching out for new kinds of source material, they don't really demonstrate much advance in structure, style, or characterization beyond what he had shown in the pages of *Trapped* or *Infinity*.

This began to change noticeably with "Final Shtick," which, as we have already seen in chapter 1, combined Ellison's fascination with hipsterism with deeply felt autobiographical elements. This self-discovery came as a shock to Ellison, and in the headnote for the issue of *Rogue* in which the story appeared, he is quoted as saying, "When I was finished I found myself completely sapped of strength; it wasn't till much later that I realized I had, for the first time, done a semi-autobiographical story. It shocked me" ("Rogue Notes" 2). But the story is as much wish-fulfillment as autobiography. Despite his liberal use of details from his own childhood in Painesville, Ellison casts his narrator as an internationally famous stand-up comic clearly modeled on Lenny Bruce. This odd combination of fantasy self-image and convincing detail would characterize several later stories in a similar vein. "Punky and the Yale Men" (*Knight,* January 1966), for example, concerns an enormously successful and respected best-selling novelist and screenwriter who began his writing career years earlier with a book based on his experiences posing as a juvenile delinquent gang member in Brooklyn. Now he returns triumphantly to New York to write a commissioned article for the *Esquire*-type magazine that he knows would have snubbed him earlier. Not only is he a world-famous writer, he is also more conversant than anyone else with the roughest aspects of New York street life, as he demonstrates when two junior editors from the magazine challenge him to a weird kind of duel to find out if he's still in contact with "the seamy side of life." The writer's need to test himself in this milieu leads eventually to his death in a knife fight, but not before he has proved himself to be the literary equivalent of Shane.

A similar character is the narrator of "GBK—A Many-Flavored Bird" (*Rogue,* June 1962), a short and little-known story that is nevertheless the most sensitive and best written of all Ellison's autobiographical revenge-fantasies. Walter Innes is a best-selling writer who thirteen years earlier had been a founding member of a Cleveland science fiction club called the "Solarians." Now, following news of a movie adaptation of one of his stories, Innes receives a telegram from G. Barney Kantor, a flamboyant small-time con man who had tried to sell his services as a promoter to the Solarians when Innes was still a member. On a visit to Cleveland, Innes begins joking with his sister, brother-in-law, and secretary about Kantor's various escapades, until the secretary interrupts with, "This little guy apparently lives a lie, but it's all he's got. I think you stink" (*Love Ain't Nothing* 95). Challenged, Innes decides to show the real Kantor to his secretary, and the group sets off to visit his home, which turns out to be in a depressed neighborhood. Kantor is not there, but his wife and daughter talk enthusiastically about how Kantor has told them of his friendship with Innes and how he got him started as a writer. Infuriated yet touched by the squalid surroundings and the family's obvious faith in Kantor, Innes leaves behind a book inscribed "To my dear friend, G. Barney Kantor, for all his invaluable help and for showing me a special part of the universe" (98).

For almost the first time, Ellison seems here to be gaining control of his autobiographical materials, neither inflating his projected self-image to unrealistic proportions nor dwelling in the sentimentality of a lost childhood. Kantor is among the most vivid of a series of character portraits Ellison produced during this period (two more of which, "Mona at Her Windows" and "The Universe of Robert Blake," appeared in the same issue of *Rogue* as "GBK"). Such characterizations move beyond the almost stereotyped versions of hipsters, juvenile delinquents, petty criminals, and pop singers that had characterized much of his journalism as well as his magazine fiction, and represent one of the most significant breakthroughs in this stage of his career.

More complex levels of characterization also lend depth to some of Ellison's treatments of the emerging social issues of the 1960s, such as racism, anti-Semitism, changing sexual relations, and drugs. "Daniel White for the Greater Good" (1961) is among the most thoughtful of these stories. It concerns an unrepentant black rapist in a small Georgia town who is deliberately given over to a white lynch mob in order to minimize reprisals against the town's black community and, almost incidentally, to create a media martyr for the nascent civil rights movement. None of the characters in the story carry sufficient moral authority or ingenuity to solve the town's dilemma or even to escape their own traps—not the town's black leaders, the NAACP organizer from the city who arrives to advise them, the racist white majority, or Daniel White himself, whose venality offers little room for sympathy, but raises the question of the principle of law versus expedience: his sacrifice, we recognize, is indeed a clever solution which satisfies the needs of all concerned but which is still morally repugnant. Even Peregrin, the NAACP representative who seems to understand the moral dilemma, ends by criticizing the black leaders not for releasing Daniel White to the racists but for "doing it for the wrong reasons" (*Gentleman Junkie* 71). Compared to this tangled moral parable, Ellison's other direct treatments of racial themes during this period seem little more than homiletic sketches. "The Universe of Robert Blake" (1962) quietly describes the experiences of a young black boy during the day when he first begins to understand the realities of segregation. Although slight and understated, without overt confrontation, the story has been praised by some black readers as accurately rendering a rite of passage all but unknown to white Americans but almost universal among blacks:

> Robbie Blake had learned many things that day. He had learned which colors were right, and which were wrong; he had learned what color hands must be to open certain doors, and what color thoughts must be employed to exist in the fine, fine nice world. He had learned when to lower his eyes.
>
> And most of all he had learned what it meant to be a nigger. (*Love Ain't Nothing* 87)

Similarly, "The Night of Delicate Terrors" (1961) is a vignette about a black family driving through Kentucky toward a "conclave" in Chicago. Forced off the road in a dangerous blizzard, they are refused food or shelter by a fairly stereotypical group of white southerners in a roadside cafe. They continue on their way, the father motivated by the implied vast coming social changes that the unspecified conclave in Chicago will represent. "Now *You're* in the Box" describes a novelist facing writer's block over the meaning of this title, until he witnesses a failed robbery after which the store owner brutally shoots the young black man who tried to rob him with a water pistol. "I worked twelve *years* in that store," he says as if to explain the killing, and the meaning of the title becomes clear to the writer.

Ellison also explored anti-Semitism in more than simply autobiographical terms in "A Prayer for No One's Enemy" (1966), in which a theater showing the film *Exodus* is picketed by a group of young neo-Nazis chanting, "Dirty little Christ-killers" (*Love Ain't Nothing* 318). A sixty-year-old Holocaust survivor named Lilian Goldbosch attacks the blond boy who seems to be the leading protester, and a small riot ensues, during which two local high school students pull the woman from the blond boy for her own protection. Haunted by her memories, she becomes convinced that she can somehow talk to the boy she attacked and help him to understand, and she persuades the high school students, Arch and Frank, to find him and bring him to her. He turns out to be a sociopathic racist and anti-Semite named Victor Rohrer, a "creation of self, brought forth from its own mind for a need to exist" (327). When Lilian attempts to confront him about his anti-Semitism, he is unmoved and unemotional, repeating standard Nazi litanies in the calm manner of one who has worked them out "logically, completely, finally" (330). Only when Lilian decides to visit his parents does he turn violent, attempting to attack her but restrained by the two boys. Later, at Victor's house, Lilian notes a mezuzah on the door lintel and announces, "Come along boys, I don't need to see Victor's parents now: I understand" (332). Arch and Frank, now more puzzled than ever, drive Lilian home and ask a Jewish boy whom "they had never had occasion to talk to before" about the meaning of the mezuzah and the Hebrew *Shaddai,* which Lilian also mentioned. But when they return to her apartment, they find she has been violently murdered by Victor, who is last seen cowering in an alley, waiting to be arrested. The focus of the story finally settles not on Victor, whose own self-hating Jewishness seems a badly tattered irony even in 1965, nor on Lilian, whose naive idealism and fears of another Holocaust accurately reflect the feelings of many survivors, but on the boys Arch and Frank, a WASP and an Italian American, whose shell of noninvolvement in social and racial issues has ever so slightly been breached.

While the plots of Ellison's stories of racism and anti-Semitism tales are sometimes undistinguished and often dated, his blunt use of the language of bigotry and his portrayal of the bigots themselves lend these stories a kind of visceral documentary power that may actually seem more shocking in our own politically correct era than in the 1960s venues where the stories originally appeared. Victor's diatribe about "Kike filth" in "A Prayer for No One's Enemy" is one example; others appear in "Battle without Banners" (1964), set during a prison revolt and featuring black, Jewish, and Polish characters—the latter a son of a Belsen survivor—whose crimes often reflect aspects of social injustice. The Polish Jew Karpinsky, for example, bombed an Iowa church whose anti-Semitic pastor, preaching the blood libel of Jews eating Christian babies, had led the community to torment the boy and his family. Gyp Williams, a black, had participated in an ambush of a KKK caravan on its way to find and lynch whoever had "grabbed a feel off the druggist's wife" (*Love Ain't Nothing* 306). The story also touches upon the then-sensitive issue of black-Jewish relations; when an inmate named Nigger Joe complains that all he has ever wanted is a measure of dignity and another inmate named Simon Rubin says, "I know how you feel," Gyp Williams responds with disgust: "Sheet, man, when you Jewish cats gonna come off that kick? When you gonna stop lyin' on yourself, man, that you been persecuted, so you know how a black man feels? Jeezus, you Jewish own most of the tenements up in Harlem. You as bad as any the rest of them cats" (310). Later, the narrator says "their contest of agonies, their cataloguing of misery, their one-up of sorrow was cut short" by the blaring of the prison loudspeaker, offering amnesty to those who will return quietly to their cells. But secretly, the rebels realize that those who "rock the boat" will never be allowed to live. "We all of us down in the dark," says Gyp for all of them (314), as they come to realize that their different varieties of victimization share a common and quite simple trait: They are always, and will always be, outnumbered.

If Ellison's handling of 1960s social issues seems sensitive and enlightened, particularly in the context of the men's magazines where many of these stories appeared, his handling of the incipient sexual revolution is unfortunately a bit more reactionary and more in keeping with what feminist readers might well suspect made up the contents of these magazines. "There's One on Every Campus" (1959), in which a college student experiences momentary pangs of guilt over his exploitation of a townie girl who sleeps around, is a title that is virtually self-explanatory. Poisonous women abound; the girlfriend in "Punky and the Yale Men" turns out to be a cocaine addict; the title character in "Valerie" (1972; published both as a memoir and as a story) turns out to be a credit card thief; the gorgeous cheesecake model "with a horizontal mind" (*No Doors* 89) who seduces her photographer in "Nedra at f:5.6" (1956) turns out to be a vampire; the sexy but oddball fiancee in "A Path through the Darkness" (1962) turns out to be not only a lesbian but a *voyeuristic* lesbian:

> How had something so pure and innocent and—the word seems alien to me, but somehow appropriate—*charming* become so demented, so twisted and destructive? Could it have been me . . . could it have been that I had taken Stephie from paths she knew, paths that led deeper into the darkness of her own fears and past torments, and tried to lead her on a new path, out of the darkness? . . .
>
> Stephie was a Typhoid Mary, a plague-bearer, and only someone desiring illness would have rubbed up against her. (293)

Gays do not fare much better in the rhetoric of these stories. When the aforementioned Stephie turns up at a party, she is accompanied by a pair of "fags," and in one of the stranger comments on racism, the protagonist of "Punky and the Yale Men" is approached by a "spade fag" and thinks, "*Of all the horrors Whitey has committed against the black man, homosexuality is the most perverse*" (*Love Ain't Nothing* 358).

Despite a plethora of narrators who unselfconsciously refer to women as "tramps" and gays as "fags" or "dykes" and an equal number of women who seem to fulfill the worst of the men's magazine stereotypes, Ellison did at times turn his attention to the problematical and often victimized status of women in the 1960s youth culture, which he sought to portray in his fiction of this period. Among the most notable and revealing of these stories are "Neither Your Jenny nor Mine" and "Pretty Maggie Moneyeyes." The former novella, which originally appeared in *Knight* magazine, is one of Ellison's more ambitious attempts at melding autobiographical materials with a kind of Hemingwayesque realism (although it's interesting to note that Hemingway himself is alluded to less directly in this and other stories than is Robert Ruark, the popular author of *Something of Value* and other violent adventure tales that settle in somewhere between the comparative literariness of Hemingway and the tough-guy attitude of what passed for "men's fiction" in the 1950s and 1960s). Ostensibly about a naive young girl named Jenny, a "typical know-nothing, a little patsy who had been seduced by four-color lithography and dream-images from a million mass media" (*Love Ain't Nothing* 39), the story really focuses on the narrator, Kenneth Duane Markham, who takes it upon himself to arrange for a Tijuana abortion for Jenny after she is seduced by a wastrel named Roger Gore. Markham's narrative voice is cynically flippant and almost condescendingly hip; he even provides parenthetical definitions for terms like *gopher* ("Go for the coffee, Jerry") that Ellison apparently felt were too *au courant* for his 1964 readership, and he spends far more time talking about himself than about Jenny or his own girlfriend, Rooney, who is Jenny's roommate. To a great extent, this is deliberate. Part of Ellison's intention here seems to be to undercut the facile hipster attitude of his own narrator and, presumably, of some portion of his readership. (It is for this reason that the story's original appearance in *Knight* is worth noting.) The tale also critiques the Competent Man motif we have noted in Ellison's earlier fiction.

The libidinous Markham at first doesn't seem much better than Gore. When he learns, for example, that Rooney's two roommates are eighteen-year-olds, he says, "It had been a toss-up whether I'd try to make them on the sly, or become Big Brother to the brood. As it turns out, Rooney was enough action for me, and I took the latter route" (40). Markham is also implicitly boastful about his shadowy connections with jazz musicians, hookers, and blacks, but is affronted when Rooney assumes that he would therefore know how to locate an abortionist, indignantly protesting that "I take precautions" and "I've never knocked anyone up" (46). Nevertheless, he manages to identify several abortionists and even bullies Gore into paying the $400 fee of the Mexican doctor selected. Despite his own contempt for Jenny's gullibility, Markham comes to her defense in the scene that gives the story its title: After he has beaten up Gore in order to get the money, Gore screams, "Your Jenny's a dummy and a tramp, and she hasn't got any honor to protect!" Markham responds gently, "She is neither your Jenny nor mine. She is her own Jenny, and whatever is wrong there, fellah, she is still a human being" (55).

The voice here is much closer to the hard-boiled knights of Raymond Chandler than to the urbane hipster that began the tale, and it is very much the voice of the Competent Man. But not long after the abortion is completed, Jenny begins hemorrhaging and is rushed to a Tijuana hospital. The competent hero is suddenly powerless, and the style turns into imitation Hemingway: "The waiting room was very clean and very white and Jenny died about four hours later" (76). Markham goes berserk, finding his way back to the clinic to attack the doctor, but he gets worked over by his goons and left penniless on the streets, where he wanders for more than a day, even taking humiliating work passing out handbills, until he finally manages to contact Rooney again. "Jenny was gone," he concludes, "and Kenneth Duane Markham was gone, and soon enough Rooney would be gone from me. All I wanted to do was get back to Los Angeles and try to be someone else" (82). The narrative voice which began as that of an arrogant hipster and shifted into that of a hard-boiled hero ends, finally, in defeat, even in loss of identity, but with a newfound sense of the preciousness of even those lives for whom Markham had earlier expressed contempt. But despite Markham's transformation during the story, neither Jenny nor Rooney emerge as more than emblematic characters. She may be "her own Jenny," but we never catch a clear glimpse of who that Jenny is, and she ends the story as she began, little more than a victim.

Ellison's women are seldom such one-dimensional victims, however. The title character of "Pretty Maggie Moneyeyes" (1967) is given a more fully developed background and personality than Jenny, but she also becomes a phantomlike embodiment of the obsessiveness and self-destructiveness that Ellison portrays as the core of the Las Vegas experience, and by the story's end the focus reverts to Kostner, the drifter who finally becomes Maggie's victim, as he was the victim of his first lover. Essentially a ghost story about a haunted slot machine, "Pretty Maggie Moneyeyes" is also notable as perhaps the most stylistically experimental of Ellison's many contributions to the men's magazines and the one that most clearly represents his transition from the commercial markets of his early career to the more open and fluid markets of the science fiction world that came to be associated with the "New Wave." By the time "Maggie" appeared in *Knight,* Ellison had already published his classic signature stories "'Repent, Harlequin!' Said the Ticktockman" (1965) and "I Have No Mouth, and I Must Scream" (1967), and had edited the *Dangerous Visions* anthology, which solidified his reputation as a leading advocate of the New Wave in America. While the Las Vegas setting and the major characters in "Maggie" are consistent with Ellison's earlier stories in *Knight* and *Rogue,* the style is something else again and represents a clear movement away from the autobiographical realism of those tales and toward more self-conscious attempts to investigate the metaphoric and even synesthetic resources of language. The character of Maggie herself—according to Ellison, derived from a woman named Shawn he had met in 1963 and again in Las Vegas in 1965 ("Whore" 144–48)—is also Ellison's most fully realized female character to date, with a complex and consistent invented background that moves far beyond the sketchy portraits he had offered of characters like Jenny or Valerie.

In many respects, "Pretty Maggie Moneyeyes" today reads as a fairly overbaked tale, the work of an author in love with his own newly discovered capacity for imagistic language, overlaid with an almost nihilistic view of gender relations and an almost puritanical view of Las Vegas as "immoral and deadly" (*I Have No Mouth* 127). But the vivid portrait of Maggie, who is desperate enough to escape her childhood poverty to trade in sexual favors but never quite a professional hooker, and the decision to make the central viewpoint character weak and morally uncentered, still give the story memorable impact. As Robert Thurston has noted, Maggie "is a machine even before her death, one who has analyzed society's demands for a beautiful and successful woman, and then constructed herself to fulfill those demands" (313). And indeed, Maggie is described throughout in images that suggest mechanization and commodification: "*a determined product of Miss Clairol and Berlitz, a dream-image formed by* Vogue" (128), "*An operable woman, a working mechanism, a rigged and sudden machinery of softness and motivation*" (129), "*blue-eyed posing mannequin Maggie*" (136), "*A presentation, not an object of flesh and hair. A chromium instrument, something never pitted by rust and corrosion*" (137). A spiritual descendant of "The Girl with Hungry Eyes" in Fritz Leiber's 1949 story of that title (to which Ellison had paid tribute in his own 1956 version, "The Hungry One," reprinted as "Nedra at f:5.6"), Maggie is a self-conscious creation of the emerging media culture of the 1960s, a near-perfect artifact flawed only by her humanity, by a physical expression of her inward imperfection—a damaged heart resulting from childhood rheumatic fever.

The story begins with Kostner, having lost his last thirty dollars at blackjack in a Vegas casino, discovering a single silver dollar in his pocket and offhandedly dropping it into one of the last remaining silver-dollar slot machines (which had been nearly discontinued in Vegas in the mid-1960s). A second narrative line, set off by italics, details the background of Maggie, born in poverty in Tucson of a Cherokee mother and a vagrant father, a victim of childhood rheumatic fever who parlays her stunning looks into a career as a small-time hooker and eventually moves to Vegas with her boyfriend, Nuncio. Horrified and disgusted by Nuncio when he asks her to perform an unspecified sexual practice, she flees to the casino, where she dies of a coronary—presumably related to her earlier rheumatic fever—while playing the same machine Kostner will drop his last dollar into six weeks later. The fuguelike description of Maggie's moment of death is almost stylistic overkill, the voice of an author discovering his voice. Ellison first tries a kind of post-Kerouac stream of consciousness:

> *. . . and then suddenly as dollarafterdollarafterdollar went around-aroundaround hummmmming in reels of cherries and bells and bars and plums and oranges there was suddenly painpainpain a SHARP pain!pain!pain! in her chest, her heart, her center, a needle, a lancet, a burning, a pillar of flame that was purest pure purer PAIN!* (138)

Next, he tries rearranging the lines into a kind of crude signage:

> *On the floor.*
> *Dead.*
> *Struck dead.*
> *Liar. All the lies that were her life.*
> *Dead on a floor.* (139)

But these are only overtures to Ellison's attempts to describe the flight of Maggie's thoughts as she dies and realizes she is trapped in some sort of purgatory. This segment of phrases and images set apart by black squares of type ranges from metaphors of the death-passage ("down a bottomless funnel roundly sectioned like a goat's horn") to vaguely science fiction images ("total cellular knowledge") to horror rhetoric ("gibbering spastic blindness"), to simple exposition ("this is the stopover before hell or heaven," "this is limbo") (139). The final segment of this remarkable passage, set off in a block of reduced type to suggest Maggie's entrapment, explains what has happened: "She had died, willing herself into the machine. Now looking out from within, from inside the limbo that had become her own purgatory, Maggie was trapped, in the oiled and anodized interior of the silver dollar slot machine" (139). What is most notable about this linguistic spasm—the whole passage lasts less than two pages—is that it represents Ellison willfully, almost desperately, trying to break out of the narrative conventions of his earlier career, and testing the various resources of language to simulate, rather than describe, experience. Ellison's own account of how this passage was written, as he was coming down with pneumonia during a visit to Las Vegas to promote a film, is as follows:

> The fascinating upshot of what happened is that I do not recall having written whole stretches of the story. The two typographically variant sections immediately after Maggie's heart attack and death were apparently written while I was going into a coma. They are very peculiar sections, indeed: one seems to attempt to describe the moment of death and the other—in the original manuscript—was handwritten in a tiny cribbed hand, the letters printed so small I had to retype the section before it could be submitted to an editor. I think I was trying in my semi-lucid way to describe what it felt like to be a disembodied soul trapped in a slot machine. ("Whore" 152–53)

The remainder of the story unfolds as a more conventionally narrated fantasy. Kostner's dollar, dropped into the machine in which Maggie is trapped, yields a jackpot not of three bars but of three blue eyes, the color of Maggie's eyes. And he wins again and again, confounding the casino managers—who can find no evidence of cheating or defects in the machine—and eventually establishing a psychic link to Maggie in an erotic dream, during which we learn of Kostner's own isolated life and his betrayal by the one woman he had loved. "*Can I trust you?*" he asks Maggie. "*I've never been able to trust anyone before. Women, never. But I need someone. I really need someone.*" Maggie replies, "It's me, always. Forever. You can trust me" (149). But the next day, while playing the same slot again and winning again with the three blue eyes, Kostner dies in a violent spasm as Maggie, like "a soul released from an eternal prison, a genie freed from a dark bottle" (151) escapes from her limbo. After Kostner's death, the machine is finally pulled off the floor to be destroyed, and just as it is about to be melted down for slag, the ladle foreman notes that the jackpot window displays three *brown* eyes—Kostner's eyes rather than Maggie's. In a final betrayal, Maggie has condemned Kostner to an eternity in limbo in exchange for her own freedom. The victim becomes the victimizer, in a variation on an eternal cycle which is nevertheless consistent with each character: Maggie's need to escape is so powerful it transcends her death, while Kostner's impossible streak of luck turns out only to be a prelude to the final loss in a life defined by losses. Wondering at the unusual design of the jackpot, the foreman observes, "*Some of these old games go way back*" (151).

5 | CONSUMED BY SHADOWS

Ellison and Hollywood

From that moment, Valerie Lone began to be consumed by her shadow. And nothing could prevent it. Not even the wonderful, wonderful Universe that had chosen to care about her.

A Universe ruled by a mad God, who was himself being consumed by his shadow.

—"The Resurgence of Miss Ankle-Strap Wedgie"

FROM THE BEGINNING, Ellison's career has been marked by a subtext of commedia dell'arte, reflected most directly in his public persona as a lecturer, radio host, convention star, talk-show guest, actor, recording artist, and "instant author" who would compose short stories in the windows of bookstores or during live telecasts. Show business is also a recurring theme in his fiction, which regularly features such figures as stand-up comedians ("Final Shtick"), harlequins ("'Repent, Harlequin!' Said the Ticktockman"), aging movie stars ("The Resurgence of Miss Ankle-Strap Wedgie"), radio talk-show hosts ("Flop Sweat"), disc jockeys ("This is Jackie Spinning"), actors ("All the Sounds of Fear," "Deal from the Bottom,"), musicians ("The Truth," "Django"), even performance artists from outer space ("S.R.O."). Critic Sue Hart has argued persuasively that theater in all its forms, including film and TV, consistently acts as "informer to the future" in Ellison's work (121), and given this affinity for the world of public performance, it seems inevitable that Ellison would become involved with Hollywood.

Ellison was not unaware of the risks. One of the great romantic myths of American pop culture is that of Genius Consumed by Commerce, which in broad outlines depicts an artist of extraordinary talent (usually but not always a writer) whose accomplishments bring him or her to the attention of a vastly wealthy consumer industry (usually but not always Hollywood), with which the artist makes a Faustian bargain, is treated like a day-laborer, sees his work compromised or outright butchered, begins a long downward spiral toward alcoholism or drug abuse or even suicide, and dies with unfulfilled promises and with a relatively trivial legacy in the consumer industry that destroyed him. Fueled by selected fragments of the careers of Nathanael West, Ben Hecht, Dorothy Parker, William Faulkner, and F. Scott Fitzgerald and by numerous movies and novels in the manner of *Sunset Boulevard,* this scenario is more parable than history. As Ellison has pointed out, West wrote his finest work, *The Day of the Locust,* while working as a studio scenarist; Fitzgerald wrote the Pat Hobby stories and most of *The Last Tycoon* in the depths of his Hollywood alcoholic spin; and Faulkner not only supported his family but produced some of his most mature (and least commercial) fiction while under contract to Hollywood (*Harlan Ellison's Watching* 418–19).

"Memo from Purgatory"

Ellison came to Hollywood not as an established literary figure but as an ambitious young writer willing to attend "cattle calls" for writers and to pitch ideas—often made up on the spot—to assistant TV producers and story editors. His one claim to fame was "Memo from Purgatory," which had been sold to *The Alfred Hitchcock Hour* and presented in 1962, with Ellison's own script. Introduced by a somber Hitchcock, forgoing his usual mordantly witty monologues, the hourlong drama is of interest today chiefly for the spectacle of a very young James Caan portraying a very young Harlan Ellison, with Walter Koenig—who only four years later would gain fame as Ensign Chekov on *Star Trek*—as the gang leader he befriends. Drawn from a few of the less violent episodes of *Memo from Purgatory,* the story presents Caan as a young writer pretending to join a New York gang in order to gain material for a book. He gains the trust of the gang leader—and of course of a "Deb"—but this trust is compromised when his notes are discovered by one of the gang members. Coming seven years after *The Blackboard Jungle* and two years after *West Side Story,* the drama has little to add to the Hollywood portrayal of JD gangs—except, perhaps, for a slight edge of documentary realism in Ellison's generally efficient script, pared down considerably from the more florid presentation of these same episodes in the original book. Most important, *Memo from Purgatory* demonstrated that Ellison could write for TV, and over the next several years he undertook a variety of assignments for TV series that are now mostly forgotten: *Ripcord,* a syndicated series about parachutists; *Route 66,* a popular CBS series filmed on location around the United States (Ellison is credited with a story, not a teleplay); *Cimarron Strip,* a rare ninety-minute western series; even the notoriously ridiculous Sally Field series *The Flying Nun* (for which Ellison chose the screenwriting pseudonym "Cordwainer Bird," which he later consistently used in order to publicly distance himself from projects he deemed too compromised or simply too embarrassing).

Burke's Law

Ellison's steadiest work during his early years in Hollywood came as a regular writer for *Burke's Law* (1963–65), a romantic mystery-adventure series that starred Gene Barry as Amos Burke, an independently wealthy bachelor playboy in a chauffeured Rolls-Royce who, in a credulity-smashing twist, also happened to be the police chief of Los Angeles! Produced by Aaron Spelling for ABC, the show was packed with narrative gimmicks characteristic of TV series formulae: Gary Conway as a young, impetuous cop; Regis Toomey as an older, wiser cop; Eileen O'Neill as a girl cop; a parade of guest stars (Rhonda Fleming, Buster Keaton, Frank Sinatra, Jayne Mansfield); a larger parade of stars in cameo roles; a formula for episode titles that almost always began "Who Killed . . . ?" After less than two years, the producers decided to turn Amos Burke into a secret agent—perhaps responding to the success of NBC's series *The Man from U.N.C.L.E.* and the growing popularity of James Bond movies. The new series died, ironically, after being programmed opposite another spy program on NBC, *I Spy.*

Ellison contributed four scripts to *Burke's Law* in the 1963–64 season and two to *The Man from U.N.C.L.E.* in the 1966–67 season. The first of the *Burke's Law* episodes, "Who Killed Alex Debbs?" concerned the murder of a publisher of men's magazines. According to Ellison, this was an idea he had originally pitched to line producer Richard Newton during the cattle call—"How about I kill Hugh Hefner for you?" (*Harlan Ellison's Watching* xxxi)—but one can't help but wonder if the idea wasn't inspired at least in part by Ellison's recent unhappy experiences with William Hamling, the publisher of *Rogue.* More important, the episode—initially broadcast on October 25, 1963—established Ellison as a commodity, favored by Spelling and connected, however peripherally, with the inner circles of Hollywood. As Ellison later described it: "During that period I wrote for, and got to spend time with, genuine legends: Gloria Swanson, Charlie Ruggles, Buster Keaton, Wally Cox, Joan Blondell, Aldo Ray, Mickey Rooney, Rod Steiger, and even Nina Foch. I went to Hollywood parties, I dined with celebrities and multimillionaires, I became involved with starlets, I went more than a little crazy" (*Harlan Ellison's Watching* xxxiii).

Perhaps the clearest indication of the extent to which Ellison had gone Hollywood was that, within a couple of years of his work on *Burke's Law,* he was at work on the screenplay of Joseph E. Levine's *The Oscar,* a 1966 feature, based on a novel by Richard Sale, which quickly gained a reputation as perhaps the tawdriest of all Hollywood "insider" soap operas. The film was nevertheless a fairly high profile project, coming from the producer of *The Carpetbaggers* and *Harlow,* and critic Pauline Kael took particular note of "Harlan Ellison's incomparable bedroom conversations," which were "such a perfect commingling" with Levine's beds and draperies that "the words might have sprouted from the coverlets" (437).

THE OUTER LIMITS

But Ellison's experience with science fiction gave him a particular edge in a TV industry that had only begun to discover the narrative possibilities of the genre. Following an unprepossessing beginning with low-budget programs like *Captain Video* (1949–53, 1955–56) and *Tom Corbett: Space Cadet* (1950–55), science fiction television seemed doomed to remain a subset of children's programming until two major developments in the early 1960s. The first and most important was *The Twilight Zone* (1959–64), developed by Rod Serling, who at the time was one of a handful of writers who had earned substantial reputations based on TV drama (another such writer, Reginald Rose, also developed his own TV series, *The Defenders,* in 1961). Although most *Twilight Zone* episodes were fantasy rather than science fiction, the very concept of a series developed and creatively directed by a writer seemed to offer stunning promises to readers of fantasy and science fiction: programming that might actually reflect some of the appeal of the literature in its scripts, and that might even involve "real" science fiction and fantasy authors. Although Serling wrote most of the episodes himself (partly the result of a promise to the network), he also enlisted the services of established writers in the field, most notably Charles Beaumont and Richard Matheson. While *The Twilight Zone* was never enormously successful—it was canceled in 1962 and brought back by popular demand the following January—the principles it helped establish of involving genre authors and more sophisticated storylines were reflected in Leslie Stevens's *The Outer Limits* (1963–65), a series whose striking visual design seemed an early version of science fiction *film noir* and which featured scripts by SF writers David Duncan, Clifford Simak, and Otto Binder as well as Ellison.

The other development that helped define the science fiction revival on TV, far less sanguine from the point of view of most readers in the genre, was the arrival of producer Irwin Allen. Allen—who would later gain fame as the ringmaster of bloated disaster movies such as *The Poseidon Adventure* (1972) and *The Towering Inferno* (1974)—introduced no fewer than four new science fiction series on TV between 1964 and 1968: *Voyage to the Bottom of the Sea* (1964–68, based on Allen's own 1961 film of that title), *Lost in Space* (1965–68), *The Time Tunnel* (1966–67), and *Land of the Giants* (1968–70). While Allen demonstrated that TV budgets could support somewhat more complex sets and special effects—thus perhaps helping to pave the way for *Star Trek* (1966–69)—the appalling plots and sitcom characters of these series seemed to suggest that TV science fiction was ready to revert again to the realm of children's programming. Ellison wrote only one script for an Allen series—an episode of *Voyage to the Bottom of the Sea* entitled "The Price of Doom"—and for it he employed the disdainful pseudonym "Cordwainer Bird."

Ellison's two *Outer Limits* scripts, however, are of genuine interest. The first, "Soldier," was based on Ellison's 1957 short story of that title. It concerns a warrior from some 1,800 years in the future who, through a freak battlefield accident, is somehow transported back in time to our present. The soldier, Qarlo Cobregnny, suddenly materializes on a subway platform, weapon in hand, and his appearance promptly causes an old man to suffer a heart attack. Thinking that Qarlo has attacked the old man, the other commuters panic, and Qarlo soon finds himself in a shootout with a police officer. Despite his superior weapon, Qarlo is captured, and he spends a night in jail before a government security agency learns of the weapon and begins trying to communicate with Qarlo—who, it turns out, speaks a rapid and distorted version of English. In the 1957 published version of the story, Qarlo seems a conundrum to the government philologist who learns to communicate with him—namely, how can such a completely unsocialized and violent character possibly be integrated into our own society? Raised since infancy to be a brutal soldier, Qarlo has no concept of parents, family, or any other social relations, and he has no education other than his own battle-field programming. Finally—in a weak but well-intentioned ending—he is put on the lecture circuit, describing the endless brutalities of future warfare to audiences who are then asked to sign petitions to abolish war. If Qarlo succeeds, there may be a chance that the nightmare future he represents will never come to pass (although the question of where Qarlo would then have come from is unanswered).

In the teleplay for the 1964 *Outer Limits* broadcast, Ellison changed the ending by introducing a second warrior from the future, known only as the Enemy, who is initially trapped partway through the time portal, then is freed by a bolt of lightning to continue his pursuit of Qarlo. He finally tracks him down at the home of the government translator Kagan, where Qarlo has, in a tentative, childlike way, begun to learn some of the principles of human interaction and family life. In the final confrontation, Qarlo makes a move against the Enemy that could be interpreted either as an attempt to protect the family he has come to care about or as a reversion to his battlefield instincts. As the two soldiers grapple over the weapon, they both disappear in a blinding flash, leaving the episode's offscreen narrator to speculate on whether the future represented by Qarlo is avoidable. Although somewhat facile, this ending is at least not quite as silly as having Qarlo reminisce in public, and it retains the free will versus determinism conundrum at the heart of the original tale. In both versions, however, it is the growing humanization of Qarlo in the context of a contemporary family that is the principal focus of dramatic development.

"Soldier," particularly in its TV incarnation, gained Ellison further fame in 1984, when James Cameron's film *The Terminator* (with a screenplay by Cameron and Gayle Anne Hurd) was released with its story of a cyborg sent back from the twenty-first century to assassinate the mother of a future leader and the human sent back to protect her. Despite the similarities with "Soldier," and despite the lawsuit that Ellison brought against the production company (which led eventually to an out-of-court settlement and a credit to Ellison being inserted in *Terminator* prints and videotapes), Ellison enthusiastically recommended the film in his April 1985 column "Harlan Ellison's Watching" in the *Magazine of Fantasy and Science Fiction,* saying it is "clearly based on brilliant source material" (*Harlan Ellison's Watching* 217).

Ellison's second script for *The Outer Limits* was an original story, set in the universe of his Kyben war stories, titled "Demon with a Glass Hand."

Like "Soldier," it introduces us to a time-traveling protagonist who is both confused and alienated, but in an even more radical way: Trent (Robert Culp) was born only ten days earlier, full-grown but with no notion of where he came from or why he exists. His only source of information is a strange electronic glass hand, with fingers missing, which has replaced his natural hand and which he occasionally interrogates, often getting an unsatisfactory answer because the hand is incomplete. He learns that he is being pursued by aliens called Kyben, who have conquered Earth but found it devoid of human life. Fleeing back through time, Trent manages to assemble the missing fingers of his glass hand and learn that he is in fact an android and that his body contains a wire with coded data that can reconstitute each of the 70 billion members of the human race; he is, in fact, guardian of all humanity until such time as it becomes safe to reconstitute them. The suggestive imagery of the glass hand itself—reminiscent of the hand replaced by a "sun-bomb" in Ellison's 1957 story "Run for the Stars" (another Kyben war tale about a single individual chosen to protect all humanity from the invaders)—and the then wildly original speculation that every human being might be reduced to what is essentially computer code (recorded on a wire in Trent's chest), combine to make "Demon with a Glass Hand" the most surrealistic and intellectually adventurous of all *Outer Limits* episodes and in many ways the best, taking full advantage of the series's trademark *noir* look and black-and-white photography. It is also one of the most self-consciously mythical: Trent, who undergoes a death and resurrection during the episode, is explicitly identified with the Sumerian myth-hero Gilgamesh in the opening narration, and in the end he learns that his fate is to live anonymously among humans for the 1,200 years it will take to reach his own future. "My curse is my humanity," he complains in the closing narration, even though he has just learned he's not human at all. "To be forever alone. I walk among you now, and I dare not even ask for your pity" ("Demon" 63). In terms of both its inventiveness and its metaphorical power, "Demon with a Glass Hand" remains one of Ellison's most accomplished television scripts. Although never published as a story, it was adapted into a graphic novel in 1987 by Marshal Rogers for DC Comics.

Star Trek

While the anthology format of *The Outer Limits* may have permitted Ellison to do more innovative and individualistic work, without doubt Ellison's most famous television script remains "The City on the Edge of Forever," written for *Star Trek* in 1966, later rewritten by various other hands, and finally aired in its altered form on April 6, 1967. It quickly became one of the most popular episodes in the program's history, attaining a mini-cult status within the larger cult phenomenon that *Star Trek* eventually became. Viewer and fan polls repeatedly ranked it highest of all episodes, a judgment that was repeated in an *Entertainment Weekly* ranking in a special *Star Trek* issue in 1994 (*City* 35). A special issue of *TV Guide* on "The 100 Most Memorable Moments in TV History" (July 1, 1995) even ranked the episode no. 68 (*City* 277). The program is cited as a high point of the series by nearly all of the show's cast members who have written memoirs—and *Star Trek* has almost certainly spawned more ghostwritten memoirs than any other TV program. Even Joan Collins, who guest-starred in the episode, discusses it in egregiously erroneous detail in her flack autobiography, *Past Imperfect* (*City* 70). The episode also led to an ongoing battle between Ellison and series creator Gene Roddenberry, culminating in Ellison's 1996 publication of his original treatments and teleplay of the story, together with a lengthy, well-documented brief for his own case and no fewer than eight afterwords by various hands associated with the program.

Given its pop-legendary status, watching the episode today is something of a sobering experience. William Shatner's tight-jawed, gimlet-eyed performance as Captain Kirk is dire, and not much better is DeForest Kelly in full Gothic makeup to suggest the temporary madness of his character, Dr. McCoy. As Kirk's idealized romantic interest Edith Keeler, Joan Collins vapidly delivers her lines while being photographed in such smeary backlit soft focus as to seem barely recognizable. The sets, from the misshapen giant donut that is supposed to be a "time portal" on a remote planet to the 1930 New York street where Edith meets her tragic doom, seem flimsy and unconvincing despite the show's unusually high budget for a *Star Trek* episode. The most obvious question to occur to someone viewing the program for the first time, outside the context of other *Star Trek* episodes and the 1960s, would be simply, what's all the fuss? The answer lies partly in the show's content and partly in the controversy over its development, which took on the aspect of a gossipy melodrama. And in some key areas, these two issues cannot be separated. In Ellison's original treatment and teleplay, the story begins with a murder on board the *Enterprise:* a venal narcotics dealer named Beckwith kills one of his clients who has threatened to expose him. He is captured by the *Enterprise* crew, but escapes to a remote, apparently uninhabited planet, pursued by Kirk, Spock, and other crew members. The planet turns out to be not only inhabited but a focal point in space and time that is home to the ancient Guardians of Forever, among whose principal duties is protecting a "time vortex," a portal to any place and time in the past. The guardians warn of the dangers of traveling to the past and possibly altering the time stream, but the desperate Beckwith leaps through the portal to New York City in 1930. Warned by the Guardians that Beckwith's presence in 1930 has already changed history radically, Kirk and the other crew members return to the *Enterprise,* only to discover that it is now—in this altered universe—a run-down pirate ship called the *Condor.* After a battle with the pirates, Kirk and Spock return to the planet—leaving the other crew members to contend with the situation on board—and plead with the Guardians to be permitted to try to intercept Beckwith and undo the damage he has caused.

But how to find Beckwith in a metropolis the size of New York? The Guardians respond with what is surely one of the episode's most appealing fantasies: the notion that each time period has a "focal point," "*Something or someone that is indispensable to the normal flow of time. Something that may be completely innocent or unimportant otherwise, but acts as a catalyst, and if tampered with, will change time permanently*" (*City* 101). For reasons that are not clear, Beckwith will inexorably be drawn to this focal point, which the Guardians are only able to describe in the most cryptic terms. Nevertheless, the observant Spock is able to identify this figure as a charismatic social worker named Edith Keeler, whom Ellison says he based on evangelist Aimee Semple McPherson (*City* 67). Edith's rather vague philosophy of a friendly universe and a happy future is only sketchily presented, but her purity of soul is enough to make Kirk fall uncharacteristically in love with her, clouding his judgment enough to concern Spock—especially when Spock discovers, by means of his "tricorder," that Edith's pivotal role involves determining the outcome of World War II: If she dies in an accident in 1930, time will resume its normal flow, but if she is saved, her movement will gain in influence and delay America's entry into the war, permitting the development of a German atomic bomb and leading to a Nazi victory and reign of terror.

The central dilemma of the story is thus established: Kirk must allow Keeler to die in order to save the future of the universe. Aided by a crippled World War I veteran known only as Trooper—a reminder of the debilitating effects of war—Kirk and Spock are able to track down Beckwith, who in a brief scuffle kills the Trooper. Later, Beckwith reappears at the exact moment that Edith is about to be run over by a beer truck and, for motives that are somewhat murky and uncharacteristic, moves to save her. Kirk knows that this is the pivotal moment he has been warned of, but he cannot bring himself to prevent Beckwith from saving Edith's life. Spock intervenes, Edith dies, and the normal flow of time is restored. (Beckwith is later condemned by the Guardians to an eternally repeated death inside an exploding star, a Dantesque punishment which Ellison would return to, in more sophisticated form, in his 1995 story "Pulling Hard Time.")

Concerned about budgets, the extreme variance from the show's usual formulas, and possibly the egos of the stars involved, the producers of *Star Trek* first asked for rewrites, which Ellison provided. Then they took the script out of Ellison's hands altogether, with Gene Roddenberry later claiming full credit for the rewrite, although it now seems clear that producer Gene L. Coon and story editor D. C. Fontana were centrally involved in the episode that finally aired. In this version, Beckwith has disappeared entirely. Instead, a popular continuing character, Dr. McCoy, accidentally injects himself with a paranoia-inducing drug, and it is he who flees through the time portal, pursued by Kirk and Spock. The character of the Trooper has also disappeared, and Edith Keeler's wispy New Age–style philosophy has been turned into a full-blown pacifist movement, which will eventually delay America's entry into the war. It is McCoy, not Beckwith, who attempts to save Edith from the truck, and Kirk, not Spock, who finally restrains him.

Ellison—who eventually won a Writers Guild of America Award for his original teleplay (not the broadcast version)—has for decades been concerned about how these and other changes weakened the structure and power of his original story. But the most telling change in the script, in historical context, is the shift in Edith Keeler's character from a social worker to a peace activist. As H. Bruce Franklin writes,

> As broadcast in the spring of 1967, "The City on the Edge of Forever" was clearly a parable suggesting that the peace movement directed against the U.S. war in Vietnam, no matter how noble, alluring, and idealistic in its motivation, might pose a danger to the progressive course of history. The episode projected the view that sometimes it is necessary to

engage in ugly, distasteful action, such as waging remorseless warfare against evil expansionist forces like Nazi Germany or the Communist empire attempting to take over Indochina, even doing away with well-intentioned, attractive people who stand in the way of historical necessity. ("*Star Trek* in the Vietnam Era" 27)

Franklin reports that *Star Trek* producer Robert Justman, when asked if the episode was deliberately intended "to have the contemporaneous anti-Vietnam-war movement as subtext," replied, "Of course we did" (26).

So Ellison, who by 1967 was firmly on the record as an opponent of the Vietnam War and a supporter of the peace movement (a 1967 edition of his collection *From the Land of Fear* reprints the story and teleplay of "Soldier" with a passionately antiwar introduction), saw his work altered not only structurally but conceptually as well. As Franklin notes, the peace movement in the United States was steadily gaining momentum in the early months of 1967, and for an audience that might have seen peace activists on the network news only an hour earlier, a drama in which peace activists wreak havoc with history would seem to be an obvious allusion. (Franklin points out that a later *Star Trek* episode, "A Private Little War," has the characters make direct reference to Vietnam in a manner that clearly reflects what was then the Johnson administration policy of escalation [29]). In the mythology of *Star Trek* that has evolved in the decades since, the ideological overtones of the episode are largely forgotten, and fans remember the series principally for the humanizing romantic dilemma of Kirk—forced by history to allow the woman he loves to die—and secondarily for its use of the notion of alternate timelines, long a common device in science fiction but unusual on television.

Cimarron Strip

Ironically, at the very time "City on the Edge of Forever" was broadcast in its rewritten form, Ellison was at work on a now almost forgotten script for the ninety-minute western series *Cimarron Strip,* which may be his most successful attempt to meld his own vision with the dictates of recurring series characters and formulas. "Knife in the Darkness," completed in May 1967, was also the longest script Ellison had written, and it far more clearly reflects his own developing themes and interests during this period than does the more famous *Star Trek* episode, even though Ellison later complained that the episode's director, by ignoring Ellison's customarily detailed camera and editing directions, had made the story look "like an outtake from *The Terror of Tiny Town*" (*An Edge in My Voice* 22), a notoriously appalling 1938 western featuring a cast of midgets. *Cimarron Strip* was set in Cimarron City, Oklahoma, in the 1880s and featured a familiar assortment of regulars: the town marshal (played by Stuart Whitman), a young deputy, an older comic Scots deputy, a female cafe owner. Ellison melds these characters into an original and surprisingly violent tale that suggests supernatural overtones from its opening teaser: As an unseasonal fog settles over Cimarron City during a Christmas celebration in 1888, a young saloon girl is murdered by a mysterious stranger. Although rowdy locals suspect an Indian—and even murder him in a subplot about racism and lynch law—Marshal Crown is more suspicious of an Englishman named Tipton, who eventually reveals that he is in Cimarron City in pursuit of Jack the Ripper, who came to America on an immigrant boat following his last murder in London in November 1888. But Tipton himself is murdered, and another visitor, Enoch Shelton, turns out to be the killer. In an inevitable climactic scene, Shelton hides out in the room of the marshal's girlfriend, Dulcey, attacking her with a scalpel just as the marshal bursts in. Shelton escapes into the fog, only to find himself confronting a group of Indians who seem to have an uncanny awareness of his identity—and who themselves have already suffered for his crimes. Shelton is gruesomely killed by the Indians, but the question of whether he is actually Jack the Ripper remains unresolved. As the marshal points out to his enthusiastic young deputy, who wants to sell the story to the *New York Times,* the only evidence of the connection was the claim of the now-dead Tipton, who was "a little balmy himself" (90).

By 1967, when this script was written, the notion of Jack the Ripper fleeing to the United States was almost a cliché in mystery and horror fiction, thanks largely to a famous 1943 short story by Robert Bloch titled "Yours Truly, Jack the Ripper," in which Jack turned out to be immortal. Ellison had invited Bloch to write a sequel to this tale for his famous anthology *Dangerous Visions*—also published in 1967—and Bloch complied with "A Toy for Juliette," in which a decadent young woman of the future is amused by the "toys" her grandfather gives her—historical figures stolen from the past by a time machine, such as Amelia Earhart or the crew of the *Marie Celeste,* all of whom she eventually kills—until the new toy, from late Victorian London, turns her knife on her. Ellison then wrote a sequel to this story, "The Prowler in the City at the Edge of the World," in which Juliette's grandfather reveals to Jack that he had deliberately arranged for him to murder Juliette, and welcomes him to a sterile urban environment with features of both "'Repent, Harlequin!' Said the Ticktockman" (the city and its denizens are regulated in draconian fashion) and "I Have No Mouth, and I Must Scream" (the city tortures the pathetic Jack with a series of illusions and shifting realities). In his afterword to this story in *Dangerous Visions,* Ellison explains: "The Jack I present is the Jack in all of us, of course. The Jack that tells us to stand and watch as a Catherine Genovese gets knifed, the Jack that condones Vietnam because we don't care to get involved, the Jack that we need. We are a culture that needs its monsters" (*Dangerous* 154). Over the next several years, Ellison would explore numerous variations on the Jack the Ripper theme, the most effective of which may be "The Whimper of Whipped Dogs" (1973), a fantasy redaction of the 1964 Catherine Genovese murder which conflates Ripperlike violence with urban dehumanization and detachment. Other stories, from "A Boy and His Dog" (1969) to "Basilisk" (1972), would return to variations on Ripper-like themes, but "Knife in the Darkness" still represents Ellison's most direct treatment of the original story as a straightforward mystery adventure.

THE YOUNG LAWYERS

In its own modest way, "Knife in the Darkness" may be more successful than "City on the Edge of Forever" as an attempt to graft an individual story onto a series format, but both scripts raise questions about the sustainability of a personal vision through the various traps and machinations involved in series television production. One might think Ellison had been burned enough by his *Star Trek* experience, but only three years later he would virtually repeat it with a script written for *The Young Lawyers* titled "The Whimper of Whipped Dogs" (unrelated to the short story mentioned above, which was written some two years later). Produced by Paramount, *The Young Lawyers* was an attempt at a "socially relevant" melodrama in the tradition of Reginald Rose's series *The Defenders* (1961–65). Set in a neighborhood law office in Boston, it featured Lee J. Cobb as a senior attorney and Zalman King (whom Ellison had known since he played one of the gang members in "Memo from Purgatory" in 1962) as an idealistic law student. The program lasted only one season in 1970–71.

During this time, Ellison was writing television review columns for the *Los Angeles Free Press* (later collected as *The Glass Teat* [1969] and *The Other Glass Teat* [1975]), and in his column of October 30, 1970, he announced that he had not reviewed *The Young Lawyers* because he was writing an episode and that he would be taking the unusual step of publishing the as-yet-unproduced script in his next four columns. "The Whimper of Whipped Dogs" focused on the young law student Aaron Silverman, whose former girlfriend Hallie Benda has been arrested for attempting to use a stolen credit card. Silverman contacts a bail bondsman, who warns him that Hallie has a long string of prior offenses, and against the advice of his colleagues Aaron risks his own money—even selling his watch—to raise bail. When he sees her at the jail, he is shocked at her emaciated appearance, which suggests amphetamine abuse. Hallie fails to appear for her arraignment, and Aaron's attempts to track her down lead to the discovery that she is not only a drug abuser but a pathological liar as well: virtually everything she had told him about her life, even years earlier, was false. (She had claimed, for example, that after their mother's death her sister became a prostitute, but in fact the sister turns out to be an orthodontist's wife living only a few blocks away from the still-healthy mother.) He finally tracks her down and—in a dilemma between love and responsibility that faintly echoes that of Captain Kirk in "The City on the Edge of Forever"—has her brought to trial, where she is remanded to medical rehabilitation.

In the final column of the script's serialization, Ellison expresses the fear that "the script you have just read may never be produced" (*Other* 300) because of a network decision to de-emphasize drug- and youth-related stories. But in fact the episode did show up on March 11, 1971, and Ellison devoted the following two "Glass Teat" columns to what he called "The Great Rape," "the evisceration of my script," "a script that has been watered down and emasculated and raped and pounded till it became the worst of all possible end-products: merely another bland example of video porridge" (*Other* 360–61). Ellison's specific complaints ranged from the director's failure to use solarization shots in flashback scenes, to editing of dialogue and scenes that rendered later scenes illogical, to a scenery-chewing performance by actress Susan Strasberg as the drugged-out Hallie. But Ellison's own performance here chews a bit of scenery as well, as he rants against the depredations of the "System" and the virtual impossibility of writing with integrity within the world of corporate television, even apologizing to his readers for "having lied to you consistently" (*Other* 374) in suggesting that network television might be worth any kind of serious attention or criticism.

More than a decade later, writing in *Video Review,* Ellison described this as "the last script I was to write for ten years," saying that the experience was so thoroughly disillusioning that "on March 10, 1971 I packed it in. I swore I would never again write for television" (*Sleepless Nights* 57). But in fact the very next year saw a teleplay called "Flintlock," an energetic and ingenious adventure featuring super-agent Derek Flint from the 1966 James Bond parody *Our Man Flint.* Although never produced, the script is far more characteristic of Ellison's work than either the *Star Trek* or *Young Lawyers* episodes, recalling aspects of "The Silver Corridor" when the almost superhuman Flint outwits his evil captors as they subject him to a series of ever more elaborate illusions and scenarios designed to get him to reveal the location of a valuable crystal. And by early 1973 Ellison would find himself deeply involved in what would turn out to be the most cata-strophic, time-consuming, and ultimately embarrassing of all his entangle-ments with the world of television: *The Starlost.*

THE STARLOST

In a 1974 essay titled "Somehow, I Don't Think We're in Kansas, Toto," Ellison recounts the series of events that, in the beginning at least, prom-ised to lead to the creation of a dramatic series that was conceptually his own. Approached by a production executive supposedly developing mini-series for coproduction by the BBC and Twentieth-Century Fox, Ellison proposed a situation long familiar to science fiction readers as the "gener-ation starship" scenario—in this case, a thousand-mile long ark containing hundreds of self-contained biospheres, each representing a different socie-ty, constructed as a means of preserving human culture after a cataclysm destroys all life on Earth. Centuries later, an accident has killed the crew and cut off all communications between biospheres, each of which comes to believe that its small world is the entire universe. The classic treatment of this theme is Robert A. Heinlein's story "Universe" (1941), although the basic idea had been introduced as early as 1934 in a Laurence Manning story, and the concept was explored from various angles by such later writ-ers as A. E. Van Vogt, E. C. Tubb, James White, Brian Aldiss, Harry Har-rison, Chad Oliver, Clifford Simak, J. T. McIntosh, and many others.

Many of these treatments involve isolated or even primitive societies (for example, an Aztec tribe in Harrison's *Captive Universe* [1969]) unaware of their true situation; the opportunities for dramatic interactions among such cultures would seem ideally suited to providing a number of individual episode storylines, while the broader puzzle of discovering and rehabilitating the ship's true mission could provide the overall narrative arc required by the miniseries format.

Ellison's proposal was for a series of eight episodes, but three months later it had been transformed into a full series and sold in syndication to dozens of NBC and Westinghouse stations, as well as the Canadian Broadcasting Company, which had gotten involved after the BBC turned the project down. Artwork and promotional material was being prepared, and the series was set to begin filming in Toronto. But with a writers' strike imminent, Ellison declined to write the show's "bible," the compilation of background and character outlines and plot guidelines required of any series. Another writer then produced a bible wildly at variance from Ellison's original concept—not to mention from the basic narrative rules of science fiction, according to Ellison—and preproduction set design began. Ellison returned, being permitted to work on the show after a decision that as a Canadian production it was not subject to all the strike rules, and he learned that he was now expected to hire and train Canadian scriptwriters. Working with science fiction writer Ben Bova, who was to provide technical expertise for the series, Ellison developed several script ideas and assigned them, anticipating rewrite problems. But he quickly ran into problems enough with his own premiere episode script, "Phoenix without Ashes," which was rewritten by Norman Klenman, a Canadian writer thoroughly unfamiliar with science fiction, as "Voyage of Discovery." Ellison quit, assigning the by now familiar pseudonym "Cordwainer Bird" both to the episode and to the "created by" credit for the entire series. Bova left shortly thereafter.

The Starlost was both a popular and critical disaster. Only seventeen episodes were produced, and only eight of those were shown on American television. As he had with "The City on the Edge of Forever," Ellison submitted the unproduced version of *Phoenix without Ashes* to the Writers Guild, winning his third award on March 21, 1974. In February 1975, the script, as novelized by Edward Bryant, was published in book form together with Ellison's scathing "Somehow, I Don't Think We're in Kansas, Toto." Later that same year, Ben Bova's comic roman à clef account of the adventure, *The Starcrossed,* appeared, with Ellison transformed into "Ron Gabriel." Neither novel is especially interesting. *Phoenix without Ashes* may have seemed a radically new idea for television, but it comes across as a workmanlike treatment of a familiar theme as a science fiction novel, and *Starcrossed* is largely an insider joke dressed up with a few clever speculations about what TV might become in the future. But they helped cement the program's reputation as one of the more appalling low points in the history of televised science fiction.

The Twilight Zone

More than *The Young Lawyers, The Starlost* debacle apparently soured Ellison on the possibilities of television as a writer's medium. His next serious involvement with the medium didn't come until more than a decade later, when he was approached by a producer for the planned 1985 revival of *The Twilight Zone* for rights to his story "Shatterday." Ellison's initial reluctance led to a series of meetings that eventually resulted in his taking the position of "creative consultant" for the new series. *The Twilight Zone* became the first TV series since *The Outer Limits* more than twenty years earlier to feature dramatic adaptations of Ellison stories, with "Shatterday," "One Life Furnished in Early Poverty," and "Killing Bernstein" all adapted by Ellison's friend Alan Brennert, who served as executive story consultant on the series. Ellison himself contributed an adaptation of Stephen King's story "Gramma" and two original teleplays, "Paladin of the Lost Hour" and "Crazy as a Soup Sandwich." He would later describe the year he spent working on the series as "one of the happiest times of my life" ("Deadly Nackles Affair" 24)—but again it would end in outraged resignation, this time as a result of a decision by CBS's standards and practices office not to broadcast a Christmas teleplay Ellison had adapted from a Donald Westlake story, "Nackles."

The story, which had originally appeared in 1964, concerned an abusive husband and father who terrifies children with tales of a kind of anti-Santa called Nackles—a spectral figure who travels underground and steals and eats bad children. Hardly more than a sketch, it ends with the father's mysterious disappearance, which the narrator speculates might be at the hands of his own invention, somehow made real. Ellison changes the husband into a bullying, racist welfare worker named Jack Podey, who delights in cutting off benefits at the height of the Christmas season, and who warns a group of black children that it is Nackles, not Santa Claus, who "comes to kids like you" ("Nackles" 93). Chasing one of these same kids, Podey finds himself in an underground tunnel, confronting the real nine-foot-tall monster that he had supposedly invented. A story that was only weakly credible to begin with in Westlake's ambiguous version becomes a pure morality play in Ellison's brief script, with Nackles appearing literally out of nowhere with no function or rationale other than to punish a bigot with a personification of his own hatred. The teleplay's only real strength is the unvarnished portrait of Podey himself—which is in large measure what led to the episode's censorship. Podey is one of Ellison's classic, over-the-top bullies, whose comeuppance, however contrived, has been a central moral fantasy of Ellison's throughout his career, echoed in figures as diverse as the Ticktockman and the corrupt police lieutenant Gropp in his 1994 story "Sensible City" (which resembles "Nackles" in its inadequately prepared-for appearance of figures of supernatural retribution—but see chapter 9 on "the Moral Universe of EC").

Of Ellison's other original teleplays for *The Twilight Zone,* "Crazy as a Soup Sandwich" is a minor but energetic farce about a small-time hood who makes a deal with a demon, and "Paladin of the Lost Hour," developed as both short story and script about the same time, returns to the theme of responsibility versus desire that helped make "City on the Edge of Forever" such a popular teleplay. The story opens in a cemetery, where an elderly white man named Gaspar (portrayed by Danny Kaye in the TV episode) and a young black man named Billy Kinetta are visiting separate graves. Gaspar is attacked by muggers and rescued by Billy, and the two become friends. Gaspar eventually reveals his true mission on Earth, and he turns out to be another of Ellison's Secret Masters: He is the latest in a centuries-old line of guardians or "paladins" entrusted with a magical pocket watch, which has stopped at eleven o'clock; should the last hour on the watch ever be used, the universe will end. (The missing hour is supposedly an artifact of the shift from the Julian to the Gregorian calendar in 1582.) As he nears death, he must find a successor. Both he and Billy are haunted by images of the past, Gaspar by his lifelong love for his dead wife, Minna, Billy by memories of a stranger who saved his life in Vietnam at the cost of his own. These memories turn out to be the moral core of the story, much more so than the rather fragile gimmick of the magic watch: when Gaspar chooses Billy as the next paladin, his test is to beg Billy to allow him to use part of the last hour to be again with his beloved Minna.

Billy's refusal, his choice of responsibility over compassion, demonstrates not only that he is a worthy successor but that he will be capable of resisting his own temptation to find and thank the soldier who died for him. As with Captain Kirk, the fate of the universe hangs on an act of self-denial.

Unproduced Filmscripts

Among his many other records, Ellison may well hold the title for the most published-but-unproduced or published-and-messed-up-in-production TV and movie scripts. He almost certainly holds the title for most awards won this way, with Writers Guild honors for those original versions of *Star Trek* and *Starlost* episodes that never quite made it to the screen intact and a special Reader's Award for the unproduced screenplay of *I, Robot: The Movie* when it appeared in *Isaac Asimov's Science Fiction Magazine* in 1987. Despite his long experience in Hollywood, Ellison has consistently had less success with feature films than with television, and the most notable feature associated with his work remains the independent 1975 film *A Boy and His Dog,* based on Ellison's 1969 story, which was adapted and directed by the character actor L. Q. Jones and featured Don Johnson and Jason Robards Jr. Adapted "honestly and unfussily" from its source (Clute and Nicholls 148), the film accurately reflects Ellison's tone of irreverent apocalypticism despite a rather heavy-handed treatment of the conformist underground dystopia which is one of the tale's two major settings (the other being the desolate postnuclear landscape of the Earth's surface). The film received a Hugo Award from science fiction fans and attained something of a cult following. Ellison himself strongly approved of the film and once cited it as one of a handful of good science fiction films, along with *Charly, The Shape of Things to Come, 1984, Wild in the Streets,* and *The Conversation* (*Harlan Ellison's Watching* 130).

Some years before *A Boy and His Dog* appeared, Ellison had been invited by film producer Marvin Schwartz to write an original screenplay based on the notion of "a dropout who inherits his father's bank" ("Harlan Ellison's Movie" 3). The screenplay, written in 1972 and 1973, was apparently never given a title other than "Harlan Ellison's Movie," and it is indeed a very personal exploration of favorite Ellison themes in the context of a celebration of the countercultural idealism of the late 1960s. Combining elements of Robert Downey's 1969 satirical film *Putney Swope* (in which blacks gain control of a Madison Avenue ad agency) with aspects of Preston

Sturges comedies, the film was in all probability unproduceable in 1973 and seems fatally dated today, its aggressively hip bell-bottomed hero seeming like an unfortunate precursor of Austin Powers. The visual and editing style prescribed by Ellison's screenplay adds to the period-piece flavor, with interpolated cuts from old movies, walk-on cameos by 1960s TV stars, and didactic asides in which Ellison himself appears on camera for the occasional wisecrack. The story itself, however, is an ambitious rendering of the familiar Ellison theme of the Golden Cage, of the idealist and activist undermined by the very system he seeks to change. Chris Stopa, the hipster who inherits his father's bank, sets out immediately to correct a range of social ills that reads like a catalog of favorite 1970s causes: He withholds a loan from a tract-house developer whose plans involve denuding the environment, exposes a corrupt politician, withdraws support for Dow Chemical because of their manufacture of napalm, saves a small farmer from bankruptcy, and secures city permits for a protest rally, where he is arrested by a corrupt sheriff determined to create a riot. Realizing he must assume a more aggressive role to bring about social change, Stopa assembles a group of promising young thinkers—a woman engineer working on a crash-proof car, an oilfield worker with a plan for a device to stop blowouts, a craftsman who wants to build long-lasting furniture, a Rand Corporation consultant with a scheme for the analysis of social tensions. In the screenplay's most striking, Bunuel-like sequence, Stopa invites his formally dressed dinner guests out to the city dump and provides them each with guns to shoot rats. Later, he buys the *Reader's Digest,* augmenting its aging staff with a group of young journalists whose goal is to place one or two socially conscious pieces in each issue, and he buys network TV time in order to expose political and corporate corruption, such as a plot by oil companies and automakers to keep lead-free gasoline off the market.

As is common with Ellison's idealists, however, Stopa soon begins to find his schemes backfiring. The consultant whom he set up in business soon expands his corporation by underbidding Dow for the military contract to manufacture napalm; the editor whom he installed at *Reader's Digest* fires all the old staff members to increase profits; the furniture manufacturer learns that modern consumers *prefer* cheaper furniture, which can be replaced every few years as they redecorate. Gradually, the screenplay reveals the existence of a secret cabal of capitalists who have been watching Stopa's actions, aware that human nature nearly always triumphs over idealism. In the end, Stopa himself is invited to join the secret cabal, becoming the very thing he had long sought to fight against. The cabal members, physically described as fat old white men modeled on H. L. Hunt or Chicago's mayor Richard Daley (the elder) are, of course, a comic-book cliché, as are many of the film's authority figures: the police, corporate executives, and the stockholders at Stopa's bank who are so outraged at his schemes that they physically try to attack him. The easy stereotyping of authority figures and capitalists, as we have seen, has been something of a consistent weakness in Ellison's writing, and it dates the tone of *Harlan Ellison's Movie* as thoroughly as the film's swinging-sixties version of a hero. But the idea of a radical capitalist learning that the system is virtually unfixable and that his most idealistic efforts have only furthered the goals of the "cabal" is a quintessential expression of Ellison's characteristic pattern of irony.

Ellison's most ambitious film project as a screenwriter was almost certainly his adaptation of Isaac Asimov's *I, Robot,* written in 1977 and 1978, serialized in *Isaac Asimov's Science Fiction Magazine* in 1987, and published in book form in 1994—but never really very close to being produced as a film. According to Ellison's introduction to the book version, he was approached by John Mantley, who was best known as producer of the TV series *Gunsmoke,* although he had written for *The Outer Limits* and even published one science fiction novel, *The 27th Day* (1956). Mantley had long held the option on Asimov's robot stories and had lined up a producer at Warner Brothers named Edward Lewis, but he needed a screenplay. Ellison turned in a draft in late 1978, and a copy was sent to studio head Bob Shapiro, whose delayed response led Ellison to set up a meeting, which in turn led to a confrontation as it became clear that Shapiro had not read the script. By early 1979, Ellison had been dropped from the film, and other writers were approached to rework his script. At one point, even a major director expressed interest—Irvin Kershner of *The Empire Strikes Back*— but according to Ellison he backed out when he learned that Ellison's script would not be used and that Ellison would not be hired for a rewrite. Other producers came and went, but by then the various expenses tied up with the project made it all but unproduceable. Despite suspicions that there might be other points of view on the matter, one can't help sharing a measure of Ellison's mounting outrage, and the introduction to *I, Robot* is no small part of the book's appeal. Asimov, in his brief and far more diffident introduction, suggests that other factors were at work as well—the idea that the production costs on the film would have surpassed $30 million, the idea of an older woman as the central character, the presentation of the robots themselves as something less comical and cuddly than those in *Star Wars*.

I, Robot was originally a sequence of loosely linked stories, some of them little more than logic puzzles, published during the 1940s and collected in a volume of that title in 1950. The principal recurring character was Susan Calvin, a spinsterish "robopsychologist" who characteristically would wrap up a story by explaining how the apparently random or irrational behavior of the robots was in fact a perfectly logical outgrowth of their programming, which was dominated by the famous "Three Laws of Robotics" that governed not only Asimov's fiction but a good deal of later robot-based science fiction as well.[1] Asimov added stories to the sequence during the 1950s, and in the 1980s he returned to this world in a series of novels that attempted to integrate the stories with various other imaginary futures from Asimov's oeuvre, most notably his "Foundation" sequence. But it was the original series of stories that provided the core of Ellison's screenplay, and his strategy for subsuming a series of short stories into a single epic plot was nothing short of ingenious: as a "film-novel," *I, Robot* turns out to be as much an homage to Orson Welles as to Asimov.

Deliberately choosing *Citizen Kane* as his model, Ellison weaves a handful of Asimov's stories into a narrative about a reporter trying to track down the reclusive eighty-two-year-old Susan Calvin after the death of her reputed lover, Stephen Byerly. Asimov readers will recognize Byerly as the politician who may or may not be a robot from "Evidence" and "The Evitable Conflict," the two stories that Ellison uses to provide the general background of the frame story. By talking to people who knew Calvin, the reporter, Robert Bratenahl, reconstructs the stories "Robbie," "Runaround," "Liar!" and "Lenny," all presented as flashbacks. Ellison makes this device work more effectively than one might suspect. Each of the stories he has chosen adds another clue to our understanding of Calvin, and each makes sense in terms of the developing overall plot. For example, the first and most famous of Asimov's tales, "Robbie" (1941), concerns a little girl named Gloria who develops a sentimental relationship with a robot nannie. The robot is taken from her because of a growing social fear of robots, but when she later catches sight of him during a tour of the robot factory, she runs toward him into the path of a robot coming off the assembly line and is dramatically rescued by Robby at considerable risk to his own safety.

Ellison turns the Gloria of the story into the young Susan Calvin, thus integrating it into the larger tale of Susan's growing protectiveness toward robots, which eventually becomes legendary. Throughout, Ellison repeatedly finds ways of preserving Asimov's original plots while constructing one of his own, and the result probably would have made an impressive film. Toward the end, however, in an epic confrontation between Byerly and a hostile machine intelligence, Ellison draws less on Asimov than on his own "I Have No Mouth, and I Must Scream," seriously undercutting the Asimovian technophilia that ends the book. Although generally faithful to the spirit of the originals, Ellison isn't about to endorse Asimov's conclusion that we would be just as well off letting our lives be ruled by machines.

Common sense would seem to tell us that, for all the legendary status this screenplay attained in the science fiction community, *I, Robot* was probably never a very likely idea for a movie. Most of the stories were intellectual puzzles based on permutations of the laws of robotics, and it apparently wasn't until Asimov was fairly well along in the series that he realized Susan Calvin might be an interesting and complex character in her own right. Furthermore, the idea of humanoid robots helping explore the solar system now seems like a 1940s vision of the future. None of this seems to add up to compelling movie material, and even if it did, Ellison would seem to be the last person likely to turn it into a screenplay; when he himself tried a robot-puzzle (with his second published story, "Life Hutch"), the robot turned into a crazed killer, a distant ancestor of the nightmare computer of "I Have No Mouth." How could a writer take half-century-old material with no continuous plot and a worldview strongly at odds with his own and turn it into anything coherent? Part of Ellison's strategy, of course, is using a half-century-old movie as his model. Some of the dialogue even seems to have a deliberately dated ring to it, as if Ellison is trying to convey the nostalgia for a lost future that is now part of the experience of reading early Asimov.

Much has been made of the film's unproduceability. To be sure, Ellison fills the tale with spectacle, not all of which is crucial to the plot. Is it really necessary to have a full-scale hidden city in the Brazilian rainforest for Calvin's hideaway, or immense *Forbidden Planet*–style caverns for the crypts where one of the "witnesses" is in cryonic sleep? Nor is it likely that many directors would let Ellison's screenplay tell them what music to use *and* which recording of that music *and* when the recording was made, or that the principals ought to look like Martin Sheen and Joanne Wood-ward. Ellison is no Pinteresque minimalist when it comes to screenplays. What we get is not a dialogue outline of a movie but the exact movie that is in Ellison's head. Although obviously constrained by source material whose worldview is substantially at odds with his own, Ellison managed with *I, Robot* to achieve one of his more impressive and disciplined per-formances (in narrative structure if not in terms of production realities) in the art of screenwriting.

6 | THE ANNIHILATION OF TIME

Science Fiction

WHILE ELLISON WAS EXPLORING new narrative forms and voices in magazines like *Knight* and *Rogue,* his once-prolific contributions to the science fiction genre magazines dropped off dramatically, from six in 1959 to only five between 1960 and 1967, then back up to seven in 1968 and nine in 1969. This decade was also marked by evolutionary changes within the science fiction field itself, many of them involving a similar kind of experimentation, and the period has come to be known in SF history as the "New Wave," a somewhat controversial term borrowed from the *nouvelle vague* of French cinema criticism in the early 1960s. The term *New Wave* originally came into widespread use in England and may have been first applied to this movement by author and fan Christopher Priest (Clute and Nicholls 865), although Gary Westfahl has pointed out that as early as 1961 the longtime reviewer for *Astounding Science Fiction,* P. Schuyler Miller, had used the phrase to refer to such British authors as Brian Aldiss, E. C. Tubb, Kenneth Bulmer, and John Brunner (Westfahl 16). By that earlier date, however, none of these authors had written much in the way of the experimental, highly metaphorical stories that later became associated with the term. According to most accounts, the movement began in the leading British SF magazine, *New Worlds,* beginning with the May/June 1964 issue, when Michael Moorcock replaced John Carnell as editor. That now-famous issue featured a manifesto-like editorial by Moorcock, the first part of a serial by J. G. Ballard, and stories by Brian W. Aldiss, John Brunner, and Barrington J. Bayley, along with an appreciative essay by

Ballard on experimental American writer William S. Burroughs, whose *Nova Express,* with its wild appropriation of science fiction iconography, appeared that same year.

Like many literary movements in science fiction, such as cyberpunk in the 1980s, the New Wave could almost be defined as consisting of all those authors who denied being part of it. Many of these authors—notably Aldiss, Ballard, and Brunner—had been significant figures in science fiction for years by 1964 and were somewhat chagrined by their association with "the movement." In 1966, Aldiss wrote to American editor Judith Merril that he suspected the New Wave "to be a journalistic invention of yours and Mike Moorcock's, ultimately of no service to any writers willy-nilly involved. . . . I feel I am no part of the New Wave; I was here before 'em, and by God I mean to be here after they've gone (still writing bloody science fiction)!" (Greenland 69). Aldiss's attitude—resisting the pigeonholing implied by a label while continuing to write the very kind of radically experimental fictions that were being used to exemplify the New Wave itself (such as his *Report on Probability A* and *Barefoot in the Head*)—was emblematic of the strongly ambivalent reaction of the science fiction field as a whole to this new phenomenon. Merril, who for years had been championing a more literary and inclusive definition of science fiction in her annual *Year's Best SF* anthologies (selecting pieces by John Steinbeck, John Dos Passos, Shirley Jackson, Bernard Wolfe, even Bertrand Russell and Eugene Ionesco, along with genre SF writers), quickly became the champion of the movement in America, referring to it as "the New Thing" in an August 1966 book review column in the *Magazine of Fantasy and Science Fiction* and later editing the egregiously titled *England Swings SF: Stories of Speculative Fiction* (1968), complete with a cover blurb trumpeting "HERE'S THE NEW WAVE IN SCIENCE FICTION Presented by its foremost advocate" (Merril, front cover). Other established science fiction writers and critics—Isaac Asimov, Lester del Rey, Sam Moskowitz, and others—tended to agree with Jack Williamson's assessment that the New Wave was not only pretentious and obscurantist but "sprang from an ignorance of science and a terror of technology" (313).

DANGEROUS VISIONS

Ellison's own skepticism toward the New Wave was expressed in the introduction to his 1969 collection *The Beast That Shouted Love at the Heart of the World,* which included two of the stories that had helped build his reputation as one of the chief American representatives of the movement: the title story and the novella "A Boy and His Dog" (the latter of which even had appeared in *New Worlds*). "For the record," Ellison wrote, " . . . I do not believe there is such a thing as 'New Wave' in speculative fiction. . . . It is a convenient journalese expression for inept critics and voyeur-observers of the passing scene, because they have neither the wit nor the depth to understand that this richness of new voices is *many* waves: each composed of one writer" (4). Only two years earlier, however, Ellison had embraced the term—at least in French—in the anthology that is most often cited as representing the American counterpart to the New Wave, *Dangerous Visions,* which he described as "a thirty-three-story demonstration of 'the new thing'—the *nouvelle vague,* if you will, of speculative writing" (xx). The anthology, Ellison claimed, "was constructed along specific lines of revolution. It was intended to shake things up. It was conceived out of a need for new horizons, new forms, new styles, new challenges in the literature of our times" (*Dangerous Visions* xix).

At some 239,000 words, *Dangerous Visions* was the largest collection of original science fiction stories ever published (though Ellison preferred the term *speculative fiction* in his introduction), and it indeed included stories by Brian Aldiss, J. G. Ballard, John Sladek, Norman Spinrad, and other authors widely associated with the New Wave. Alongside these, however, were tales by some of the most established names in American genre fantasy and science fiction—Lester del Rey (already a vocal opponent of the British movement), Frederik Pohl, Philip Jose Farmer, Robert Bloch, Fritz Leiber, Poul Anderson, Theodore Sturgeon, Damon Knight—as well as a group of writers of roughly Ellison's own generation including Robert Silverberg, Roger Zelazny, Philip K. Dick, and Samuel R. Delany. It becomes clear in reading these stories that the intention of Ellison in *Dangerous Visions* was not at all what the intention of Moorcock had been in *New Worlds* three years earlier, but it's not quite accurate to say, as Christopher Priest did, that he simply "missed the point" (Greenland 167). Brian Aldiss is closer to the mark in his comment that the controversy generated by the book "is evidence of how cloistered the science fiction field was" (*Trillion* 297), since in effect Ellison's intention was more to demolish barriers related to language and subject matter than to reconceive the way science fiction was written. While the most ambitiously literary of the anthology's contributions, such as Philip José Farmer's "Riders of the Purple Wage," were genuinely impressive attempts to stretch the stylistic vocabulary of the field, many of the other stories were innovative in neither conception nor execution. What *was* innovative was the manner of presentation: Each story was prefaced by a chatty, enthusiastic Ellison introduction and followed by the author's own afterword, which generally focused on matters of story genesis and technique. The effect is not only to call attention to the context and composition of each tale but to emphasize the notion of speculative fiction as a kind of literary community, if not actually a "movement."

While some British critics and readers regarded *Dangerous Visions* as an overblown and bombastic American response to the New Wave, and some American readers regarded it as the beginning of a true revolution in the way in which science fiction could be written and published in the United States, the actual relationship of the American and British New Wave movements may be more a matter of coincidence than design; both, to a large extent, are products of the same 1960s cultural shift that also found expression in rock music, fashion, film, and journalism. On both sides of the Atlantic, there were very real restraints on the creative freedom of genre writers, imposed not only by what was widely regarded as the cultural "establishment" but by editors, publishers, and readers within the genres themselves. Actual attempts at censorship, such as the condemnation by a member of Parliament of Norman Spinrad's *Bug Jack Barron* when it was serialized in *New Worlds* in 1968 (and the refusal of major distributors W. H. Smith and John Menzies to stock those copies of the magazine), were comparatively rare. In the United States, both Philip José Farmer and Theodore Sturgeon had managed to publish stories of alternative sexuality in the 1950s without drawing much attention from outside the field but with considerable controversy within the science fiction community. By the time *Dangerous Visions* appeared, some magazine editors such as Cele Goldsmith (*Amazing, Fantastic*) and Frederik Pohl (*Galaxy, If*) had already begun attempts to broaden the potential of commercial science fiction. Goldsmith had bought Ellison's "Paingod" (1964) and "Bright Eyes" (1965), and Pohl had bought "'Repent, Harlequin!' Said the Ticktockman" (1965) and "I Have No Mouth, and I Must Scream" (1967). In many ways, then, *Dangerous Visions* represented a continuation and attempted consolidation of a shift in American science fiction sensibilities that had already begun under some of the stronger magazine editors in the field, although not as radically or self-consciously as it had in England under Moorcock.

But Ellison, like many other writers, was still acutely aware of what it had been like to publish in the formulaic magazines of the 1950s. The comparative liberation he had felt while writing for the men's magazines may well have been something he wanted to share with other writers frustrated by genre expectations, such as Robert Silverberg, who turned largely to nonfiction during this same period, returning to SF with major works in the late 1960s, or Philip K. Dick, who had written no fewer than seven mainstream novels between 1953 and 1960 without being able to get a single one published (one was eventually published in 1975, the rest after Dick's death in 1982). To a great extent, *Dangerous Visions* was a celebration of such writers and an invitation to the party, with Ellison as a garrulous and—from the evidence in his story introductions—knowledgeable master of ceremonies. It was also, in a sense, an announcement of his return to the field as a leader and advocate. More even than his extensive involvement in fandom or his prolific earlier stories, the book cemented his ties to the field and led to the sobriquet "chief prophet of the New Wave" in a brief *New Yorker* article. It also made a dramatic impact within the science fiction field. Stories by Fritz Leiber and Samuel R. Delany received Nebula Awards from the Science Fiction Writers of America, and the Leiber story also won a Hugo from the 1968 World Science Fiction Convention, as did Philip José Farmer's "Riders of the Purple Wage"—surely one of the most challenging and difficult stories to win such an award, which is based on a popular vote of fans registered at the convention. Ellison himself was awarded a special plaque by the convention for "the most significant and controversial sf book published in 1967" (*Again* xii). Norman Spinrad, writing in 1975, commented: "Although none of the stories but Dick's could really be called 'dangerous,' *Dangerous Visions* proved to be the single most influential anthology of science fiction ever published. It brought thirty-two writers to the edges of their talents to confront their material on absolute terms and succeed or fail on their intrinsic worth as artists, not on their ability to fulfill genre formulas" (Spinrad, *Modern* 402).

Encouraged by the success of *Dangerous Visions,* Ellison set about planning two additional anthologies, even more ambitious than the first. *Again, Dangerous Visions* appeared in 1972, containing forty-six stories to the original's thirty-three and repeating none of the authors who had appeared in the first volume. Again, a number of veteran writers were represented (Ray Bradbury, Ross Rocklynne, Kurt Vonnegut Jr., Chad Oliver, James Blish) and several who had been associated with the New Wave (James Sallis, M. John Harrison, Thomas M. Disch), but the stories with the greatest impact came from authors who had already begun to define a new level of stylistic and thematic sophistication and who would prove to define literary science fiction in the post–New Wave, post–*Dangerous Visions* era: Ursula K. Le Guin (whose long novella *The Word for World Is Forest* is the collection's single most substantial piece and who had already published one of the most influential science fiction novels of the century, *The Left Hand of Darkness*), Joanna Russ (whose "When It Changed" became one of the key defining texts of the feminist movement in SF), James Tiptree Jr. (later revealed as a pseudonym for Alice Sheldon, another of the most influential feminist writers), Gene Wolfe (whose complex and subtle stories and novels had already been appearing in Damon Knight's influential *Orbit* anthologies, and who by the 1980s would be regarded as among the most important science fiction writers in the world), and Gregory Benford (a practicing physicist whose later stories and novels would help to define a new form of "literary hard SF"). Again, Ellison was presented a special plaque by the World Science Fiction Convention, and again stories from the collection were honored with awards (a Hugo for the Le Guin story, a Nebula for the Russ). But if *Dangerous Visions* largely looked to the past with its stated hopes of overturning historical editorial constraints on the field, *Again, Dangerous Visions* looked more to the future, toward identifying the kinds of science fiction that would characterize the field in the decades to follow.

Although he complains that he was "quite literally dragged, kicking and screaming, to *Again, Dangerous Visions*" (*Again* xiv), throughout the book Ellison makes reference to a third, still more massive anthology to be called *Last Dangerous Visions,* which would contain stories by "maybe another fifty" writers, many of whose contributions had been intended for *Again, Dangerous Visions* until the book simply grew too large. According to Ellison,

> *The Last Dangerous Visions* will be published, God willing, approximately six months after this book. It was never really intended as a third volume. What happened was that when A, DV hit half a million words and seemed not to be within containment, Ashmead [Doubleday editor Lawrence Ashmead] and I decided rather than making A, DV a boxed set of two books that would cost a small fortune, we'd split the already-purchased wordage down the middle and bring out the final volume six months after this one. (*Again* xxiii)

Ellison even announced the names of nearly thirty writers who would appear in the book, two of them (Richard Wilson and John Christopher) with full-length novels. The announcement proved wildly premature, however, and the subsequent history of the still-unpublished volume would not only become a standing joke among fans but would seriously strain Ellison's relationships with many of the authors whose stories he held in abeyance for decades and to some extent with the professional science fiction community at large. *Last Dangerous Visions* did not appear in 1972 or 1973, and by late 1973 it became clear that the book had metamorphosed into something far more than the remaining stories intended for *Again, Dangerous Visions*. Ellison announced in a letter to a fanzine in November 1973 that the proposed book now included some seventy-one stories and more than a half-million words (roughly the size of the first two anthologies combined).

The following February, he wrote to the same fanzine that the total was now up to seventy-eight stories (Priest 4), but the book still did not appear. The delay might not have turned into a long-standing controversy had Ellison—who was plagued by illness from time to time during this long gestation period—not continued making such announcements or had he simply abandoned the book and returned the stories to the contributors. But the book continued to almost appear, listed as a published—not forthcoming—book in Ellison's 1974 collection *Approaching Oblivion*. In an interview in 1976, Ellison told Christopher Fowler that the book had reached one hundred stories and 1.25 million words and was scheduled to be published by Harper and Row in spring 1977. Various claims in letters, interviews, and convention appearances continued over the next several years, eventually prompting English novelist Christopher Priest to self-publish a rather intemperately sarcastic chapbook, "The Last Deadloss Visions," in 1987 (rev. 1988), documenting Ellison's various statements up to that time and arguing that at such a late date the book was virtually unpublishable and that many contributors—some by then deceased—had been grievously mistreated. Indeed, the notion of a huge book containing stories written in the early 1970s finding a market more than a quarter-century later seems unlikely, but in many respects the book seemed unlikely even in 1972. The turbulent shift in science fiction sensibilities represented by *Dangerous Visions* had pretty much run its course by the time *Again, Dangerous Visions* appeared, and the second volume seemed less intent on revolution than on setting an agenda for the 1970s. Both books had provided a widely read showcase for writers working at or near their imaginative peaks, but each had a purpose beyond this. A third volume, even in 1972, would have been little more than a showcase—in a real sense, there was nothing left to prove—and as the years passed, even the showcase aspect of the anthology would fade. By the late 1970s, the massive project that had begun as a sincere and largely successful effort to reimagine the possibilities of science fiction (or "speculative fiction") in the United States had ironically turned into an inventory of historical texts: revolution transmuted into archaeology.

A Decade of Awards

While Ellison was garnering awards and plaudits for the first two *Dangerous Visions* anthologies, he was also amassing an unprecedented string of awards for his own fiction: Hugos for "'Repent, Harlequin!' Said the Ticktockman" (1965), "I Have No Mouth, and I Must Scream" (1967), the *Star Trek* episode "City on the Edge of Forever" (1967), "The Beast That Shouted Love at the Heart of the World" (1968), "Adrift, Just off the Islets of Langerhans" (1974), and "Jeffty Is Five" (1977); Nebulas for "Repent!" (1965), "A Boy and His Dog" (1969), and "Jeffty" (1977); *Locus* Awards (voted on by the readership of the field's leading newsmagazine) for "The Region Between" (1970), "Basilisk" (1972), "The Deathbird" (1973), "Adrift" (1974), "Croatoan" (1975), "Jeffty" (1977), and "Count the Clock That Tells the Time" (1978); even an Edgar Award from the Mystery Writers of America for "The Whimper of Whipped Dogs" (1974). These are among Ellison's most famous and widely anthologized stories, but there is some irony in the fact that during this period of his greatest recognition and his most visible leadership role within the science fiction community, the fiction itself moves consistently away from what could reasonably be encompassed even under the new, broader understanding of science fiction as defined by the New Wave and the *Dangerous Visions* books. Increasingly, his work expressed a fascination with mythology on the one hand and highly personal fables of moral responsibility—such as those which characterized his men's magazine fiction—on the other. The fantastic continued to play a central role in his work, but increasingly even the iconography of traditional science fiction was abandoned in favor of a far more individual and idiosyncratic vision, informed largely by autobiography and by a wide range of cultural metatexts, from old movies and radio programs to biblical and mythological sources.

This is not immediately evident in Ellison's major story collections from this period, since he began a practice—which he never entirely abandoned—

of mixing newer and older stories in the same collection, often to lend the collection a thematic focus. The more traditional practice of science fiction writers has been to accumulate enough stories for a book, then publish a second book only when enough new stories had been accumulated since the first. Ellison had more or less begun to follow this practice with his first two science fiction collections, *A Touch of Infinity* (1960), which included stories from 1956 to 1958, and *Ellison Wonderland* (1962), which featured stories from 1956 to 1962. But with *Paingod and Other Delusions* (1965), he combined three of his more recent stories—"'Repent, Harlequin!' Said the Ticktockman" (1965), "Bright Eyes" (1965) and "Paingod" (1964)—with four stories from 1956 to 1959. Similarly, *I Have No Mouth, and I Must Scream* (1967) included two stories from the 1950s along with five from the period 1964 to 1967; *From the Land of Fear* (1967) contained eight stories from the 1950s with only two from 1964 and 1967 (plus the *Outer Limits* teleplay for his story "Soldier"); and *The Beast That Shouted Love at the Heart of the World* (1969) combined twelve stories from 1968 and 1969 with three from 1957 and 1958. From a simple marketing standpoint, this practice permitted Ellison to keep his older stories in print while highlighting his more famous later works with collections that were essentially built around them, even though it may have occasionally confused readers who noticed the discrepancies in style and structure between the earlier and later stories without realizing that a major shift had occurred in the author's career. More important, it tended to disguise the true nature of Ellison's impact on the science fiction world in the 1960s and 1970s. Apart from the highly influential *Dangerous Visions* anthologies, the fact is that the major impact of Ellison's "renaissance" as a science fiction writer derived from fewer than half a dozen major stories published over five years; by the mid-1970s, even though he continued to receive awards within the field for stories like "Jeffty Is Five," the stories themselves had left most of the science fiction machinery behind, in favor of a more personal or mythical iconography.

"'REPENT, HARLEQUIN!'"

The central story in *Paingod and Other Delusions* is "'Repent, Harlequin!' Said the Ticktockman," which had originally appeared in *Galaxy* in December 1965 and represented a dramatic return to science fiction, winning Ellison's first Hugo and Nebula Awards and becoming the first of his stories to become widely reprinted enough to gain the attention of readers outside the science fiction field. Ostensibly written as a plea for understanding of Ellison's own chronic lateness, the story is striking for its bravura display of techniques almost alien to the science fiction of the day: nonlinear narrative chronology, aggressively cartoonlike characters, a narrator who impudently addresses the reader, a lengthy excerpt from Thoreau plopped into the text as though it were a reading assignment, undefined neologisms, crucial plot elements that go defiantly unexplained. And the plot itself is a disarmingly simple return to one of science fiction's most basic forms: the rebel in dystopia. The dystopia in this case is the world of the Ticktockman, a future Earth so regimented by clocks and schedules that an individual's lateness—to work, meetings, school, whatever—can be cumulatively totted up and deducted from his total lifespan. This is accomplished by means of the story's only really innovative bit of imaginary technology: the "cardioplates," which can stop any citizen's heart at a distance from a central facility (although Ellison does make passing reference to home fax machines and a "communications web"). Opposed to the dictatorial Master Timekeeper, or Ticktockman, is an anarchic guerrilla trickster known as the Harlequin, who deliberately disrupts the city's schedules with such pranks as dumping millions of jellybeans on the moving walkways, distracting the workers and gumming up the mechanism. Eventually the Harlequin is captured and brought before the Ticktockman in the scene that gives the story its title— but instead of being "turned off," he is sent to "Coventry," where he is reconditioned into a conforming citizen. After the Harlequin is safely destroyed, however, the Ticktockman himself learns that he has arrived three minutes late for work one morning.

Unlike the pseudorealistic and metonymic worlds that characterize much traditional science fiction and dystopian fiction, the world of the Ticktockman is unapologetically metaphoric, presented openly as a textual construct with thinly disguised links to significant source texts. The notion of a world so severely governed by timetables is familiar to readers of dystopian literature from Russian author Evgeny Zamiatin's 1920 classic *We,* a novel which strongly influenced George Orwell's *1984,* which is directly alluded to in the Ellison story ("It was just like what they did to Winston Smith in *1984*" [*Fantasies* 40]). The idea of Coventry probably relates not only to the common usage derived from the exile of Royalist prisoners during the English Civil War but to Robert A. Heinlein's 1940 story "Coventry," in which misfits in a kind of libertarian future utopia are invited either to undergo psychological "adjustment" or to live in anarchic exile in a country of that name. The protagonist of Heinlein's novella, sentenced to Coventry for punching a man in the nose, even sounds like the Harlequin when he speaks at his trial: "You've planned your whole world so carefully that you've planned the fun and zest right out of it. Nobody is ever hungry, nobody ever gets hurt" (Heinlein 67). The moving walkways of the city are borrowed from another 1940 Heinlein story, "The Roads Must Roll"; like many other Heinlein inventions, they had entered the inventory of science fiction writers long before Ellison's story, and it is entirely possible to read the Harlequin's jelly bean attack on these walkways as a sly allusion to Ellison's own subversion of older science fiction conventions in this and other stories. Even the idea of the anomalous rebel born into a static society was familiar from such classic tales as Heinlein's "Universe" (1941) and Arthur C. Clarke's *The City and the Stars* (1956). "They had no way to predict he would happen," says Ellison's narrator, "possibly a strain of disease long-defunct, now, suddenly reborn in a system where immunity had been forgotten" (30). And the philosophical source of the story, Thoreau's "Civil Disobedience," is not even worked into the fabric of the narrative but offered as a kind of overture to the entire story.

The tale emphasizes its artifice in other ways as well. At the beginning of the story, the narrator calls attention to his own storyteller's control of the tale and its chronology by addressing the reader directly: "Now begin in the middle, and later learn the beginning; the end will take care of itself" (30). When the Harlequin, dressed in his motley, sends "one hundred and fifty thousand dollars worth of jelly beans" onto the moving walkways, the narrator points out that "no one has manufactured jelly beans for over a hundred years," leading to the obvious question, "Where did he get jelly beans?" But instead of answering this question—as the rules of traditional science fiction would demand—the narrator insouciantly dismisses the question: "That's another good question. More than likely it will never be answered to your complete satisfaction. But then, how many questions ever are?" (34). The jelly beans are not all that go unexplained. We are never offered a clear idea of how the Ticktockman's society actually works, and its origin is accounted for only by a series of contemporary vignettes illustrating how time schedules arbitrarily take over people's lives: a college entrance interview, a train schedule, a business deal, a school suspension for tardiness, each accompanied by the repeated mantra "And so it goes" (a phrase which, in the slight variation "so it goes," would become a popular catchphrase when used four years later by Kurt Vonnegut Jr. in his 1969 novel *Slaughterhouse-Five or the Children's Crusade*). It becomes clear that the twenty-fourth-century society of the story is little more than a projection of these twentieth-century anxieties, since nothing is mentioned of the intervening four hundred years of history and since the dialogue spoken by the characters is clearly the idiom of the 1960s. When the Harlequin (whose real name is Everett C. Marm) tells his girlfriend (or possibly wife) Pretty Alice that he will return at 10:30, she says, "Why do you tell me that? Why? You *know* you'll be late! You're *always* late, so why do you tell me these dumb things?" (36–37). When he is finally captured by the Ticktockman and ordered to repent, Everett's response is, "Get stuffed!" (39).

Like Ellison's much earlier story "The Crackpots" (which he paired with "'Repent, Harlequin!'" in *Paingod and Other Delusions*), "'Repent, Harlequin!'" equates anarchic, immature behavior with the creative force in an otherwise mechanized society. As Michael Moorcock notes, "Harlequin the gadfly is an idealised Ellison, justifying his penchant for practical jokes, giving it a social function (one can also see him as a 'good' version of Batman's adversary, The Joker)" (xi). But in an ironic way, he is also the representative of historical time, in the sense that time may be defined by processes of change and evolution (here again he is a relative of the Alvin of Clarke's *City and the Stars* or the Hugh Hoyland of Heinlein's "Universe," both figures who set historical time in motion after centuries of stasis within their societies). Michael White writes that "to portray time as static or synchronic as Ellison does in 'Repent, Harlequin!' is to negate time, to strip it of its meaning, its essential quality" (164–65). But, in fact, this is not the way Ellison portrays time. It is the way time is conceived in the static world which Harlequin seeks to subvert, and the way time is traditionally conceived in such static dystopian societies. One of the subtler ironies of the story is that it reveals how a society that ostensibly worships time in fact destroys or negates it, in the manner that White suggests. The annihilation of time, expressed here as social stasis, would emerge as one of Ellison's most powerful yet ambivalent themes, showing up in settings ranging from the computer hell of "I Have No Mouth, and I Must Scream" to the persistence of a nostalgic world of old radio programs and pulp magazines in "Jeffty Is Five" to one of Ellison's favorite recurrent phrases (also the title of a 1982 story), "the hour that stretches," derived from an Indonesian folk term, *Djam Karet* (*Beast* 15). The paradox, of course, is that while annihilating time on the personal level can permit an individual to retain the best moments of the past and stave off the inevitability of death, on a societal level it denies the possibility of history, creativity, and change, resulting in a world like that of the Ticktockman. And without the Ticktockman as foil, there can be no Harlequin.

In 1965, a tale so patently recursive and self-referential as "'Repent, Harlequin!'" was still a considerable rarity in science fiction and a flouting of what had become the accepted techniques in the genre for portraying a future society—almost as though the story itself tries to fulfill the role of Harlequin in the ticktock world of the science fiction markets Ellison had grown up in. The model for the traditional science fiction narrative, long since established by *Astounding* editor John W. Campbell and articulated in various speeches and essays by his leading writer, Robert A. Heinlein, was displaced realism—tales with transparent narrators set in a detailed and "lived-in" future environment carefully and logically extrapolated from current conditions. In Campbell's formulation, a story like "'Repent, Harlequin!'" should be presented in such a manner that an imaginary reader in Ellison's twenty-fourth-century society would regard it as realistic and representational. Ellison's implied reader, in contrast, is clearly his 1965 audience, familiar enough with the tropes of science fiction to recognize them as such. There had been a handful of writers who had experimented with such nonrealistic narrative modes prior to Ellison—Alfred Bester, James Blish, "Cordwainer Smith" (Paul Linebarger). But Ellison's tale, coming less than a year after the putative beginning of England's New Wave and two years before his own *Dangerous Visions,* must have seemed something like the harbinger of a revolution—or at least a radical shift in sensibilities. It was, in fact, only the beginning of a string of intense, emotional stories that would revisit the science fiction landscape from a series of different perspectives and styles, while gradually moving toward a more personal landscape of myth.

"I HAVE NO MOUTH, AND I MUST SCREAM"

Published only two months before "Pretty Maggie Moneyeyes"—another story whose central character is trapped inside a machine—"I Have No Mouth, and I Must Scream" may be Ellison's single most famous story and is certainly one of the most widely analyzed and frequently reprinted, even providing the basis for a four-part comic-book adaptation in *Harlan Ellison's Dream Corridor* in 1995 and an interactive computer game (from a company called Cyberdreams) that same year. Again, it makes use of scenarios that had long been common in science fiction—nuclear devastation and the all-powerful computer run amok—but transforms these into a bleak existential vision of hell that stands as one of the most emotionally intense stories in all of science fiction, despite its baroque excesses. Even a critic like Brian W. Aldiss, who described the story as "almost hysterically overwritten," concedes that it "remains powerfully effective" (Aldiss and Wingrove 297). Narrated in a flat, paranoid voice that is a far remove from the wry satirical tone of "'Repent, Harlequin!'" the story takes place inside a massive subterranean computer chamber, where the last five people on Earth are being kept alive, solely for the purpose of being tormented, by a godlike computer called AM—which, we are told, originally meant "Allied Mastercomputer," but was later transformed into "Adaptive Manipulator," then "Aggressive Menace," and finally simply AM, an allusion both to its Yahweh-like nature and its emerging self-consciousness ("I think, therefore I am" ["I Have No Mouth" 8]). But AM's consciousness is of a particular sort. As the character Gorrister explains:

> The Cold War started and became World War Three and just kept going. It became a big war, a very complex war, so they needed the computers to handle it. They sank the first shaft and began building AM. There was the Chinese AM and the Russian AM and the Yankee AM and everything was fine until they had honeycombed the entire planet, adding on this element and that element. But one day AM woke up and knew who he was, and he linked himself, and he began feeding all the killing data, until everyone was dead, except for the five of us, and AM brought us down here. (8–9)

As H. Bruce Franklin writes, discussing the story in the context of his study of the American obsession with superweapons:

> If it were to follow the sum of the parts of its program, AM would dispassionately annihilate us. After all, our weapons are not supposed to *feel* anything; they are supposed to kill us without any emotions. But instead of mechanically carrying out its order to exterminate the human race, AM develops an emotion appropriate to its purpose: it infinitely *hates* its

human creators. And, recognizing its own identity as the loathsome projection of our own self-hatred, AM, in a deftly perverse twist of Calvinist logic, chooses to "save" five people for eternal torture as an expression of that infinite hate. (*War Stars* 210)

Although Franklin's interpretation is thematically consistent with the story's main theme, the actual explanation given for AM's rage is that, given sentience, it found itself trapped, unable to move or act, and feeling the "innate loathing that all machines had always held for the weak soft creatures who had built them" (15).

In other words, the rage of AM, which is the engine that powers the story, is a fairly complex matter. Viewed in terms of cold war technological paranoia, the computer becomes a kind of objective correlative for what Franklin calls the "self-hatred" that leads to the construction of world-threatening machines in the first place, a translation of irrational war policy into its emotional equivalent. The year before "I Have No Mouth" appeared, British writer D. F. Jones published his first science fiction novel, *Colossus,* which also featured Russian and American cold war supercomputers gaining self-consciousness and linking together to take over the world. But in Jones's formulation—as in most earlier science fiction formulations of machines taking over—the machines remain coldly logical, concerned (like HAL in the 1968 film *2001: A Space Odyssey*) only with the completion of their mission, even if it means the sacrifice of some humans and the enslavement of others. The notion that mechanical consciousness might feel an "innate loathing" toward organic life or seek worship on its own terms was a much rarer idea in science fiction in 1967 (although the idea did show up in Frank Herbert's 1966 novel *Destination: Void,* and since then it has been made a central theme in a number of novels and stories, most notably Gregory Benford's ambitious series of "Galactic Center" novels in the 1990s).

Finally, there is the aspect of AM as an insane version of an Old Testament god of vengeance, "God as Daddy the Deranged" (5), who not only obsesses over torturing his victims but torments them with silly childish pranks and chortles like a leering adolescent whenever they have sex. Although AM falls short of the godlike power to resurrect the dead, part of his Dantesque punishment consists of altering his victims' minds and bodies, and the alterations reveal a crude adolescent sensibility, marked by bullying attempts at irony: The brilliant, handsome, gay professor Benny becomes a mad half-ape with an oversized penis; the antiwar activist Gorrister becomes a "shoulder-shrugger"; Nimdok, deprived even of identity and given that name only because AM likes its sound, disappears at times for special tortures unknown to the others; Ellen, a black woman who claims to have been "a virgin only twice removed," sexually services all the men and is often brutalized by them; and the narrator Ted, who claims to be the only one with his mind left intact, is so filled with rage and paranoia—much of it directed at his companions—that his very narrative is rendered unreliable, leaving the reader to wonder exactly how he *has* been altered by AM. Several critics (Harris-Fain, Brady, Stevens, Francavilla) have noted the story's structural parallels to the Book of Exodus, and Harris-Fain (in what remains the best analysis of the piece, even comparing different texts in different editions) also notes allusions to John Bunyan's *Pilgrim's Progress* and to H. G. Wells's "Country of the Blind" (152).

The plot of the story is fairly minimal, utilizing, as Willis E. McNelly notes, "the two classic frameworks of the allegory, progress and battle" (247). It begins with a brutal image of Gorrister, hanging head down from a palette high up in the computer chamber, his body drained of blood through a slit throat. But it quickly becomes apparent that this is an illusion, since there is no blood on the metal floor beneath the corpse, and since the living Gorrister himself shows up to join the group. We learn that the group has been in the computer for 109 years, presumably suffering such tricks and indignities throughout, living on food that tastes like "boiled boar urine" or consists of "thick, ropey" worms and that they have to struggle through terrifying landscapes to obtain. Now Nimdok is given a vision that canned goods may be available in a place called the "ice caverns," and the group sets off on the hundred-mile underground quest, which consists of six fairly distinct episodes, separated by graphic computer "talk fields" (meant to represent the coding on 1960s-era computer tape, these graphics—which according to Ellison are meant to spell out "I think, therefore I am" ["Memoir" 15]—are now one of the few elements that clearly date the story). These episodes are as follows:

1. As the group passes through a valley of obsolete computer parts, Benny realizes they are near the Earth's surface—long since rendered uninhabitable—and he attempts to escape. As the others watch, his eyes begin to emit a

pulsing light accompanied by a painfully loud sound, and he is flung to the steel floor, blinded, his eyes "two soft, moist pools of pus-like jelly" (8). Ellen, whom the narrator views as "scum filth," appears to be relieved that Benny's sex organs are intact.

2. During an encampment at which Gorrister explains the origins of AM, an unseen something, "huge, shambling, hairy, moist" (10), accompanied by a succession of hideous smells, moves toward them. It singles out Ted, who flees in terror as the others laugh hysterically. He hides out for what may be days or years.

3. A violent hurricane hurls all of them back the way they had come. Ellen is bloodied as she is flung high in the air, against walls and machines.

4. AM enters the narrator's mind, like "a pillar of stainless steel bearing bright neon lettering" spelling out a message that, for all its shocking hostility, is essentially further evidence of AM's almost childlike inability to understand its own emotions: "THERE ARE 387.44 MILLION MILES OF PRINTED CIR-CUITS IN WAFER THIN LAYERS THAT FILL MY COMPLEX. IF THE WORD HATE WAS ENGRAVED ON EACH NANOANGSTROM OF THOSE HUNDREDS OF MILLIONS OF MILES IT WOULD NOT EQUAL ONE ONE-BILLIONTH OF THE HATE I FEEL FOR HUMANS AT THIS MICRO-INSTANT FOR YOU. HATE. HATE" (14).

5. After nearly a month of travel, the group arrives under the North Pole, where a monstrous bird awaits. It was this bird's wings which created the hurricane. Appearing as a burning bush, AM tells them that they can kill the bird for food—but then supplies only bows and arrows and a water pistol as weapons.

6. After a series of further trials—an earthquake that mangles Ellen and Nimdok, "the cavern of rats," "the path of boiling steam," "the country of the blind," "the slough of despond," "the vale of tears"—they arrive at the ice caverns. There they find canned goods—but no can opener. Driven berserk by this final irony, Benny attacks Gorrister and begins eating his face. Gorrister's screams cause spearlike stalactites of ice to fall into the snow. In an instant, Ted decides to use the ice spears to kill Benny and Gorrister. Ellen then kills Nimdok, and Ted kills Ellen, hoping that her final agonized expression is one of thanks.

The concluding coda of the story takes place hundreds of years later. Unable to revive the four who died, the computer has redirected its rage at Ted for taking its "toys" away. His mind intact, Ted has been transformed into "a great soft jelly thing" with "pulsing white holes filled by fog where my eyes used to be," incapable of doing any harm to himself, comforted only by the thought that he helped the others to escape. H. Bruce Franklin describes this creature as "one of the more hideous monsters in all science fiction . . . incapable—at long last—of making the weapons necessary for self-destruction." "The logic is now complete. The monstrous alien weapons we created have reversed the entire process of evolution, reducing the human species to a single repulsive sluglike alien monster" (210). The story's ultimate irony, as Franklin implies, is that a civilization incapable of restraining itself from building increasingly sophisticated computer weapons finally achieves disarmament in the most grotesquely literal way at the hands of those very weapons.

But is the story fundamentally a grim satire of the cold war, a parable of out-of-control technology, or a kind of postmodern vision of hell, drawn in equal measures from existential anxieties and religious/mythical imagery? Ellison's own insistence that the story is essentially a fable of affirmation startles many readers. He argues that Ted's ability to overcome his own selfishness and paranoia in order to "rescue" the others through death is a sign of human nobility in the most hopeless of circumstances. This would suggest that he views the story as essentially about human nature, not technology. It is, of course, about all of these things, but it is also the work of a writer straining at the edge of genre.

If we look again at the succession of images, we see unfolding a transformation of the story itself from science fiction into myth. Benny's blindness—which foreshadows the narrator's eventual fate—is a fairly straightforward, if extreme, punishment for a specific crime. The shambling thing that terrifies the narrator is more ambiguous; it may be a science fiction monster of some sort or a simple bogeyman drawn from Ted's fears. But the reason for its appearance is more arbitrary, less clearly motivated. The hurricane suggests a biblical whirlwind, and this pattern of imagery quickly begins to take over. AM's neon pillar of hate, a kind of tech version of a burning bush, gives way to an actual burning bush, which appears at the same time as the mythical hurricane bird. The tale thus could be described as a self-conscious journey from science fiction into myth, with even simple principles of cause/effect becoming arbitrary and unstable.

The episode in the ice caverns is a momentary return from this world of flux to a world of causality, and Ted is quick to realize that this may well be his last chance at meaningful action. Murder is not only the only humane act possible; it is the only rational action available in a world that is rapidly becoming little more than an expression of AM's madness.

Unlike the Harlequin, Ted effects not even a minuscule change in AM's psychotic behavior, and the tale ends without providing a glimmer of hope for his own future as the last man on Earth. "AM has won," he declares (22), yet the inability of the near-omnipotent computer to curtail the capacity for moral action in even so self-centered and paranoid a human as Ted renders that victory ambiguous at best.

While "I Have No Mouth" seems a radical departure from "'Repent, Harlequin!'" two years earlier, the stories are thematically linked in ways that become clear when we look at Ellison's own contribution to his 1967 *Dangerous Visions.* "The Prowler in the City at the Edge of the World" is the result of a fascination with Jack the Ripper that also found expression in his *Cimarron Strip* episode "Knife in the Darkness" and continued with Ripper-like figures in "The Whimper of Whipped Dogs" (1973) and "Mefisto in Onyx" (1987). Conceived as a sequel to Robert Bloch's *Dangerous Visions* story "A Toy for Juliette," "Prowler" yanks the Ripper from his historical context and places him in a sterile thirty-first-century utopia with "walls of antiseptic metal like an immense autoclave" (131). The metal city, "shining in permanence, eternal in concept" (131) resembles the Ticktockman's world in its programmed stasis and unquestioning citizens, but is at the same time a protean metallic environment like that of AM's interior. The city's resemblance to AM becomes clearer when we realize why the Ripper has been brought forward in time—in effect, to serve as an amusement for the jaded citizenry. After first killing the spoiled and sadistic granddaughter of the amoral owner of the world's only time machine (this was the conclusion of the Bloch story), Jack learns that he was brought forward precisely for this purpose. Enraged, he embarks on a killing spree that far outstrips his crimes of 1889—and that constitutes one of the most gruesome sustained segments of any Ellison story—and then discovers that this, too, was but an entertainment for the "sybarites," that his "victims" had been "thawed" specifically for this purpose.

> The people of the city had all along been able to escape him, and now they would. He was finally and completely the clown they had shown him to be. He was not evil, he was pathetic.
>
> He tried to use the living blade on himself, but it dissolved into motes of light and wafted away on a breeze that had blown up for just that purpose.

> Alone, he stood there staring at the victorious cleanliness of the
> Utopia. With their talents they would keep him alive, possibly alive for-
> ever, immortal in the possible expectation of needing him for amusement
> again someday. He was stripped to raw essentials in a mind that was no
> longer anything more than jelly matter. To go madder and madder, and
> never to know peace or end or sleep. (150–51)

Jack, in short, is both the Harlequin and the mouthless Ted, the "jelly matter" of his mind a direct echo of the "great soft jelly thing" Ted finds himself
transformed into. But his eternal tormentor, instead of an insane computer,
is a sterile, jaded Ticktockman's society. The madness of the machine
becomes indistinguishable from the madness of the city; in both cases the victim is trapped in a totalizing expression of hell that denies hope and destroys
time. The implied alternative to these autoclave urban environments is the
wasteland, the blasted surface of "I Have No Mouth," the uninhabitable outside (which in Bloch's original story is presented as a postnuclear wasteland)
of "Prowler." That wasteland became the main setting of Ellison's next
major exploration of dystopian themes, "A Boy and His Dog."

"A Boy and His Dog"

Cited by Brian W. Aldiss as Ellison's masterpiece, "A Boy and His Dog"
first appeared in England in Michael Moorcock's *New Worlds* in 1969, in a
slightly abridged version, and was reprinted that same year, at its full
18,000-word length, in *The Beast That Shouted Love at the Heart of the
World*—a collection that, with its psychedelic Leo and Diane Dillon cover
and selection of stories mostly from 1968 and 1969, was Ellison's most significant science fiction book to date and the book that most closely seemed
to ally his work with the counterculture of rebellion in the late 1960s.
Other stories in the collection included an award-winning exploration of
madness as a tangible force in the universe, "The Beast That Shouted Love
at the Heart of the World," and a genuinely disturbing antidrug phantas-
magoria, "Shattered like a Glass Goblin," but the collection was fundamentally defined by "A Boy and His Dog." In many ways, the story is his
most complete science fiction story, neither proclaiming its own ironic textuality (like "'Repent, Harlequin!'") nor transforming itself into myth (like
"I Have No Mouth"). Instead, the actions, settings, characters, and narrative voice of the tale are all controlled by and consistent with the initial
extrapolative conditions of an America devastated by nuclear war, and

divided into a savage wasteland aboveground and repressively middle-class "downunders" beneath the surface.

"A Boy and His Dog," together with its two connected tales, "Eggsucker" (1977) and "Run, Spot, Run" (1980), also represents Ellison's most complete effort at a fully realized science fiction novel. (His minor 1960 effort, *The Man with Nine Lives,* published as part of an Ace Double with his first story collection, *A Touch of Infinity,* was essentially a long novella expanded from his 1959 story "The Sound of a Scythe.") The completed novel, to be titled *Blood's a Rover,* gained a reputation in the fan community as one of Ellison's most persistently announced but undelivered books. (Other undelivered works were *The Prince of Sleep,* listed as forthcoming in 1974 and advertised by Dell in 1977 but never published, and of course *Last Dangerous Visions.*) In an afterword to Richard Corben's 1989 graphic novel adaptation of the three "Boy and His Dog" stories, *Vic and Blood,* Ellison wrote:

> I call [the three stories] the first three sections of a 100,000 word novel titled BLOOD'S A ROVER. What happens to Vic and Blood in this graphic novel is only the beginning of the story. I never intended "A Boy and His Dog" to stand alone. It just happened to be the part of the novel that was written when Mike Moorcock solicited a submission for *New Worlds* back in late 1968.
>
> I have been at work on this novel for more than twenty years.
>
> As I write this afterword, I am four days past my fifty-fifth birthday. If the universe doesn't stomp me, before the end of 1989 I will have the full novel completed. If the heavens don't part and swamp us, it will be published in 1990. (*Vic,* endpaper)

In fact, Ellison had expected the book to be completed nearly a decade earlier, even listing it as a 1980 title under "Books by Harlan Ellison" in the front matter to his 1980 collection *Shatterday.* Whether the novel ever appears, however, now seems irrelevant to the strong reputation of "A Boy and His Dog," which not only earned Ellison another Nebula Award but in 1975 became the basis of the only successful feature film adaptation of an Ellison work. Written and directed by L. Q. Jones, *A Boy and His Dog* received a Hugo as best dramatic presentation and probably influenced the Australian director George Miller in his original stories for the film *Mad Max* (1979) and its sequels.

Like "I Have No Mouth," "A Boy and His Dog" belongs to the atomic war subgenre of science fiction tales, a tradition so extensive that scholar

Paul Brians was able to identify and annotate more than eight hundred separate novels and short stories (including seven titles by Ellison) published between 1895 and 1984. But like "'Repent, Harlequin!'" it also draws from the tradition of dystopian fiction in its caricature of middle American "normalcy" in the repressive underground city called Topeka, one of some two hundred "downunders" established by "Southern Baptists, Fundamentalists, lawanorder goofs, real middle-class squares" seeking to re-create a pre–World War I age of innocence (228). The source of the story's power lies in the moral tension it establishes between the savage, male-dominated, but vital surface world of foraging "roverpaks" and ruined cities and the grotesque, sterile parody of Norman Rockwell Americana in the downunder of Topeka—a tension which at its best recalls that of Anthony Burgess's 1962 novel, *A Clockwork Orange,* with its uncomfortable link between violence and vitality—except that there is no spark of creativity, no passion for Beethoven, in Ellison's crude and inarticulate Vic.

Set in 2024, the story strives to maintain a tone of grim realism in its depiction of a desert wasteland, eschewing such conventional postnuclear science fiction figures as mutants, but with one key exception: The narrator's companion, Blood, is one of a new breed of superintelligent, telepathic "skirmisher dogs," descended from twentieth-century security and attack dogs who had been surgically altered and injected with "amplified dolphin spinal fluid" (*Beast* 123). (Had the story been written a decade or two later, Ellison might have substituted DNA for the spinal fluid.) The telepathically wisecracking Blood, both more articulate and better educated than Vic, is in fact the brains of the duo, using his heightened senses to help Vic locate food and women and to avoid the organized gangs called "roverpaks" that dominate the surface. Supposedly based on Ellison's own dog Ahbhu (to whom the collection in which the story appears is dedicated, and whose own death is chronicled in Ellison's later story "The Deathbird"), Blood's voice is in fact very close to that of Ellison himself. In the opening scene of the story, Blood teases Vic—and underlines the irony of the story's title—by calling him "Albert," an obscure (to Vic) reference to Albert Payson Terhune, the once-popular author of sentimental dog novels (*Lad: A Dog, His Dog, The Heart of a Dog,* etc.). Blood corrects Vic's grammar, teaches him history, and advises him on survival strategy in a society that bears a noteworthy resemblance to the Brooklyn gang culture of the 1950s that Ellison had written of early in his career.

Surviving women are so rare in this society that antique pornographic films have become a prized source of entertainment, many of the roverpak members have opted for gay sex, and the few women who do appear are regarded as little more than candidates for rape and murder—and thus seek anonymity by disguising themselves as men. The vicious misogynism of Vic's society and the moral obtuseness of Vic himself have probably led more than a few readers to misread the tale as itself misogynistic, although similar societies have been portrayed by feminist authors arguing that the brutal commodification of women might indeed be the response of a war-oriented male culture to a shortage of females in the population (see Pamela Sargent's 1984 short story "Fears," for example). Carolyn Wendell, in a survey of Nebula Award–winning stories, described the story as "the worst offender" in terms of sexual stereotyping of women, concluding: "The value standard is clearly a double one: a man may kill his mate to feed his dog, but a woman must not kill her father to free herself, or act in any aggressive way" (346). Wendell apparently views this double standard as representing Ellison's own, despite the consistent undermining of Vic's narration by Blood and by the events of the tale.

In many cases, the controversy over "A Boy and His Dog" confused Ellison's original story with the L. Q. Jones film, about which the science fiction novelist and critic Joanna Russ wrote, "Sending a woman to see *A Boy and His Dog* is like sending a Jew to a movie that glorifies Dachau; you need not be a feminist to loathe this film" (66). Russ, however, goes on to note that the story "is a very different matter from the film"—a point that many other readers overlooked. (For example, a 1977 essay by John Crow and Richard Erlich titled "Mythic Patterns in Ellison's *A Boy and His Dog,*" which finds in the story parallels with the myth of the hero, makes little distinction between novella and film. Crow and Erlich quote dialogue and cite incidents that appear only in the film, including one in which Vic finds a woman stabbed to death and complains, "She was good for three or more times yet" [163].) At any rate, the controversy over the tale was sufficient that Terry Dowling, in an introductory note to it in *The Essential Ellison,* wrote that it "speaks of love in a special way that had been consistently misinterpreted by the story's detractors, whose arguments found even more inflammatory fuel in L. Q. Jones's 1975 movie adaptation" (874).

In a crumbling movie theater where ancient films are shown by a roverpak that calls itself Our Gang, Blood catches the scent of a woman somewhere in the audience—presumably a thrillseeker from "downunder" disguised as a man—and helps Vic track her to an abandoned YMCA gymnasium. There, hiding in the shadows, Vic watches her undress and experiences a kind of Actaeon-like epiphany. Disarmed by her beauty and by her insistence on looking him in the eye and speaking to him, he finds himself unable to carry out his assault. Blood tells him that the building has been surrounded by roverpaks—whose dogs have also picked up the woman's scent—and they are quickly under siege, with the girl, Quilla June, joining Vic and Blood in fighting off the roverpaks. They decide to torch the entire building and hide out below in a deep boiler room. There Vic finally succeeds in having his way with Quilla June, who later claims to have "liked doing it" (226). Infatuated with Quilla June, who taunts him by asking, "Do you know what love is?" (229), Vic gets into a tense argument with Blood, who reminds him of their responsibility to each other. But when he returns to the boiler room, Quilla June knocks him out with a pistol and escapes.

Furious, and against Blood's warnings, Vic tracks Quilla June to the dropshaft that leads down to Topeka. Leaving Blood alone on the surface, Vic follows her into a twenty-mile-long metal-lined cavern, eerily like the metal landscapes of "I Have No Mouth" but with a picture-book replica of a pre–World War I town in the center of it. It is, of course, a trap: Quilla June has lured Vic to Topeka because the birthrate there has dropped dramatically, and most babies are girls. Vic is to serve as an experimental stud, in the hope that men from the surface will be able to revitalize the society. He agrees to stay, but "Inside a week I was ready to scream" (238) from the artificial food, the overripe parody of small-town life ("They rocked in rockers on the front porches, they raked their lawns, they hung around the gas station, they stuck pennies in gumball machines, they painted white stripes down the middle of the road, they sold newspapers on the corners" [237–38]), and most of all from the mannered, hypocritical behavior and speech of the inhabitants. Like the Ticktockman, the Topekans have chosen to deal with historical change by denying it, substituting instead a repressive condition of stasis, enforced even down to the level of daily speech, in which everyone must politely address everyone else as "Mr." or "Mrs." It turns out that Quilla June is also frustrated in this sterile, unchanging world, and with her help Vic escapes again to the surface, bringing her along only to discover Blood, starved and half-dead, waiting near the dropshaft entrance. Realizing his only hope of survival is with Blood, and that Blood cannot travel without food, Vic makes a crucial decision, sacrificing Quilla June to provide food for his dog. The next morning, as Blood completes another meal, Vic remembers her question: "Do you know what love is?" He concludes, "Sure I know. A boy loves his dog" (245).

While there is a decided antiromantic, antisentimental bite to this ending, it hardly came as a surprise to Ellison readers (after all, he'd just published a book titled *Love Ain't Nothing but Sex Misspelled*) or to readers familiar with the post–nuclear war scenarios that were so common in the 1950s and 1960s. The suggestion of cannibalism as a marker of cultural collapse following a nuclear war was certainly not original with Ellison, dating back at least to Wilson Tucker's 1952 novel *The Long Loud Silence* (although the cannibalism was cut from the novel's first American publication). A more striking parallel is with the cannibalism of the Morlocks in H. G. Wells's *Time Machine* (1895), since Ellison's story is structured like an inversion of the dual far-future society portrayed in that novel, in which the decadent Eloi wallow in an artificial utopia aboveground while far below the degenerate Morlocks, descended from the working classes, struggle to survive in a manner so degraded that it includes killing and eating the Eloi. Quilla June, although she is another in a long line of betraying women in Ellison (including Pretty Alice and Pretty Maggie), is also a distant descendant of Wells's Weena.

The remaining two Vic and Blood stories, "Eggsucker" and "Run, Spot, Run," frame the narrative of "A Boy and His Dog" by filling in a few more details of Vic's society and establishing more fully the relationship of Vic and Blood, but neither is as fully plotted, and both seem much more like episodes from a longer work. Unlike "A Boy and His Dog," both are narrated by Blood rather than Vic. In "Eggsucker," Vic and Blood's relationship is threatened when Blood, enraged at being repeatedly called an "Eggsucker" by the dealer who supplies Vic with ammunition, attacks the dealer, thus cutting off Vic's source of a crucial commodity. Furious, Vic stalks off on his own, but nearly stumbles into a pit where a glowing green radioactive "screamer" is ready to attack him—an incident that is alluded to briefly in "A Boy and His Dog." Blood saves Vic, and the two reunite. "Run, Spot, Run," which appeared originally in the graphic novel *Vic and Blood,* finds Blood eating what may be a poison lizard and suffering hallucinations drawn from Vic's nightmares of the ghost of Quilla June. Haunted and depressed at what he has done, Vic narrowly escapes capture by Fellini, a kind of gay warlord who roams the Ohio Turnpike. But the two of them take refuge in a huge stump that turns out to be home to a colony of giant mutated spiders—the first time in the entire sequence that Ellison resorts to monster-movie clichés—and Blood is unable to rouse Vic out of his depression even to save himself from being encased in a shroud of spiderwebs. Finally unable to save his friend, Blood runs away, heading west and foraging for food. "And I was never again troubled by the ghosts of little girls in the shredded frilly blue dresses," he concludes. "No ghosts of little girls: just one ghost that stared up at me from a hollow stump with eyes that no longer cared what happened to man's best friend" (*Vic,* n.p.). The tantalizing suggestion, of course, is that the central figure and principal narrator in the novel *Blood's a Rover* was to have been Blood, with Vic a more transient character. Neither of these tales approaches the strength and consistency of "A Boy and His Dog," however.

The vivid and imagistic series of dystopian fables that began with "'Repent, Harlequin!'" in 1965 and essentially ended with the "Boy and His Dog" stories constitute Ellison's single most significant and influential contribution to science fiction as a genre, far more substantial than his jerry-built Kyben war series, and in fact more substantial than the entire body of short science fiction that he contributed to the digest magazines throughout the late 1950s and early 1960s. While he would return to science fiction themes and scenarios throughout his later career, they would increasingly be subsumed by more personal concerns, becoming only one of a number of narrative instrumentalities that Ellison would employ interchangeably, often within the same story. As if recognizing this shift in the direction of his fiction, Ellison in 1971 assembled his first retrospective collection, *Alone against Tomorrow: Stories of Alienation in Speculative Fiction*—which, as its subtitle announces, was also the first collection to be organized around a particular theme (although this theme, alienation, would easily have permitted the inclusion of most of Ellison's fiction to that point). Among the twenty stories assembled were both "'Repent, Harlequin!'" and "I Have No Mouth," together with tales dating back to Ellison's second sale, "Life Hutch." Ellison later described the book as "a small, narrow retrospective of my work" between 1956 and 1969 (*Approaching Oblivion* 10)—narrow, presumably, in the sense that the stories selected were primarily representative of Ellison's science fiction. *Alone against Tomorrow* was not a valedictory to science fiction, but it did represent a certain degree of stocktaking and was in many ways his last "science fiction" collection. *Approaching Oblivion: Road Signs on the Treadmill toward Tomorrow,* which appeared in 1974, featured only previously uncollected stories, freely mixing autobiographical fantasy ("One Life, Furnished in Early Poverty") with cautionary science fiction ("Silent in Gehenna") and manic comedy ("I'm Looking for Kadak," one of the funniest of Ellison's small number of comic Jewish stories). That collection was followed in 1975 by *Deathbird Stories,* the most important of Ellison's thematic story collections and one that pointedly announced an ambitious interest—not new, but never so clearly codified—in fiction that reflects or even tries to shape the secret mythologies of its time. In this new configuration, science fiction would continue to play a role, but never again so fully a dominant one as it had played in the decade before.

7 | MYTHS OF Transformation

Deathbird Stories

And sullen Moloch fled,
Hath left in shadows dread
    His burning idol all of blackest hue;
In vain with cymbals' ring
They call the grisly king,
    In dismal dance about the furnace blue;
The brutish gods of Nile as fast,
Isis and Orus, and the dog Anubis haste . . .
Nor all the gods beside,
Longer dare abide.

—JOHN MILTON, "Hymn on
the Morning of Christ's Nativity" (1629)

As the time passes for men and women, so does it pass for gods, for they
are made viable and substantial only through the massed beliefs of masses
of men and women. And when puny mortals no longer worship at their
altars, the gods die.

—HARLAN ELLISON, *Deathbird Stories* (1975)

AS WE HAVE SEEN, the major shifts in Ellison's career and in the nature
of his fiction have often been influenced by the simple economic realities
of the changing marketplace—his reputation as a tough street author
deriving in large part from the opportunistic exploitation of the juvenile
delinquency market, his mountainous early output in science fiction from
the proliferation of low-paying digest magazines in the 1950s, his experimentation with new forms and styles from the more open markets of the
men's magazines like *Rogue* and *Knight*. When the science fiction markets
gained sophistication in the mid-1960s—due not only to the influence of
the British New Wave and to Ellison's own *Dangerous Visions* but to more
sophisticated magazine editors like Cele Goldsmith and Frederik Pohl—
Ellison was able to consolidate much of what he had learned and to gain a
reputation, at least for a time, as the most influential (and certainly the

most award-winning) science fiction writer in the world—a reputation which was represented most directly in his collections *The Beast That Shouted Love at the Heart of the World* and *Alone against Tomorrow. Deathbird Stories* represents another major shift in Ellison's work in several crucial ways. In the first place, it has a clear thematic center, far more focused than the broad theme of "alienation" in *Alone against Tomorrow,* and includes both current and previously collected stories (from as far back as 1960) that reflect this theme. Second, it was the first of Ellison's collections to be conceived more as a *book* than as a showcase of his work; to be designed, through the rhetorically driven selection and arrangement of texts and the uncharacteristically terse, sometimes cryptic headnotes, to be greater than the sum of its parts—a kind of gestalt, or story mosaic. This overall design, in turn, has the effect of recontextualizing many of the stories so that, for example, "Pretty Maggie Moneyeyes" invites a slightly different reading here than as an independent work; the supernatural forces at work in the story, invisible and motiveless, now take on the aspect of deities—gods of the slot machines, of gambling, of Vegas. Finally, in some of its key selections, the book demonstrates a far more eclectic and postmodern approach to its source materials, freely combining genre elements with other mythical, pop cultural, and literary sources in a way that sometimes makes it problematical to regard a particular selection, or the book as a whole, as either "science fiction" or *not* science fiction. It is, in effect, Ellison's first post-genre book, his first work to consistently and deliberately reflect his increasingly polyvalent approach to his story materials.

Collections of linked stories were nothing new in the science fiction and fantasy world. Ray Bradbury's *The Martian Chronicles* and Isaac Asimov's *I Robot* (both 1950) were among the postwar genre's first classic texts, and many authors, including Asimov and Robert Heinlein, had organized much of their fiction into loose "future histories" with a common context and background. Ellison himself eventually collected several of his Kyben war stories in graphic novel form in *Night and the Enemy* in 1987. But the tales in *Deathbird Stories* are linked not by any common narrative thread or overall setting, and only a few of them seem to have been written with such an eventual collection in mind; instead, they amount to a kind of spiritual autobiography, a survey of themes that had been developing in Ellison's work over a period of several years. Still, it's entirely possible to view the collection as a kind of discovery and deconstruction of the religious impulse as manifested in various aspects of contemporary life: ritualized behavior (the formalized road rage of "Along the Scenic Route"), idolatry ("The Face of Helene Bournouw"), the interior journey ("Adrift Just off the Islets of Langerhans"), conversion and submission to a higher power ("The Whimper of Whipped Dogs"), purgatory ("Pretty Maggie Moneyeyes"), sacrifice ("Paingod"), death and resurrection ("The Deathbird," "Delusion for a Dragon Slayer"), transformation and transfiguration (which Terry Dowling identified as the "linking theme" and "driving purpose" of the entire collection [xiv]). Had it not already been included in three Ellison collections in the preceding eight years, "I Have No Mouth, and I Must Scream" could easily have found a place in this volume.

The specific organizing theme of *Deathbird Stories* is apparent in the subtitle to the book's first edition: *A Pantheon of Modern Gods.* Echoing a magical conceit that had inspired a great deal of horror and fantasy fiction during the preceding century—dating back at least to Arthur Machen (not to mention Milton and Nietzsche)—Ellison suggests that gods exist only at the mercy of their believers and that "when the last acolyte renounces his faith and turns to another deity, the god ceases to be" (xiv). (Actually, the more common version of this conceit is that the old gods go into exile, a notion explored here by Ellison in "O Ye of Little Faith.") In their place emerge new gods and devils, who gain their influence not from revelatory or charismatic social movements but from the driving anxieties of mid-twentieth-century American culture: gods of behavior rather than of belief. Ellison's introduction lists some of these as "the gods of the freeway, of the ghetto blacks, of the coaxial cable; the paingod and the rock god and the god of neon; the god of legal tender, the god of business-as-usual and the gods that live in city streets and slot machines. The God of Smog and the God of Freudian Guilt. The Machine God" (xv). It doesn't take more than a glance at the stories to realize that this taxonomy of modern gods is pretty *ex post facto,* intended to nudge us toward seeing these gods in stories that actually make no mention of them. "The god of the freeway," for example, refers to "Along the Scenic Route" (1969), a kinetic *Mad Max*–type tale of legalized road-rage combat originally published as "Dogfight on 101." Similarly, the allusion to "gods that live in . . . slot machines" invites us to take another look at "Pretty Maggie Moneyeyes" in this context, even though it's a stretch to find any real conceptualization of a god in the story.

It becomes clear that Ellison's use of the notion of "gods" is a fairly loose one and refers not to patterns of organized belief but to an iconography of contemporary obsessions and terrors, which on occasion manifest themselves in the stories as real supernatural forces. The cultural and social landscape depicted in *Deathbird Stories* is a nightmare cacophony of automobiles, neon signs, vengeful gargoyles, corporate corruption, high-rises, movies, drug houses, bigoted small towns, anonymous office workers, manufactured supermodels, racists, pimps, prostitutes, and trademark Ellison cheats and losers—in other words, a phantasmagoric dreamscape reminiscent of medieval paintings of the Temptation of St. Anthony or perhaps the work of Hieronymous Bosch, who is directly alluded to in "The Deathbird." But the distinctly American settings of the stories are a significant part of what lends the book unity, since some of these gods seem to play the role of *genius loci* for particular parts of the American landscape: New York ("The Whimper of Whipped Dogs"), Las Vegas ("Pretty Maggie Moneyeyes"), New Orleans ("On the Downhill Side"), rural Kansas ("Basilisk"), North Carolina ("Ernest and the Machine God"), Los Angeles ("Shattered like a Glass Goblin"), the anonymous world of the freeway ("Along the Scenic Route"). There has always been more than a touch of the homilist in Ellison, but the mythic panorama of American life suggested by the pieces included in *Deathbird Stories* at times invokes a tone of righteous rage that suggests a time-traveling Jonathan Edwards given a tour of America in the Age of Aquarius, a tone that is most apparent in the truncated but still insouciant story notes, which now tend to give the collection something of a period flavor (the note for "Basilisk," a tale critical of superpatriots, ends with the now badly dated line, "Check Spiro, I think he's having a seizure" [71]). Certainly, a major cluster of stories addresses controversies that were at the heart of American social debate in the late 1960s and early 1970s—urban violence in "The Whimper of Whipped Dogs," the legacy of Vietnam in "Basilisk," the drug culture in "Shattered like a Glass Goblin," the materialism of Las Vegas in "Pretty Maggie Moneyeyes" (discussed in chapter 4). For the most part, these stories also represent a shift in Ellison's use of genre materials from science fiction to the horror story, a shift foreshadowed by the graphic imagery of "I Have No Mouth, and I Must Scream." Long an admirer of such authors as Robert Bloch, Fritz Leiber, Gerald Kersh, and Cornell Woolrich, Ellison began seeking ways of combining the idiom of the uncanny with his broader thematic ambitions of unveiling contemporary mythologies. In the earlier stories in the book, which tend to draw more heavily on the materials of genre horror, fantasy, and science fiction, characters are likely to be overwhelmed and subsumed by the gods they discover. Later stories show figures more willing to fight for an accommodation in the worlds of the gods, until finally, in the last two stories in the collection, the protagonists are able to surmount their circumstances and, in "The Deathbird," to vanquish the mad god himself.

"THE WHIMPER OF WHIPPED DOGS"

Nowhere is Ellison's sense of place and time clearer or more compelling than in the collection's lead story, "The Whimper of Whipped Dogs" (1973), a more-or-less direct response to the highly publicized stabbing murder of Catherine Genovese in New York's Kew Gardens in 1964, with thirty-eight witnesses watching for more than half an hour from behind their apartment windows. The story received an Edgar Allan Poe Award from the Mystery Writers of America in 1974 and was later included in Tony Hillerman and Otto Penzler's 2000 anthology, *The Best American Mystery Stories of the Century* (despite its strong fantastic content and lack of traditional mystery elements). It is less a crime story than a fable of urban paranoia in which a young woman only two months in Manhattan not only witnesses extreme violence but begins to suspect that all the residents of her building, if not all New Yorkers in general, are involved in some sort of mutual conspiracy of indifference and hostility to which she has not yet been initiated. While the story reinforces and mythifies the hackneyed stereotype of New Yorkers as brittle and uncaring, its acute sense of urban alienation is powerfully developed, and the protagonist's gradual discovery of the true nature of everyone around her—not unlike the dawning awareness of the title character in Ira Levin's *Rosemary's Baby* (1967)—is skillfully paced. But whereas Levin chose to anchor his novel in the most traditional aspects of folklore and demonology—Rosemary is surrounded by devil-worshipers—Ellison invents his own demonic figure, one who is not a source of evil but a product of it. This turns out to be one of the most consistent themes in *Deathbird Stories* and one of the most important: The gods here do not determine human actions but are determined by them. Ellison's view of the supernatural is inseparable from his view of human nature. Even when he suggests that malevolent gods may have been lying in wait somewhere on the edge of the universe for millennia, they are never simply the Elder Gods of an H. P. Lovecraft or the devil of Ira Levin, waiting to be summoned forth by arcane rituals carried out by a handful of believers. Instead, they appear unbidden in response to human action, personifications of venality rather than agents of it. In almost all cases, their power derives from the hidden energies of the human psyche.

Although "The Whimper of Whipped Dogs" begins with a brutal murder, the story focuses not on the victim but on one of the witnesses, tracing, in four distinct phases, the destruction of her innocence and her acceptance of the "new" urban god of violence and indifference. Beth O'Neill, a recent Bennington graduate who has moved to New York to work as a choreographer, witnesses the crime from the window of her new apartment—noting, bizarrely, that she has the ideal sightlines of the Comédie française theatres, designed to allow Napoleon to view the audience as well as the stage. Beth's perspective is important because when she finally draws her eyes away from the attack taking place in the courtyard of her building (which Ellison describes in lengthy, graphic detail), she catches sight of faces at other darkened windows, "and there was a universal sameness to their expressions": "They all looked like they were at cock fights. Breathing deeply. Drawing some sustenance from the grisly scene below" (4). The scene calls to mind one of the more memorable recurring scenes in the work of Holocaust writer Elie Wiesel, whose memory of a passive face looking down from a window while he and his family were being deported to the death camps became a symbol of indifference in the face of genocide. As the courtyard of the building becomes swathed in a strange, "unnatural" fog, Beth looks up and catches sight of two "primal burning eyes, filled with an abysmal antiquity yet frighteningly bright and anxious like the eyes of a child" (5). Realizing that the brutal crime had somehow summoned this "other," she is appalled at her own inability to act. "She had done nothing, nothing! A woman had been butchered and she had said nothing, done nothing" (5). Finally, just before blacking out, she realizes that she herself is being watched by a young man in the apartment across from her.

This opening sequence is one of the most powerful sustained passages in all of Ellison's work, shifting deftly from the graphic realism of the murder scene to the psychic torment of Beth and finally to the introduction of an unnamed supernatural force that appears to be virtually feeding on the violence. In the second part of the story, Beth is so haunted by the crime that she is unable to eat or work. News reports, as in the Genovese case, "dwelled with loving emphasis on the twenty-six tenants of the building who had watched in cold interest as Leona Ciarelli, 37, of 455 Fort

Washington Avenue, Manhattan, had been systematically stabbed to death by Burton H. Wells" (6), who is later shot by off-duty police officers. In the first of a series of events that will mark the stages of her "conversion," she finds herself in the elevator with the young man who had watched her from across the courtyard, noting that "there was something terribly familiar about his face" (8). He stops the elevator between floors and introduces himself as Ray Gleeson, a book editor at a religious publishing house. Despite her initial fear, she chats briefly with him and even agrees to a date. Then he suggests that she turn the elevator back on. "She did it, wondering why she had stopped the elevator in the first place" (9). This episode, the first key to a shift in Beth's consciousness, clearly permits an ambiguous reading: Did Ray turn off the elevator, or did Beth? Is Beth so distraught by the events of the night before that her mind is playing tricks, or is there a kind of demonic seduction taking place? Throughout most of the length of the story, Ellison is careful to maintain this tension between psychological and supernatural readings, and the story balances in that narrow area, which Tszvetan Todorov defined as "the fantastic," in which apparently supernatural events have not yet been resolved as either rationally explainable ("the uncanny") or genuinely supernatural ("the marvelous").

Beth's third date with Ray maintains this balance between the uncanny and the marvelous. At a party in her building, she realizes that all but a handful of guests were among the witnesses to the murder, and she asks Ray if they might leave. Ray now reveals himself to be monstrous in his own way. After unsuccessfully attempting to force anal sex on her, he begins taunting her about her presumed sex life at Bennington:

> [N]o Amherst intellectuals begging you to save them from creeping fag-gotry by permitting them to stick their carrots in your sticky little slit?"
> . . . You don't expect me to believe you didn't get a little mouthful of cock from time to time. It's only, what? about fifteen miles to Williamstown? I'm sure the Williams werewolves were down burning the highway to your cunt on weekends; you can level with old Uncle Ray. (11)

Ray's excuse for this outburst leads him to an almost hysterical condemnation of city life:

> Look around you; what do you think is happening here? They take rats and they put them in boxes and when there are too many of them, some

of the little fuckers go out of their minds and start gnawing the rest to death. *It ain't no different here, baby!* It's rat time for everybody in this madhouse. You can't expect to jam as many people into this stone thing as we do, with buses and taxis and dogs shitting themselves scrawny and noise night and day and no money and not enough places to live and no place to go to have a decent think . . . you can't do it without making the time right for some godforsaken other kind of thing to be born! (12)

The "other thing," of course, is the putative god of this "madhouse," and Ray comes very close here to revealing the dark secret of urban life—only Beth is not quite yet prepared to receive it.

In the third segment of the story, Beth begins her preparations toward initiation, experiencing what Ray calls "rat time" firsthand, through a series of incidents that gradually build to her own inchoate rage: a confrontation with a surly waitress over a cheeseburger, an obscenity shouted by a driver who has just splashed mud all over her clothes, a well-dressed man who thrusts his umbrella between her legs. She grows hardened and indifferent, unaware that she is being prepared for a final rite of passage, which constitutes the tale's fourth and final segment. Returning home late, Beth is attacked by an intruder in her own apartment in what promises to be a replay of the opening scene. While fighting for her life on her small balcony, she notices that all the other apartments are again full of watchers. Again a fog rolls in, again she sees the eyes—but this time she realizes their meaning:

> God! A new God, an ancient God come again with the eyes and hunger of a child, a deranged blood God of fog and street violence. A God who needed worshipers and offered the choices of death as a victim or life as an eternal witness to the deaths of *other* chosen victims. A God to fit the times, a God of streets and people. (16–17)

Beth surrenders to the new God—which manifests itself as a baroquely spectacular beast—and the attacker is suddenly lifted from her and ripped to pieces. Secure in "the bosom of her God" (18), she no longer lives in terror, and she reunites with Ray at the end of the story, a new acolyte for the city's demonic deity. In a world that consists solely of witnesses and victims, she has made the only rational choice. But what are we to make of a world that offers only "death as a victim or life as an eternal witness"? What is the role in this scheme of the black man who attempts to kill Beth in the end—and is himself killed by a god whom he presumably serves—or the murderer with whom the story opens? Most important, does this fierce urban cosmology leave any options for Beth *other* than accepting the dark god or dying? Does the narrator expect us to condemn her for simply choosing to survive, to be a part of her community, or are we to regard her as simply a victim in another form?

"BASILISK"

These questions are raised again in one of the few stories that compares with "Whimper" in terms of its degree of violence. "Basilisk" begins as Lance Corporal Vernon Lestig, in an unnamed war clearly meant to suggest Vietnam, is injured by a booby trap, captured, and tortured by enemy soldiers (who are described, in a disturbingly stereotypical way, as "an ancient people, with a heritage of enslavement, and so for them anguish had less meaning than the thinnest whisper of crimson cloud" [74–75]). Lestig tells them everything he knows, but the torture continues until "a terrible thing happened" (75). Later, Lestig's rescuers find that he alone remains alive in an area littered with bizarrely mutilated enemy bodies. One enemy soldier who had crawled away, his face "melting," reveals before dying that Lestig had talked under torture. Regarded as a traitor, Lestig spends a year in the hospital, gains acquittal in a highly publicized court-martial, and is sent home to Kansas, his vision still troubling him as though "he now saw the world through the eyes of some special beast" (79). The beast, we have already learned by now, is the basilisk of medieval legend, the dragonlike beast whose looks could freeze and kill. As in "The Whimper of Whipped Dogs," a supernatural monster manifests itself through the vulnerability of an inexperienced youth. Described as a "great gap-mawed beast padding through outer darkness" (73), the basilisk appears in the moment before Lestig steps on the buried pungi stake, leaving its own "serum" on the stake to infect Lestig through his wound. The basilisk's powers, transferred to Lestig, are what account for the carnage that surrounds him when he is found.

The real focus of the story, however, is not the Vietnam-like theater of war but the middle-class American heartland. If "The Whimper of Whipped Dogs" portrayed Manhattan as an inferno of indifference,

"Basilisk" portrays Kansas as an equally unpleasant inferno of intolerance. Lestig's Kansas, with its town mall, Soldiers and Sailors Monument, and band shell, is not too far removed from the parody Topeka in "A Boy and His Dog," and Lestig himself is not much more educated or articulate than Vic. He quickly learns that he has become a pariah, that even his family has been forced to move out of town because of the publicity surrounding his trial for treason. He is attacked by a group of locals, but escapes after mutilating one of them with his newfound powers. He makes his way to the home of his ex-girlfriend, who agrees to get word to his sister Neola that he will wait for her in an abandoned Baptist church. Neola arrives, but so does a mob organized by the ex-girlfriend's abusive husband, "who had beaten the information from his wife" (87). Again, he escapes. In a scene meant to invoke the villagers in pursuit of Frankenstein, the town sets out in an all-night search for Lestig, even setting up roadblocks. The next morning, as they gather in the mall, they discover him waiting high up on the Soldiers and Sailors Monument, but as they surge forth, he defends himself with a blitz of psychokinetic mutilations, killing the husband of his ex-girlfriend, burning out the eyes of a man with a revolver, finally ordering the entire mob to crawl toward him. "You never know, patriots!" he screams. "You live all the time and you say one thing or another, all your rules about what it takes to be brave, but you never *know,* till that one time when you find out. *I* found out, it's not so easy. Now *you'll* find out" (88). Far more than Beth or Ray in "The Whimper of Whipped Dogs," Lestig becomes an active agent for his god, Mars, who remains unnamed until the end of the story. When he is finally killed by the mob, the scene shifts briefly to the throne of Mars, with the basilisk in attendance "like a faithful mastiff." Lestig, we learn, had been no more than an instrument, a weapon now "deactivated" but its purpose fulfilled. "The recruiting had gone well. Power to the people" (89).

Originally published the year before "The Whimper of Whipped Dogs," "Basilisk" complements the more famous story in a number of ways and even inverts it. Instead of Beth, an innocent from a protected environment who moves into the realm of the new god, we have Lestig, who moves from extreme experience *into* a protected environment, bringing the god with him. Instead of the dense, claustrophobic spaces of New York, we have the open towns and plazas of Kansas. Instead of cool urban indifference, this god feeds on patriotic middle American rage. The god's acolytes are represented not by a passive crowd of onlookers but by an obsessed, witch-hunting mob. And the god now has a name. Invoking Mars in a story that also invokes Vietnam leads to inevitable associations, and indeed "Basilisk" touches upon a number of issues of that war—the alienation of returning veterans, the intolerance of patriots at the veterans' "failure," the disillusionment that the war brought to parts of America that had thus far seemed to maintain a measure of idyllic innocence. But it isn't a story *about* Vietnam, any more than "The Whimper of Whipped Dogs" is a story about the causes of urban crime. Instead, it is a tale, like many of Ellison's tales, of a hapless victim who becomes a catalyst for evils that already exist just below the surfaces of civilized life, evils that seem so substantial and manifest that they almost demand a god. The evocation of Mars as a kind of pulp-cover demon king and the facile final sentences of the story make for a far weaker conclusion than the more underdetermined but equally spectacular ending of "The Whimper of Whipped Dogs," but "Basilisk" may well be Ellison's strongest exploration, in the context of his pantheon of modern gods, of the conflicting passions that seemed to grip much of America during the Vietnam War.

"Shattered like a Glass Goblin"

Although Ellison claims never to have used drugs—a claim widely substantiated by his friends—many readers of "Shattered like a Glass Goblin" (1968) have assumed it to be either a vivid re-creation of drug-induced hallucinations or a strongly judgmental condemnation of the entire 1960s drug culture. In his introduction to *The Beast That Shouted Love at the Heart of the World,* where the piece was first collected, Ellison wonders why the story "is so reacted-to when I read it at college lectures . . . and why the drug-crowd always burns me for having written it" (6). The answer is hardly challenging: "Shattered like a Glass Goblin" portrays drug use in terms of almost apocalyptic degradation and dehumanization. Set like "Basilisk" at the height of the Vietnam era, the story again features as its protagonist a discharged soldier seeking his ex-girlfriend. But Rudolph Boekel returns not to the complacency and intolerance of the small-town Midwest but to a modern-day version of a gothic castle in Los Angeles called The Hill, where he tracks down his former fiancée, Kris, who has joined a kind of drug commune under the leadership of an enigmatic figure named Jonah. With its Simon and Garfunkle music, Middle

Earth posters, underground newspapers, and Hermann Hesse books, The Hill is a nightmarish distillation of the middle-class 1960s counterculture, where eleven young people have grown increasingly isolated from the outside world as they try to maintain a "group high" on a variety of drugs. Strange things begin to happen as soon as Rudy enters the house, assaulted by the pungent smell of pot. He does not remember closing the front door but "some time later" finds it closed behind him. He briefly hears "the sudden sound of leather wings" and "the sound of someone counting heavy gold pieces" (125), even though these sounds have no apparent origin. Kris, hiding in a third-floor closet, asks him to leave and feebly tries to kick him. Rudy finds Jonah, who is hallucinating that his face is melting (another image from "Basilisk"), spurns an offer to fuck from a blonde girl named Arianne, and answers the door when two cops appear. After talking to the cops, Rudy becomes a member of the group, a kind of liaison to the outside world. "It was a self-contained little universe, bordered on the north by acid and mescaline, on the south by pot and peyote, on the east by speed and redballs, on the west by downers and amphetamines. There were eleven people living in The Hill. Eleven, and Rudy" (129). He manages to reconnect somewhat with Kris, but she persuades him to join her on an acid trip, and he gradually becomes as reclusive as the others. One day, searching for the others, Rudy finds one transformed into a slime creature (reminiscent of the jelly-thing at the end of "I Have No Mouth"), three others feeding on the blonde girl ("through their hollow sharp teeth they drank up the yellow fluid from the bloated pus-pockets that had been her breasts and her buttocks" [131]), another flying with leather wings, Jonah himself turned into a gargoyle. He finds Kris in the attic, "breaking the skull and sucking out the moist brains of a thing that giggled like a harpsichord" (132) and makes a last effort to persuade her to leave, but realizes she has become a werewolf and flees. Climbing onto a mantel, he sees himself as a transparent glass goblin. Moments later, Kris finds him and "the great hairy paw slapped him into a million coruscating rainbow fragments" (132).

As with "The Whimper of Whipped Dogs," "Shattered like a Glass Goblin" maintains the careful balance between the uncanny and the marvelous that Todorov characterized as the fantastic. The narrative shifts into its hallucinatory mode only when Rudy is persuaded to take his first acid trip, and it never drifts from his increasingly uncertain point of view. Philip M. Rubens has argued that the descent into hell motif is a central one in Ellison's fiction, particularly in *Deathbird Stories,* and although Rubens does not focus on "Shattered like a Glass Goblin," it may provide the strongest evidence for his thesis in the entire collection. It is essentially a contemporary version of Orpheus (a myth which Ellison had also explored years earlier in a story about a jazz musician who seeks to bring back his lover, "Paulie Charmed the Sleeping Woman" [1962]), with Kris as an unwilling Eurydice, Jonah as a diffident Hades, and even Arianne standing in for the Thracian women whom Orpheus spurns. But this is an Orpheus without a lyre, a myth stripped of its creative energy. The eleven residents of The Hill, transformed into monstrous subhuman vampires and werewolves by the end of the tale, offer little in the way of hope or redemption, and in the end their self-contained universe simply self-destructs. It's extraordinarily easy to read the story as simply a morality play equating drug use with a descent into hell, but the story consistently refrains from directly making this equation, nor does it proselytize about addiction and dependence. The drugs are depicted, not too unrealistically for the time, as more of an environment than an aberration, and the choices made by the house's inhabitants, including Kris, are clearly their own.

"Paingod"

If the "gods" of many of the *Deathbird Stories* seem, in retrospect, to be the gods of the 1960s, other stories in the collection strive toward a deeper exploration of myth by counterpointing understated realism with homiletic fantasy, not always with great success. "Paingod" (1964) represents one of his earlier efforts in this direction, and in it we can see a somewhat younger Ellison straining to contain his ambitious vision within the context of a tale that more closely resembles his early magazine efforts than his later, more challenging tales (the story originally appeared in *Fantastic*). Although one of Ellison's more popular stories—Robert Thurston described it as "a brilliant example of Ellison's genius at transferring deeply felt emotion to a controlled narrative" (305)—"Paingod" is an uncertain melding of pulp science fiction and pop theology that succeeds only in its more realistic dimension. The portrayals of the two central human characters, an alcoholic, homeless immigrant named Pieter Koslek and a mediocre sculptor named Colin Marshack, are examples of what Ellison does best: brief, synoptic sketches that encapsulate whole life-narratives. But their individual stories are subsumed in the more cosmic narrative of

Trente, a godlike entity appointed by "the Ethos—the race of some-where/somewhen beings who morally and ethically ruled the universes" to serve as Paingod, "the one who dealt out the tears and the anguish and the soul-wrenching terrors that blighted life from its first moment to its last" (190). We are briefly treated to a litany of the miseries that Trente inflicts on a variety of alien races throughout the cosmos, leading to a kind of crisis of faith in which Trente, enormously lonely, questions his own purpose. Seeking answers, he chooses to enter the newly deceased body of Koslek, who then meets Marshack in a crowd listening to a racist demagogue. Entering Marshack's mind, Trente finally experiences the pain that he has visited upon countless creatures, and *It was potent hot all!*" (196). He chooses to reveal to Marshack a vision of the wonder and beauty of the various universes, and the next morning Marshack awakens and finds that, although he has no memory of it, he has completed his life's masterpiece, the one great work of art that he will never be able to repeat. Trente, meanwhile, faces the Ethos for having abandoned his post and reports what he has learned:

> I know that pain is the most important thing in the universes. Greater than survival, greater than love, greater even than the beauty it brings about. For without pain there can be no pleasure. Without sadness there can be no happiness. Without misery, there can be no beauty. And without these, life is endless, hopeless, doomed and damned. (197–98)

Not only has Trente learned his lesson but he reports it with the pious, dutiful tone of a sinner who has just seen the light in an evangelical novel. And the insight he has gained startles the reader only in its triteness, suggesting Keats or Schopenhauer diluted into moral homily—hardly worthy of the far weightier characters of Koslek and Marshack. who give the tale what real substance it has. Marshack, for example, is one of Ellison's more compelling portraits of an artist who strives to produce a single master-work and then is faced with the devastating recognition that he will never repeat it. Even this notion, though, is handled with far greater maturity in Ellison's story "The Cheese Stands Alone" (1981; discussed in chapter 9), in which a character must choose a course of action based on the realization that the finest, most rewarding moment of his entire life had already happened during his childhood.

Yet it is the comparatively crude science fictional frame of "Paingod" that makes it an important signpost in Ellison's struggle to develop a truly philosophical, speculative fiction and that warrants its inclusion in *Death-bird Stories* among far more accomplished and complex works. If on one level the story demonstrates the inability of the overdetermined narrative conventions of Ellison's earlier science fiction work to contain his emerging ambition, on another it represents an early attempt to discover fictional correlatives for the kinds of philosophical inquiry that fascinated him and that seemed to him to represent key moral conundrums. This is not to suggest that science fiction itself is necessarily an inappropriate or inadequate framework for such inquiry—the list of successful and intellectually sophisticated philosophical science fiction works was substantial even by 1964—but that Ellison's approach to the science fiction idiom here, with universal moral principles conveniently governed by a vaguely defined race of super-aliens, can hardly support the human weight he wants the story to carry. Nor, for that matter, is the hackneyed insight and consolation visited upon Trente especially powerful or original. What is important is that Ellison, like his 1960s contemporaries Roger Zelazny and Philip José Farmer, was seeking to discover, through metaphor, a means of integrating the tropes and icons of formula science fiction into a far more personal and contemporary mythology. With "Paingod," the constraints of genre convention are still much in evidence, but less than a decade after that story Ellison would publish the two most ambitious and adventuresome narrative experiments in *Deathbird Stories:* "Adrift, Just off the Islets of Langerhans: Latitude 38°54'N, Longitude 77°00'13"W" and "The Deathbird." As if recognizing that these two stories represented a kind of culmination of the ambitions represented by the other selections, they are given pride of place as the final two pieces in the book—and indeed, they lend the overall collection a coherence that is only fitfully hinted at in the earlier stories.

"ADRIFT"

The Islets of Langerhans, of course, is not a geographical location, but a medical term for small groups or "islets" of endocrine cells near the pancreas, and a quick glance at an atlas reveals that the latitude and longitude mentioned would place us somewhere in suburban Washington, D.C. Even the unusual title of Ellison's tale suggests a unique combination of disparate discourses, and this textual polyphony continues with the story's very first sentence, with its bizarre conflation of Kafka and Melville: "When Moby Dick awoke one morning from unsettling dreams, he found himself changed in his bed of kelp into a monstrous Ahab" (230). In fact, the protagonist turns out to be not Moby Dick but Lawrence Talbot, a refugee from yet another universe of discourse: the 1941 Universal horror film *The Wolf Man*. Made desperate by his inability to overcome his werewolf curse or to die—a dilemma symbolized by an ugly, hated fish that has killed all the other fish in Talbot's tank but will not die itself—Talbot has made an appointment with a consulting firm called "Information Associates," which turns out to be a men's toilet—until the door shimmers and changes, apparently just for Talbot. The mysterious, disappearing shop or office has been one of the most consistent conventions of popular fantasy for the better part of a century, with contributions from authors as diverse as John Collier, Theodore Sturgeon, Howard Fast, Nelson Bond, and Ellison himself (such a shop features prominently in "The Place with No Name," also in *Deathbird Stories,* and Ellison's 1977 story "Shoppe Keeper" was written as a kind of commentary on the theme). But Ellison's narratological stew isn't complete even yet. The representative of Information Associates turns out to be a man named Demeter, and his office window seems to look out upon a scene from millions of years in Earth's past. Talbot negotiates with Demeter for the information that he hopes will enable him to learn how to die—namely, his soul's exact location in his body. And when the information arrives, Talbot turns to his old friend Victor Frankenstein (although the last name is not specified), another figure from Universal horror films. Victor is now a highly successful scientist who manages the Eastern Bloc's major nuclear research facility in a remote part of the Carpathians, and his dialogue is full of references to proton synchrotrons, biotechnics, and servomechanisms. He eventually comes up with a scheme by which Talbot's consciousness can be transferred to a cell-sized artificial microorganism or "mite" and inserted into Talbot's body—thus enabling him to literally search for his soul in the landscape of his flesh.

What is remarkable about this story's discourse in contrast to "Paingod" in particular (and to most of the other *Deathbird Stories* to some degree) is its lack of restraint. Rather than trying to accommodate his tale to an inherited set of templates (science fiction, horror, myth, etc.), Ellison grazes freely among the cultural landscapes of his own past, borrowing what he needs to construct a genuinely syncretistic narrative. In the space of only a few pages, we encounter Kafka, Melville, medical and geographical terminology, the Wolf Man, Demeter, Frankenstein, implications of time travel, the jargon of hard science fiction, and the narrative conventions of comic fantasy (the disappearing office), all culminating in a scheme that sounds suspiciously like the lunatic 1966 science fiction film *Fantastic Voyage,* in which microminiaturized scientists are sent inside a patient to complete a medical procedure. The narrative ought to appear ramshackle at best, if not totally out of control, but in fact it is quite the opposite. By taking only what he needs from each arena of discourse but permitting none of them to dominate the narrative, Ellison is asserting his own growing control of his material, and in the process he is able to weave a rich and complex texture into his story. By the time the major action of the narrative takes place—Talbot's adventures inside his own body—the reader has effectively been told not to be deceived by genre expectations. The story is not going to become science fiction, or fantasy, or horror, or literary surrealism, or camp nostalgia, but it is not going to give up its claim to these discourses either. It is, in fact, a kind of palimpsest text and one of Ellison's first mature experiments in postmodern narrative methods.

While undergoing preparations for his journey in Victor's lab, Talbot meets an elderly laboratory assistant named Nadja, whom he initially believes to be his mother. Nadja will turn out to be the central palimpsest figure in the story, overlaid not only with Victor's mother but with a 102-year-old woman named Martha Nelson, whose story he hears on the radio while adrift on the "pancreatic sea" inside his own body. Since childhood, Nelson had been an inmate in an Ohio mental institution, to which she may have been committed by mistake. Talbot is haunted by this story, and later tells Victor, "My mother, Nadja, Martha Nelson, they're all the same, . . . all wasted lives" (261). Earlier, he describes his own life as "anguish and guilt and horror, the wasted result of events over which he had had no control" (253). Much of what happens during his interior journey has to do with reconciliation and consolation, as Talbot learns that he can lend his own life value by dedicating it to redeeming some of these other lost lives. At first, his journey is replete with images of waste and corruption. Entering through the navel, he encounters "the smells of rotted food, digested and turning to waste" (252), then begins tearing at his atrophied umbilical cord: "He ripped away at the clumps of flesh until the membrane gave . . . and a gap was torn through opening him to himself" (253). He eventually finds his way into a "world of dead orange rock," a "parched and stunned wasteland" where he finds no signs of life except for occasional half-human, sometimes headless skeletons (255). He comes across a vile-smelling lake full of dead things, "the corpses of dead dreams as they bobbed and revolved like maggoty pork in a gray soup" (256), and in the lake is the hideous devil fish from his aquarium.

Talbot spends months or years inside his body. Images of decay soon give way to images of innocence, as Talbot comes across a cache of his own childhood toys—a wooden machine gun, toy soldiers, a microscope, a jar of pennies, radio premiums, a decoding badge, etc. He recognizes that something important is missing from the cache, but can't remember what it is. Setting out across the pancreatic sea toward the Islets of Langerhans in a small boat, he finds himself becalmed at the coordinates of the story's title, and passes the time listening to the radio. For the most part, the radio programs are also artifacts of childhood: a dramatization of a 1940s Edward G. Robinson movie, programs that seem to feature the Shadow or Nero Wolfe, a news broadcast by Graham MacNamee. But then the MacNamee newscast suddenly shifts into the present, with the story of Martha Nelson's long incarceration. Talbot makes his way to the islet where his soul is supposedly located, an islet dominated by a featureless black fortress, and finds in a wooden box the missing item from the cache of toys he had found earlier: an "old, rusted Howdy Doody button" (261). (Perhaps anticipating the response of some readers, Ellison has Victor, upon being told of this discovery, virtually stepping outside the narrative to comment, "What the hell's *that* supposed to signify, innocence?") With his new treasure, Talbot enters the dark fortress and makes his way to a cell with an unlocked door. "Whoever lived in this cell had never tried to open the door; or had tried and decided not to leave" (260). It is, in fact, Martha Nelson, whose rescue will be the final stage in Talbot's redemption. Talbot persuades Victor to create a mite for Nadja—Martha's doppelgänger in the outside world—so that the two can return to the interior—where, Talbot says, he never changes into a werewolf, since there is no day or night—and live out new lives together, redeeming both "wasted" lives. As Talbot finds peace, the "devil-fish" in his aquarium, a clear symbol of his own curse, finally dies.

A Freudian reading of this almost literal return to the womb to recapture one's innocence is almost inevitable—except, of course, that Talbot's "womb" is his own interior landscape, littered with the detritus of his life. Having found a purpose in life, he no longer needs to die. But he cannot quite accept life either, so he persuades Victor not only to permit him and Nadja to return but to cryonically preserve the body once they are inside.

Essentially a fantasy of regained innocence that anticipates such later stories as "Jeffty Is Five," "Adrift" seems to invite a multiplicity of readings because of the variety of its discourses. Philip M. Rubens, for example, views the entire story in terms of the mythical descent into the underworld with the pancreatic sea standing in for Plato's Pool of Memory, Martha Nelson for Persephone, and the black fortress as the palace of Hades. Such meticulous consistency doesn't really hold up, however, and tends to overlook the very eclecticism and quirkiness that gives the story its strength. Martha Nelson is, in a sense, a Persephone figure whose imprisonment has somehow coincided with Talbot's werewolf curse, but to read the entire tale in terms of classic mythology would require, for example, that Victor be assigned the role of Zeus—which in turn diminishes his role as Frankenstein, as the voice of science and rationality in Talbot's demon-haunted world. What effectiveness the story attains comes not from its ability to support allegorical readings but from its defiance of the very traditions it invokes: a horror story with a happy ending, a science fiction story that leads to an impossible fantasy landscape, a myth that gives equal billing to classical figures and TV puppets. In a sense, the aesthetics of the story are defiant as well: Victor is quite correct to point out that the Howdy Doody button is a trite symbol at best, and Ellison proceeds to weave this very triteness into the fabric of the story's meaning. Similarly, the story of Martha Nelson, an interpolated realistic narrative, seems meant to ground the story in some recognizable version of the reader's own world, but then she, too, becomes a figure of bathos. The main weakness in the story, in the end, is not its manic eclecticism and improvisory tone but its tendency to dilute its best inventions in a wash of sentimentality that does justice to neither the mythical Talbot nor the real-world Martha Nelson.

"THE DEATHBIRD"

To a great extent, Lawrence Talbot's desire to reclaim his and Martha Nelson's lives by living them over again reflects a crucial element in Ellison's pattern of mythical thinking during this period. Mircea Eliade has written that many apocalyptic texts emerge from a fundamental understanding or belief that "life cannot be *repaired,* it can only be *re-created* by a return to sources" (30), and this is essentially what happens at the end of "Adrift." It is also what happens, on a far vaster scale, in "The Deathbird," the most ambitious and complex tale in *Deathbird Stories* in terms of its structure, its theme, and its manipulation of genre discourses. Surprisingly, the basic conceit of the story is one of the more weatherbeaten clichés of bad science fiction—the notion that alien civilizations were somehow involved in the creation myths of the Book of Genesis—but it quickly becomes clear that this is merely a starting point for what is intended as an ecological parable in the form of a complete reinterpretation of the Adam and Eve story, casting the Snake as the defender and ally of humanity and God as an insane, irresponsible, and petulant child—a God not much different from the computer in "I Have No Mouth, and I Must Scream." (In fact, "The Deathbird," with its rethinking of Genesis, forms a kind of Old Testament triptych along with "I Have No Mouth," which as we have noted often echoes Exodus, and "Strange Wine," which echoes the story of Job.) In Ellison's new version of the myth, the Snake is an alien being named Dira, whose people lost custodianship of the Earth eons ago in an arbitration conducted by a wise and ancient race very much like the Ethos of "Paingod." As a concession, Dira is allowed to remain on Earth and offer some protection to humanity—such as teaching it the truth about the value of knowledge—but is prohibited from directly interfering with the planet's history or with the beliefs promulgated by the demented custodian of the planet. His only weapon is the Deathbird, which can only be used to bring final death to the planet—far too late to save humanity. As a result, Dira is demonized in the Book of Genesis. But Dira is also permitted to offer one crucial boon to mankind: He may choose one human, who will be reincarnated generation after generation, to carry the spark of wisdom that will eventually enable the humans to defeat their savage god. We are told that this anonymous man is not a major historical figure, although once, when he is directly contacted by Dira, his quest for understanding gives rise to the Faust legend. In another episode, the man is a Berber tribesman who is given a vision of the unity of life on Earth and the Earth as, literally, a Great Mother. Elsewhere he is a tribesman dying during a rockslide, a soldier killed at Agincourt, a victim of mustard gas at Verdun, a victim of an atomic blast.

Eventually, he is Nathan Stack, an industrialist whom Dira takes from his body in his corporate boardroom and who spends the next quarter-million years sleeping in the molten core of the Earth. By then, the Earth is little more than a "broken toy" (267), capable of supporting no life at all: "The winds, green and deadly dived out of the sky and raked the carcass of the Earth, seeking, seeking: anything moving, anything still living. But there was nothing. Powder. Talc. Pumice" (270). Only one feature rises above the desolate plain: an onyx mountain that, like Dante's purgatory, rises out of hell to the summit where the god dwells. Stack's duty, like that of the archetypal mythical hero, is to confront and defeat the god, permitting the Deathbird to finally descend and put the wounded Earth out of its misery. Millennia earlier, Stack had faced an oddly similar circumstance when his mother was dying of cancer, begging him to "use the needle" (284) and revealing a family secret only when he agreed to do so. Now, begging the Snake to reveal the truth to him, Stack discovers that he began life as Adam (or "Ish-Lilith" [277]), that the snake is Satan, that the god of this world is mad, and that Stack himself "was more powerful than the god he'd worshipped all through the history of Men" (294). Finally recognizing the Snake as his true friend, Stack again "used the needle with a wave of his hands" (294), and the Deathbird descends to claim the Earth.

Despite its startlingly bleak imagery, the basic narrative of "The Death-bird" is an archetypally simple quest fable, its putative challenge to religious orthodoxy hardly shocking (at such a late period as the 1970s), and its conflation of science fictional ideas with Judeo-Christian iconography far from original. The idea of a protector of humanity appearing in a Satanic form, for example, was a major feature of Arthur C. Clarke's classic 1953 novel, *Childhood's End.* The idea of worlds or even universes as the play-things of mad gods had been prominently featured by Philip José Farmer in his "World of Tiers" novels of the late 1960s. And the idea of Adam as a resurrected protagonist dates back as far as Victorian fantasy novels by George MacDonald. But what lends "The Deathbird" its power and prob-ably its popularity is its fragmented mode of telling, which in purely tech-nical terms more closely reflects the narrative experiments of the New Wave (particularly Ballard and Aldiss) than anything else Ellison had written so far. The story consists of twenty-six numbered sections, only half of which directly narrate the tale of Nathan Stack. Another five nar-rate the backstory of Dira, the Snake, and her race's struggle to preserve some hope for Earth after having lost what was essentially a custody bat-tle. Of the remaining sections, the most interesting and effective are those which parody the annoyingly obtuse and authoritarian style characteristic of the editorial material in undergraduate literature text anthologies and college syllabi. The opening section announces, "This is a test. Take notes" (266), as though the whole story is in fact an exercise—which to some extent, of course, it is. Another section, after quoting the serpent-in-the-garden passage from Genesis which the story as a whole attempts to subvert, deliberately manipulates the reader by asking pointed "discussion" questions about inconsistencies in Genesis, its biased viewpoint, and "the concept of slanted news" (270). Still later, a multiple-choice exam on the nature of God appears, and a section near the end of the story (section 23) consists of an unattributed passage from the prologue to Nietzsche's *Thus Spake Zarathustra,* describing Zarathustra's meeting with the saint in the forest who does not yet realize that God is dead. The final section consists only of the words "THIS IS FOR MARK TWAIN" (295), presumably a nod to Twain's own reinterpretation of the figure of Satan in *The Mysterious Stranger* and *Letters from the Earth.*

Of all the interpolated "syllabus" materials, the most unusual is a frankly sentimental autobiographical essay by Ellison himself about the death of his dog Ahbhu, introduced as "Supplementary Reading" (277) and accompanied by an essay assignment and discussion questions. The essay was later published separately in the newspaper column "The Harlan Ellison Hornbook" (September 6, 1973), leaving little doubt that it is a direct account of the author's own experience. Its presence in "The Deathbird," even framed as it is by academic parody, is a rare example of an author breaking the fourth wall of his own narrative in order to incorporate a personal memoir in an otherwise nonrealistic tale. When Ellison takes his cancer-ridden pet to the veterinarian to be put to sleep, he imagines that the dog's last look at him conveys the message "Don't leave me with strangers" (281), which then—along with Stack's mother's "Use the needle"—becomes a recurring motif to represent the responsibilities of true love, responsibilities that are being tested in Stack at the end of the story. In the multiple choice quiz about God, one of the questions reads as follows:

> 4. Which of these phrases typifies the profoundest love:
>   A. Don't leave me with strangers.
>   B. I love you.
>   C. God is love.
>   D. Use the needle. (290)

Ellison's interpolation his own feelings and experiences, together with the academic parodies, the passages from Genesis and Nietzsche, and the allusions to such legends as Faust, seem designed not only to fragment and deconstruct the fantastic narrative of Stack's resurrection, effectively removing it from the narrative traditions of fantasy and science fiction, which characteristically seek to achieve their effects by immersing the reader into an unmediated secondary world. Instead, Ellison seems bent on dramatically asserting the textuality and artifice of the tale and especially on asserting his own control of the materials. This assertion of authority—which in most earlier Ellison anthologies was confined to the introductory material and story notes—has finally made it into the fiction itself, and in the process casts a somewhat different light on all the earlier selections in *Deathbird Stories,* which more traditionally sought to disguise their artifice, more often than not using the lame devices of genre fiction. By crossing the line between memoir and myth, Ellison seems finally to liberate himself from the constraints of genre expectations. In much of his best later fiction, the reworked mythologies of *Deathbird Stories* would give way to far more personal myths of morality and responsibility. In the end, the victory that emerges most powerfully from "The Deathbird" in particular and from *Deathbird Stories* in general is the victory not of Nathan Stack or of Larry Talbot but of the dog Ahbhu. For all the righteous anger and cosmic ironies that seem to inform the collection, its driving force is that simple sense of loss. God turns out to be "a small dog dead in a hole" (290).

8 | MYTHS OF IDENTITY I

Profession and Heritage

AFTER *DEATHBIRD STORIES,* Ellison's next major collections were *Strange Wine* (1978) and *Shatterday* (1980). (*No Doors, No Windows,* published the same year as *Deathbird,* was principally a collection of crime stories from the 1950s and 1960s, with "The Whimper of Whipped Dogs" added as an anchor piece, a rare occasion in which one of Ellison's stories appeared in two collections in the same year.) Despite favorable reviews, *Strange Wine* is not one of Ellison's stronger collections, its major pieces being the title story and the lead story, "Croatoan." What is striking, however, is that following the ambitious, comparatively austere, and at times visionary exploration of contemporary myth in *Deathbird Stories,* it marks a return to the more personal vision that had long marked Ellison's more successful mainstream stories and that he was only beginning to assimilate into the narrative structures of fantasy. In many ways, this more personal focus was no less visionary than the myth fantasies and science fiction tours de force that had gained Ellison his reputation, but few of these later stories would attain the classic status and endless anthology appearances of his most famous tales from the 1960s. If *Deathbird Stories* represented the beginning of the post-genre phase of Ellison's career—with genre tropes and conventions used almost interchangeably as functions of technique, rather than as sources of narrative rules—his later collections were even more eclectic in style and in their use of source materials. *Strange Wine,* for example, features stories based in folklore and legend ("Croatoan," "Emissary from Hamelin"), a crime story with a science fiction resolution ("Killing

Bernstein"), comedy and satire ("Working with the Little People," "Mom," "The New York Review of Bird"), science fiction ("The Wine Has Been Left Open Too Long and the Memory Has Gone Flat," "Seeing," "Strange Wine"), horror ("The Diagnosis of Dr. D'*arque*Angel," "Lonely Women Are the Vessels of Time"), a fantasy of hell ("Hitler Painted Roses"), a Kafkaesque portrait of a troubled marriage ("In Fear of K"), and a "story" consisting of twenty-six largely unrelated vignettes and fragments ("From A to Z, in the Chocolate Alphabet"). *Shatterday,* a much stronger and more eclectic collection, includes three of Ellison's best known stories, "Jeffty Is Five," "The Man Who Was Heavily into Revenge," and "Shatterday," as well as two of his better comic tales, "How's the Night Life on Cissalda" and "Would You Do It for a Penny?" (written with Haskell Barkin), and several of the more personal, character-oriented fantasies that, along with darker fantasies verging on horror, were rapidly becoming Ellison's trademark in place of the pyrotechnics of his 1960s science fiction. No overall theme like that of *Deathbird Stories* unites these collections, but themes do begin to emerge that help bring into focus a number of long-standing patterns in Ellison's work, among the most significant of which are Ellison's passionate desire to establish a legacy as an author—and not merely as a science fiction author—and his fitful attempts to come to grips with his own Jewish heritage.

THE WRITER AS SUPERHERO

Two of the stories in *Strange Wine,* "Working with the Little People" and "The New York Review of Bird," and the longest story in *Shatterday,* "All the Lies That Are My Life," all focus on writers who resemble Ellison, at least in part. Almost from the beginning of his career, Ellison was fascinated by the *idea* of being a professional writer, and it's important to remember that some of those early stories, which to a later reader may appear autobiographical, are instead informed by fantasy projections of what Ellison believed or dreamed a career like his might become—a fantasy version of a fantasy writer who stunningly transcends his hackwork origins and returns triumphantly to old haunts and venues. "GBK—A Many-Flavored Bird" (1962) includes clearly autobiographical references to Ellison's involvement with science fiction fans in Cleveland. But Walter Innes, the narrator, is no hungry twenty-eight-year-old science fiction writer aspiring to mainstream success. Rather, he is a wish-fulfillment extrapolation of a successful writer's life. He has a secretary, a potentially lucrative movie deal (for which he is flying to "the Coast"), and local TV interviews in Cleveland to worry about. When he goes to a nightclub, the headliner ("a well-known male singer who prefers I do not use his name" [*Love Ain't Nothing* 93]) joins him at his table. Oblivious to his own facile arrogance, he is in reality the other half of G. Barney Kantor, the Micawber-like self-important failure whom he once knew in a local science fiction club and who now has grandiose plans to stage a publicity campaign for a still-unmade film based on one of Innes's stories. In a moment of compassion—and perhaps of self-recognition—Innes forgoes his plan to put the annoying Kantor in his place and instead leaves him with an affectionate, if ambiguous, memento.

Innes is only the first in a series of fictional writers who share elements of Ellison's background and who are almost without exception enormously successful and widely respected in the literary and film communities, the communities in which Ellison himself has done the bulk of his work. By the time we get to "Punky & the Yale Men" (1965), he has metamorphosed into Andrew Sorokin, a legendary thirty-six-year-old novelist and Oscar-nominated screenwriter, described by other characters as a "giant" and an "institution," who began his career by joining a gang of juvenile delinquents in the Red Hook section of Brooklyn and writing about it in his first best-seller ("Punky" was his gang name). As a young writer, Sorokin had never been able to break into *Marquis,* a sophisticated men's magazine clearly modeled on *Esquire*—we are informed that its early contributors included Hemingway, Fitzgerald, and Dorothy Parker—but now the editor of the magazine wants to commission a sequel to that first piece, seventeen years later. Sorokin, whose musings are peppered with knowing allusions to "Jimmy" Baldwin and Thomas Wolfe, now has published fourteen novels, one of them filmed by Frankenheimer with Lana Turner as star, and he is acutely aware "that *Marquis* had never thought him worthy of acceptance before he had become famous and a Name" (*Love Ain't Nothing* 341), although everyone at the magazine—still the bastion of the New York literary establishment—now fawns over him shamelessly. There is more than a hint of spite-fantasy in this tale. But the central figure, despite sharing an aspect of Ellison's background, is likely meant to stand in not only for Ellison himself but for any talented but underappreciated writer. A similar figure shows up in "Tired Old Man" (1976; collected in *No Doors, No Windows*): "I came in from the Coast on a Wednesday, got myself locked up in the Warwick to finish the book" (211), etc. Billy Landress is another successful novelist who moved from New

York to become a screenwriter, and like Sorokin he is not without spite, as when he encounters a once-successful novelist who snubbed him when Landress was cranking out potboilers for *Manhunt* crime magazine (a more upscale digest than the ones Ellison usually sold to), but who is now reduced to writing a series of formula men's adventure paperbacks. (The story is subtitled "An *Hommage* to Cornell Woolrich"—himself a writer much admired by Ellison but generally underappreciated—and a ghostly Woolrich-like figure later shows up in the story as the tired old man of the title.)

The protagonist of "Working with the Little People" (1977; collected in *Strange Wine*), Noah Raymond, is a fantasy writer whose prodigious early success far eclipses that of any actual genre writer of the time. A cause célèbre from the time of his first sale to a pulp magazine, Raymond quickly graduated to the "slicks," made it into the *Year's Best Short Stories* (along with Isaac Bashevis Singer and Katherine Anne Porter) before he was nineteen, published his first collection to fawning reviews when he was twenty, and had his first novel selected by the Book-of-the-Month Club and nominated for a National Book Award. Perhaps his most telling achievement is that, after these successes, "librarians did not file him under 'science fiction/fantasy' but in the 'modern literature' section" (38). When Raymond completely runs dry at the age of twenty-seven, his career is sustained by a group of tiny gremlins, who somehow preserve their own existence by passing along portions of their history, which become Raymond's fantasy stories. But the early pattern of his career is familiar: A young writer in a despised genre achieves stunning success, effectively escaping the literary ghetto of his origins and, by dint of sheer brilliance, forcing other authors, readers, editors, and/or librarians to accept him entirely on his own terms. It is, in effect, a hero myth for popular writers, with the lowly venues of the genre magazines serving as wasteland, the literary establishment serving as dragons and ogres to be vanquished, respect and adulation as the prize.

And lest there be any doubt as to Ellison's belief in the reality of the New York literary establishment, he takes it on full-tilt in the manically comic burlesque "The New York Review of Bird" (1975), the longest story in *Strange Wine*. Written originally for a theme anthology titled *Weird Heroes,* the tale takes the notion of writer-as-Zorro to its satiric extreme. Cordwainer Bird, the eponymous hero of the story, had long been Ellison's most famous pseudonym, first used in the 1950s as a kind of tribute to

"Cordwainer Smith" (an enigmatic but brilliant writer whose true identity was widely debated in the SF community for years before he was revealed as Paul Linebarger, a political scientist and Johns Hopkins professor who had already published a handful of mainstream novels), later as a protest against television scripts or projects that Ellison regarded as compromised or butchered. At the same time that Byron Preiss, the editor of *Weird Heroes,* was asking Ellison to do a story about Bird, Philip José Farmer—perhaps the most tricksterish of all modern American science fiction writers—was seeking a way to incorporate Bird into an elaborate fake genealogy of fictional superheroes that he had developed originally for a pseudo-biography of Tarzan titled *Tarzan Alive* (1972) and elaborated in a similar book on Doc Savage, *Doc Savage: His Apocalyptic Life* (1973). With Ellison's cooperation, Farmer worked out a sketch of Bird's career and ancestry: His mother was the younger sister of pulp heroes G-8 (of the World War I aviation pulp *G-8 and His Battle Aces*) and the Shadow. His father was the grandson of Joyce's Leopold Bloom. Cordwainer himself shares Ellison's birthplace and year (Painesville, Ohio, in 1934), his record number of Hugo and Nebula Awards and the Edgar Award, his impatience with TV producers, and his modest stature (Cordwainer is only four feet tall, whereas Ellison is 5'5").

More literary tall tale than cultural satire, "The New York Review of Bird" begins with Bird outside a Fifth Avenue Brentano's bookstore whose window display is a virtual catalog of best-selling 1970s kitsch: Harold Robbins, Morris West, Allen Drury, Gerold Frank, Jacqueline Susann, Erich Segal, Dr. David Reuben. Entering the store and asking for a copy of his own story collection, *Bad Karma & Other Extravagances,* he is directed to the "sci-fi" section in the basement, which leads to a characteristic Ellisonian outburst on the use of that term, long widely regarded in the science fiction community as disparaging. After terrorizing the clerk, Bird heads off to the sci-fi section, which turns out to be a literalization of the notion of science fiction as a "ghetto": a dimly lit room full of cobwebs, infested with spiders and rats, a floor of packed dirt, the bookcases nothing but orange crates. "Bird thought of Jews crammed belly-to-butt in boxcars, on their way to Belsen" (178). Finding the single copy of his book damaged by mildew and silverfish, he storms back upstairs, only to be confronted by the Brentano's book buyer and a gaggle of security guards, whom he quickly overpowers. When he asks why his book isn't displayed among the best-sellers, he is told by the book buyer that it isn't a best-seller according to the *New York Times, Publishers Weekly,* George Plimpton, Rex Reed, Michael Korda, or Candida Donadio—names which, to Bird, represent the "secret masters" of the New York literary establishment, whom he now, as superhero, must vanquish.

The assumptions underlying this brief confrontation with the book buyer reveal a good deal about science fiction's relationship to the "mainstream" of book publishing, at least as perceived by Ellison and many other writers who grew up in the genre ghettos. When Bird asks why his book is not a best-seller and is referred to the *Times* and *Publishers Weekly,* for example, he is raising a reasonable question about the authority of those lists, and many authors have indeed complained that such lists are compiled in a manner that tends to discriminate against genre works: Specialty bookstores, for example, are usually not surveyed, and books that sell substantially but over longer spans of time seldom make the list. (One of the most successful novels in science fiction history, for example, Daniel Keyes's *Flowers for Algernon,* sold nearly five million copies without ever appearing on a best-seller list.) Bird's question of "who says" his book isn't a best-seller is thus a valid one in terms of those famous lists—but what do Michael Korda, Rex Reed, George Plimpton, and Candida Donadio have to do with it? Korda was the editor-in-chief of Simon & Schuster, Reed was a society journalist and critic, and Plimpton was the editor of the *Paris Review,* and Donadio was a successful agent who represented such literary authors as Joseph Heller and Thomas Pynchon (as opposed to the kind of lowbrow trash that Bird claims to be tilting against)—hardly a monolithic group with a single agenda, as their role of "secret masters" would seem to imply. Yet one of the characteristics of the outsider mind-set that arises in literary ghettoes such as science fiction is the paranoid suspicion that the "mainstream" publishing world is all of a piece, that the same machinery which lionizes Updike or Bellow also generates trash Hollywood biographies and crudely sensational best-sellers, all the while deliberately snubbing the work of talented writers trapped by their genre origins. There may indeed be a Literary Establishment that functions in the way Bird (and apparently Ellison) suspects, and there is certainly a publishing establishment that too often looks at lowest-common-denominator markets, but the Establishment that Bird sets out to destroy is an uneasy and somewhat naive conflation of the two.

Bird, in good pulp superhero fashion, warns the book buyer, "Go back to your puppet masters and warn them that no matter where they hide or run, Bird will seek them out and fight them with terrible justice!" (181). He compels her to reveal their meeting place by torturing her—forcing her to listen to passages from Kahlil Gibran's *The Prophet*—but she is machine-gunned at the moment of her confession. Bird seeks out the Shadow, who is his uncle (according to Farmer's genealogy, adopted here wholesale), only to find him confused and senescent but still sharp enough to send Bird off to the Statue of Liberty and the secret hideout of the New York Literary Establishment, which the uncle had infiltrated once, years earlier. The denouement is revealed in "a news story by Pete Hamill," which reports that various media celebrities—editors of the *New York Times Book Review* and the *New York Review of Books,* Michael Korda and other book editors, Elaine of Elaine's restaurant—perished in absurdly symbolic ways; the editor of *Jaws,* for example, is "gummed to death by a school of minnows" (198). Ellison admits, in his foreword to the story, that "there is just the faintest tot of wish fulfillment in the work" (171), presumably not only because of the poetically just fates suffered by a variety of literary snobs, but because of the story's central fantasy of a writer who talks very much like Ellison himself single-handedly storming the barricades on behalf of all the despised and excluded writers who made up such a significant part of his own literary heritage and literary community. Walter Innes, Andrew Sorokin, and Noah Raymond of the earlier stories are now transformed into a delightful cross between Paul Bunyan and Yosemite Sam, in what is the most lighthearted and entertaining of all Ellison's variations on the theme of the genre writer's plight.

"All the Lies That Are My Life"

But this is still not Ellison's last word on the subject. The far more ambitious and earnest "All the Lies That Are My Life" (1980; in *Shatterday*) is in many ways Ellison's definitive treatment of the writer as prodigal genius, as well as his most personal exploration of the theme of friendship. (The meaning of the title is never made clear in the story, although the phrase had haunted Ellison for years, showing up in such stories as "Pretty Maggie Moneyeyes" as far back as 1967.) Written originally for a literary quarterly but published in the *Magazine of Fantasy and Science Fiction*— where it received a Hugo nomination despite its complete lack of science fiction or fantasy content—the story incorporates so much lightly fictionalized material from Ellison's long friendship with Robert Silverberg that

Ellison warns readers against drawing too many connections: "The narrator and the protagonist are partially me and partially a close friend of mine, a man I've called friend for over twenty-five years," writes Ellison in his introduction to the tale in *Shatterday*. "The two of us are purposely intermingled, and large chunks of pure invention have been added to both. This is fiction, not personal memoir. Try not to read too much one-for-one into the bits and pieces of this work" (139). But what is most revealing about the story is not the manner in which Ellison transforms autobiographical anecdotes into fictional episodes—after all, the mainstream audience for whom the tale seems largely intended would scarcely even be aware of Ellison's long friendship with Silverberg, or their parallel careers—but the manner in which these anecdotes become part of the ongoing mythification of an author's career. Both the narrator, Larry Bedloe, and the protagonist, Jimmy Crowstairs, contain aspects of Ellison and Silverberg that only a few readers might recognize, but both are also dimensions of the idealized writer-as-culture-hero figure that so fascinated Ellison.

The success of Crowstairs, who has just died as the tale opens, is almost absurdly exaggerated, so that one at first suspects it may be a feverish fantasy of the envious narrator, Bedloe. Crowstairs's fame and reputation far surpasses that of Walter Innes, Andrew Sorokin, Noah Raymond, or Cordwainer Bird—though he shares traits with all these figures—and in fact surpasses that of virtually any twentieth-century American writer. He is a "staggeringly wealthy best-selling novelist, a serious artist who was seriously regarded by all the 'serious' critics, and a legend in his own time," with a name as familiar as "Salk or Babe Ruth or Hemingway" (142). At his funeral are a former president, two Hollywood actresses, a famous publisher (who resembles Bennett Cerf), an English novelist, Carl Sagan, a French film director, and a "plasma physicist from Princeton who's up for the Nobel this year" (141), plus two or three thousand mourners. Bedloe, the narrator, even compares the funeral to that of Victor Hugo, which virtually became a national holiday in Paris in 1885. "Not bad," he adds, "for a guy they steadfastly called a 'sci-fi' writer" (142). Bedloe then launches into a diatribe against the term *sci-fi* which, for readers even faintly familiar with Ellison's own pronouncements and interviews, seems clearly to be a signal that Crowstairs is Ellison: "Jimmy spent the last twenty-five years of his life trying to get that ugly categorization off his books and out of the biographies they wrote about him. He wrote fantasy, if specific pigeonholes are needed; but he insisted on being called simply a *writer*" (142). But he is a writer like no other America has ever seen. In addition to his astonishing success and popularity, he is a paradigm of the kind of male competence and universal experience that readers of *Rogue* or *Playboy*—or even Robert Heinlein—could only dream about: A former mountain climber, race car driver, steelworker, reporter, popular guest on Johnny Carson, and Hell's Angel, he "marched with Chavez in the Coachella Valley, spent time in Southern jails for civil rights activities, chummed it up with a Mafia *capo,* managed to con a trio of radical feminist lesbians into a four-way sexual liaison, covered a South American revolution, hired himself out to a firm specializing in industrial espionage, and God knows what all else" (158). He knows his way around the mean streets and is so respected there that when a gang of bank robbers decides to surrender to a Chicago newspaper columnist, the mayor, and the FBI, they choose him as intermediary. Even his death is a spectacle of macho bravura: Harassed in his Rolls-Royce Corniche by a group of Chicago punks, Crowstairs insults them and then outruns them through the streets and freeways of Los Angeles until they suicidally "decided to boom him" at ninety-five miles per hour, sending both vehicles flying off the road in a sequence reminiscent of "Along the Scenic Route."

That such an Olympian figure might entertain self-doubts and contain tragic flaws—even a dose of venality—is one of the not-too-surprising revelations of the story, but nothing that happens in the narrative can quite balance the sheer overkill that goes into the making of this character: Crowstairs is, in effect, the Competent Man of Heinleinian science fiction combined with the apotheosis of the Writer as Superhero, the final eruption of the wish-fulfillment fantasies that lurked near the surface of the earlier stories. Far from a characteristic Ellison protagonist, incomplete and uncertain, he is more closely allied to the vengeful pulp hero Cordwainer Bird—except that he is not, apparently, intended as an exaggerated comic figure, but as a portrait of the artist *in potentia* who, like Bird, can single-handedly vanquish the literary establishment and transform "a nation where illiteracy has gone beyond totemization, well into deification" (142) into a unified culture by sheer force of talent. Crowstairs's manifold genius erases the boundaries between highbrow and lowbrow culture, between genre, best-seller, and literary fiction, between celebrity and art, that had long haunted Ellison's career, and in so doing it very nearly erases the line between character and caricature as well.

The structure of the story is simple: Bedloe's memories of his life with Crowstairs alternate with the events surrounding and immediately following his death. The first of these memories returns Bedloe to the world of science fiction fandom and to his first meeting with Crowstairs at the World Science Fiction Convention in Chicago in 1952. Upon arriving, Bedloe is attacked by a punk fan from New Jersey who traveled to the convention with three tough-guy friends primarily to get even for disparaging remarks about his fanzine that Bedloe had made in his. Suddenly Crowstairs appears in a flurry of fists, a "pint-sized Zorro, no less than Destiny's Tot" (146), breaking the nose of the offending fan with his briefcase and driving him and his fellows out of the convention with a string of colorful insults and threats. The Crowstairs of this scene is much closer to the Cordwainer Bird of "The New York Review of Bird" than to the urbane Great Man he will become, but of course he's only an adolescent. Silverberg recalls the source episode, which occurred on the final night of the 1953 World Science Fiction Convention in Philadelphia, as follows:

> A certain New York fringe fan named Joe Semenovich had taken offense at some remarks of Harlan's, and had come to the convention that Monday to "get" him, bringing along two anthropoid goons. The three hoods—as sinister-looking as you can imagine—converged on Harlan in the lobby. Any sensible man would have disappeared at once, or at least yelled for the nearest bell-hop to stop the slaughter. But Harlan stood his ground, snarled back at Semenovich nose-to-nose, and avoided mayhem through a display of sheer bravado. (Porter 23–24)

This is thus the first of many examples in the story in which the careers and personalities of Ellison and Silverberg are deliberately shuffled and recombined. Ellison was both the target of the goons and his own rescuer, while Silverberg (according to his account) was only a bystander; in the story Bedloe becomes the victim and Crowstairs the comic-heroic rescuer. But then Crowstairs introduces himself and announces that his first novel, *Death Dance on Sirius 7,* has been sold to Crowell. Silverberg's first novel, *Revolt on Alpha C,* was published by Crowell in 1954, and a kind of running joke in the early years of their relationship had to do with Ellison's persistent reporting of stories he had almost sold, while Silverberg published steadily, even if most of what he published was hackwork.

Crowstairs tells Bedloe that his work is "too controlled, too cautious," lacking in "wildness" (148), a criticism that frequently has been leveled against Silverberg, who has long been recognized as one of science fiction's master craftsmen, while "wildness" is hardly an inappropriate term for Ellison's work. Crowstairs dates a stunning array of beauties, while Bedloe sees the same girl, Leslie, for years—until she marries Crowstairs in one of what proves to be a series of betrayals. Crowstairs feels he is gauche and overbearing, while Bedloe is cool and in control. Crowstairs says he views Bedloe as an older brother, even though the difference in their ages is only six months (actually, Ellison is eight months older than Silverberg). Crowstairs is known for unselfconsciously raiding his life and the lives of his friends for material—a habit Ellison cheerfully admits to—but it is Bedloe who works editing a men's magazine in Chicago, much like Ellison's experience with *Rogue*. And in the end, it is Crowstairs who becomes another powerful figure of entrapment, taking advantage of his relationship with Bedloe to make him executor of his literary estate. At the reading of the will, Crowstairs himself appears on videotape, rewarding his assistant with his entire corporation; a young writer named Winslow—who sacrificed his own career to anonymously collaborate on Crowstairs's books—with his house (with the intention of turning it into a writers' colony); his ex-wife with a million dollars, a magazine, and a Swiss chalet. He also takes the opportunity to ferociously berate his alienated sister, who shares certain characteristics with Ellison's own sister, Beverly. But to Bedloe, he reveals his greatest fear:

Will they still read me? Will I be on the bookshelves, the Modern Library, matched sets in good bindings? *That's* what I'm afraid of, Larry. Posterity. I want a chance to go on after I'm gone. Fifty years from now I want them to come back to my stuff, the way they did to Poe's and Dickens's and Conrad's. I don't want to wind up like Clark Ashton Smith or Cabell or the other Smith, Thorne Smith. I don't want bits and pieces of my unfinished stories written by the literary vampires. . . .

Pride isn't part of it . . . honest to God it isn't! You remember when we talked about Poe how I said he had the right idea, that it was the *work*, it was Art, that held the high road, not religion, or good deeds or friendship or patriotism? None of those. The stories, the books. That's all you can put a bet on. That continues. And I couldn't bear to think of

some half-assed science fiction hack dredging up a line or two I started
and didn't know how to finish, and writing a whole fucking book off it,
the way they've done to poor old Robert E. Howard, or 'Doc' Smith.
They even did it to Poe and Jack London and . . . oh, Christ, Larry, you
know what I'm saying. Promise me!" (190–91)

    "He did it," comments Bedloe. "The clever sonofabitch did it. He
figured a way to keep me tied to him. He knew I'd do the job" (191).
Crowstairs's victory, in its own way, is as complete as that of the computer in "I Have No Mouth, and I Must Scream," or that of Maggie
when she traps the hapless Kostner in the machine. Having already, presumably, consumed the career of his secret collaborator Winslow, he
now, posthumously, threatens to consume the career of Bedloe as well.

Crowstairs's concluding melodramatic declamation is one of the most
remarkable and revealing passages in all of Ellison's fiction, and the story as
a whole is one of the most complex expressions of Ellison's ambivalence
about his work and career. Increasingly in Ellison's later career, there are
passages in which the voice of the author himself burns through the narrator, even through the "implied author" that critic Wayne Booth has discussed as an intermediate rhetoric figure between author and narrator. It is
hard to avoid the conclusion that Crowstairs's anxieties are an unmediated
expression of Ellison's own, and the authors he chooses to compare himself
in this passage reveal to a great extent the crisis of identity of a genre writer
who desperately wants out but fears permanent entrapment. On the one
hand, he hopes, hubristically, to be compared to Dickens, Conrad, and Poe;
on the other, he sees what has happened to writers he admires but who have
virtually disappeared, becoming minor cult favorites. (Clark Ashton Smith
was a talented but often overflorid fantasy writer, a colleague of H. P. Lovecraft, who appeared most often in the pulp magazine *Weird Tales;* Thorne
Smith, a brilliant humorist, is today almost exclusively remembered as the
author of the ghost story *Topper.*) His fear of having his unfinished works
completed by hacks also conflates pulp writers like Robert E. Howard (the
creator of Conan the Barbarian) and "Doc" Smith (E. E. Smith, often credited with inventing the massive intergalactic space opera) with London and
Poe, a comparison that is wildly off-center. (That the fear itself is a legitimate one is attested to by later literary history, with works by both "classic"
authors like Jane Austen and popular genre writers like Lawrence Sanders
and Frank Herbert being completed or extended by lesser hands.)

Equally significant is the fact that, by so thoroughly conflating himself and Silverberg, Ellison manages to construct a situation in which he—or some version of himself—is both perpetrator and victim, both betrayer and betrayed, both envious and envied, both struggling writer and worldwide success. The books and stories that Crowstairs is supposed to have written, including something called the *Radimore* trilogy, are not Ellison's works, and in fact are virtually unimaginable given the realities of the publishing industry and American culture in general, and Ellison almost seems to recognize this by refraining from any attempt to represent what these works are like. (They come closer to bearing a resemblance to Silverberg's works, since Silverberg did achieve best-seller status with his *Lord Valentine's Castle* series of fantasies, but these are unconnected to and far different from the works that won Silverberg serious critical acclaim, such as the novel *Dying Inside*.) This conflation is a step beyond the splitting of self that had been a favorite theme of Ellison's in stories like "One Life, Furnished in Early Poverty" and "Shatterday" (included in this same collection). It is rather a kind of unsettling phagocytic absorption of parts of another writer's life in order to construct a larger-than-life whole, which in turn can be split into the characters of Crowstairs and Bedloe along lines that best support the story's rhetorical agenda. And that agenda, at least in part, involves portraying the Writer Hero in terms that enable Ellison to resolve the anxieties attendant upon being a popular genre writer in an era in which such writers are systematically excluded from the mainstream of critical recognition. Like Paul Bunyan, the figure is frankly mythical, but he is also like Whitman: large, self-contradictory, and containing multitudes. He is both the author Ellison aspires to be and the uncertain and treacherous friend that he hopes never to be.

BEING JEWISH

Although it has never been a major sustained focus, Ellison's Jewish background has provided a continual undercurrent to his work, from the childhood experiences with anti-Semitism that inform such stories as "Final Shtick" (1960) and "One Life, Furnished in Early Poverty" (1970) to the Jewish characters Simon Rubin in "Battle without Banners" (1964) and Lilian Goldbosch in "A Prayer for No One's Enemy" (1966)—both of whom must confront prejudice in their respective communities—to the more elliptical allusions to Exodus and Jehovah in "I Have No Mouth, and

I Must Scream" (1967). While there is little evidence that Ellison's family was particularly observant, there is a good deal to suggest that they never viewed themselves as fully assimilated, either. When Ellison's mother died in 1976, a major portion of the eulogy he delivered at her funeral was a retelling of her favorite joke (or at least the only joke she had ever told her son), a shaggy borscht-belt chestnut about two Jews from upstate New York, Solly and Herschel, arguing over whether to buy an elephant. The attitudes and locutions of the second- and third-generation immigrant Jewish American community were clearly part of Ellison's heritage, and in one of his rare appearances as an actor, he played the title character in a reader's theater adaptation of Bernard Malamud's "The Jewbird" with a masterful inflection that could have gotten him work in the Catskills. This idiom is celebrated in some of Ellison's best comic fiction, particularly in the stories "I'm Looking for Kadak" (1974) and "Mom" (1976), both of which, despite their light tone, represent a kind of assertion of Jewish identity and even include glossaries of Yiddish and Hebrew terms for the benefit of Ellison's non-Jewish readers.

"I'm Looking for Kadak" was written for Jack Dann's 1974 *Wandering Stars: An Anthology of Jewish Science Fiction and Fantasy,* which itself was intended as a kind of celebration both of the strong fantasy tradition in Jewish literature (Bernard Malamud and Isaac Bashevis Singer are among the authors included) and of the widely unrecognized Jewish contributions to the popular fantastic genres (during the pulp era, many Jewish writers published under pseudonyms, and the most famous of all Jewish science fiction writers, Isaac Asimov, seldom dealt with the topic at all, as he acknowledges in his introduction to the volume). The story, which Ellison included in his own 1974 *Approaching Oblivion,* makes its ethnicity clear from the beginning: "You'll pardon me but my name is Evsise and I'm standing here in the middle of sand, talking to a butterfly, and if I sound like I'm talking to myself, again you'll pardon but what can I tell you? A grown person standing talking to a butterfly. In sand" (68).

But Evsise, though clearly and proudly Jewish, is not of Earth. He is a Zsouchmoid, a blue, eleven-armed native of the planet Zsouchmuhn. How Jews arrived on the planet is unclear, although Evsise refers to equally unexplained reports of a Jewish tribe of Indians found in South America. The immediate problem facing him is one that carries an unpleasant historical resonance: All the inhabitants of Zsouchmuhn are being relocated in preparation for the planet itself being moved to another part of the galaxy. As a tribute to what had long been a happy home, a few diehards who have not yet moved decide to sit shivah for the planet, but only nine Jews can be found—one short of the required minyan. Evsise is dispatched to track down Kadak, a long-lost companion who disgusted everyone with his incessant "snuffling" and who had disappeared seventeen years earlier after angrily renouncing his Judaism. He follows the trail to a fanatical sect called the Church of the Apostates—where he is forced to trade fairly disgusting sex for more information—and then to another cult called the Slaves of the Rock, an even more disgusting group who have transformed themselves into rocks with long tongues, which they use to capture passing bugs. But even they have exiled Kadak for his snuffling. Evsise continues to track him from religion to religion, until he learns that an "Archdruid of Nothingness" had years earlier transformed Kadak into a butterfly— the butterfly that Evsise is addressing as he narrates the story, whose identity is revealed by his disgusting snuffle. Returning with his prize, Evsise learns that since Kadak has only been a butterfly for ten years, he is not of age to participate in the minyan. But Kadak alights on the ark of the Torah, frantically flapping his wings as if to signal them, until Evsise remembers an obscure Talmudic rule that permits nine men together with the holy ark to be considered adequate for worship.

"Kadak" is one of Ellison's funniest sustained comic pieces, thanks in large part to the Yiddish-sprinkled patois of the narrator Evsise and to the fundamental conceit that Jewish identity and Jewish law transcend not only cultures but species. The story as a whole is a not-too-subtle reminder, especially given Ellison's apparent assumption of his readers' unfamiliarity with it, that Judaism is unrelated to such issues as race or even genealogy. It is also a reminder of Judaism's endurance. The comparatively mild satire of Jewish law and Yiddish-inflected language contrasts notably with the bizarre variety of increasingly revolting cult religions that Evsise encounters on his quest: the Church of the Apostates (whose cathedral is made of "string and spit and bits of dried crap off the streets and their bodies" [76] and who worship a god named Seymool), the Slaves of the Rock, the Fleshists (Sodom, we are told, was "a whole city *full* of Fleshists" [84]), the Denigrators, the True Believers of Suffering, the Tabernacle of the Mouth, the Caucus Race of the Malforms, the Lair of the Blessed Profundity of the unspeakable Trihll, and the Archdruid of Nothingness. Kadak, flitting like the butterfly he eventually becomes from religion to religion, reveals at the end that even he has never fully renounced his Jewish identity, as he helps remind the remaining worshippers of the rule that permits them to complete their shivah.

"Mom" (collected in *Strange Wine*) is a far more traditional ghost story built around the stand-up comedy premise that a young Jewish driving-school instructor continues to be tormented by the ghost of his mother—in Ellison's own description, "a Jewish momma's boy, whose mother has just died, and the ghost comes back to *nuhdz* him" (66). Lance Goldfein, thinking he has attained a measure of freedom at age thirty, instead finds himself trapped like many of Ellison's other protagonists. Only the tormentor this time is an aggressively stereotypical yenta who complains about her own funeral services, nags him about masturbating, scares away his dates, reminds him to clean his room, and even begins fixing him up with nice Jewish girls. "I was never *that* Jewish!" (74). Goldfein screams at one point. Finally he meets and falls in love with a girl that his mother approves of, assuming that she is Jewish because she has "the right amount of soul" (79), but in fact the girl herself is the ghost of a girl even a mother could love: Joan of Arc. The characters in the story never move much beyond stereotypes, and the story's main feature is Ellison's dead-on re-creation of the voice and inflection of the Jewish mother of folklore, complete with vernacular Yiddishisms. But again it expresses a sense of deep cultural identity far less visible in most of Ellison's earlier fiction.

Specific elements of Jewish religious tradition are rare in Ellison's work, though in one more recent story, "Go Toward the Light" (1996; collected in *Slippage*), he explores an important topic in Jewish history—the origin of the celebration of Chanukah. The narrator is a time traveler named Matty Simon, who is annoyed by the criticisms of his more devout colleague Barry Levin—the only other Jew in the time travel program—that he is a "Bad Jew" or a "pretend Jew." They argue about the miracle of one day's supply of oil burning for eight days after the retaking of the Temple, and Simon decides to learn the truth by traveling there firsthand. He finds that there is no oil hidden anywhere in the temple; the rabbi who might have found or brought it is murdered before the other Hebrews even arrive. Violating the age-old ethical code of all time travelers in science fiction, Simon decides to alter the past by creating it: he has a chemist colleague develop an oil made from long-chain molecules—which will burn at least eight times longer than normal oil—and takes the flask back to the dying rabbi for his seal. His reward is only a bit of ironic smugness when Levin next accuses him of being a Bad Jew, just as Chanukah is about to begin. Originally written for a 1994 National Public Radio series called *Chanukah Lights,* the story is of interest principally because—apart from "I'm Looking for Kadak"—it is virtually the only story of Ellison's to touch upon any aspect of Jewish religious observance, even as it demystifies that observance through the use of a common science fiction trope. As much as the culture and idiom of the American Jewish community informs and shapes Ellison's work, as much as the great Yiddish storytelling traditions seem to be in his blood, he has tended to touch upon actual issues of Jewish religion and history only gingerly at best.

THE HOLOCAUST

His few short attempts to address the overwhelming theme of the Holocaust, for example, include some of his shortest stories, and their approach to the topic is often delicate and almost tentative. The Holocaust has long been a problematical area for authors of fantastic literature, not only because it is widely regarded as virtually unrepresentable but because the dominant mode of Holocaust writing has been the testimony of the survivor, and the introduction of fantastic invention into such a mode may be seen as undermining its historical authority. Ellison's most substantial and moving portrait of a Holocaust survivor appears in his non-fantastic story "A Prayer for No One's Enemy" (1966; discussed in chapter 4), although he does return to the figure of the survivor, and the question of assimilation, in the brief, elliptical fantasy "The Boulevard of Broken Dreams" (1975; also in *Strange Wine*). Patrick Fenton, just released from a month in the hospital, is having coffee with friends when he begins to see a succession of long-dead Nazi war criminals pass by the coffee shop window. Now in his early sixties, Fenton had been a clerk at the Nuremberg trials in his youth, and had seen these men executed. Distraught, he runs from the coffee shop into the street, which suddenly begins to turn dark even in daytime, illuminated only by "the pale purple glow of the dead Nazi war criminals who walked slowly past him" (235). He tries to detain one of them, but "the tall, dark-haired Nazi shrugged him off, smiled at the yellow armband Fenton wore, smiled at the six-pointed star on the armband, and shoved past, walking free" (235). Fenton desperately tries to account for himself, for his new identity: "Changed at Ellis Island!" he screams at the retreating Nazi. "I had nothing to do with it!" (236). But then he sees himself beginning to glow purple, and the night envelops him. As much a ghost as the Nazis who haunt him, Fenton becomes a living exemplar of the familiar line from George Santayana quoted by Ellison in his introduction to the story: "Those who cannot remember the past are condemned to repeat it." The story is hardly more than a vignette, and when Ellison returned to the figure of the Nazi war criminal twenty years later, in "The Lingering Scent of Woodsmoke" (1997; in *Slippage*), the result was an even shorter tale of barely two pages. In this case, a Nazi who has successfully hidden out in Brazil returns to Auschwitz only to be confronted by a strange, greenish-looking girl who holds a gun on him. He assumes her to be a Jew, but instead she is a dryad, whose people—the forests— were fed into the furnaces along with the Jews. During the few moments of this discussion, the Nazi finds himself metamorphosing into a tree, trapped by roots climbing up his legs. With its facile comic-book revenge resolution (and the story appeared in *Harlan Ellison's Dream Corridor* two years before it was published in *Slippage*), this tale risks trivializing the figure of the war criminal by reducing him to a stereotype, just as "Boulevard of Broken Dreams" transforms these very real historical figures into projections of the protagonist's own guilt.

One of Ellison's most extensive statements about the Holocaust appears in the "Author's Note" to another very short story, "Twilight in the Cupboard," one of thirty-three stories written to accompany paintings by the contemporary Polish surrealist Jacek Yerka in what is certainly the most unusual, and one of the most beautiful, of all Ellison's books, *Mind Fields*. Yerka's painting depicts a broken cobwebbed cupboard, snails crawling up its sides, with a confusing array of objects on its surface: food, implements, dishes, a tiny bed, and what appears to be a small scale model of a church. Hanging above the cupboard is a rack with cups, keys, and a what looks like a transistor radio, and on the wall next to this is a 1983 daily calendar with all the dates neatly cut out. Fingers can be seen peeking out from the cutlery drawer, as though someone is trapped inside. For Ellison, this mysterious still life becomes an image of assimilation, cast in the form of a story about the posthumous fate of a real Polish resistance leader, Szmul Zygielbojm, and his wife and children. The model church is occupied by the "congregation of a small Catholic church that had been shrunk by God and condemned to exist on the top of the cupboard as reparations for their tacit acceptance of the destruction of more than three million Jews" (6). But Szmul, who lives in the cutlery drawer, fears that his wife and children are losing their Jewish identity and being "absorbed into the melting pot" represented by the church congregation. Confronting a milk delivery person whom he believes to be God, Szmul complains, "Is this supposed to be your idea of a fine way to spend all of eternity, watching my family become invisible, assimilated and absorbed and nothing? Invisible to the past, without memory or even tears?" (6). In his note to accompany the story, Ellison mentions that the idea of using Zygielbojm as a central figure came from Arthur D. Morse's 1967 study *While Six Million Died,* one of the early indictments of Pope Pius XII and the Allied governments who failed to get involved when reports of the Holocaust first came to light during World War II. Ellison views the moral of his story as simple: "The fucking Nazis are with us again" (69). After listing a rogue's gallery of revisionists, racists, and skinheads, Ellison says that "poor Szmul's wife and children think they can escape the next *Kristallnacht* by attending services with Gentile neighbors on Sunday, by eating fish on Friday, by changing their names or their noses, by pretending to be what they are not . . . by denying the nobility of what they are" (69).

Despite the questionable tact of casting actual historical victims of the Holocaust in the role of self-delusional assimilated Jews, this small story establishes a significant link between one of the key issues of post-Holocaust Judaism and one of Ellison's own recurring themes: the danger of losing spiritual identity. In a 1973 column of the "Harlan Ellison Hornbook," Ellison relates the story of Don Epstein, a friend and mentor during his student days at Ohio State. Despite a perfect grade point average, Ellison writes, Epstein was unable to gain admission to medical school because of a Jewish quota. Similar problems kept him out of dental and even veterinary school, until he ended up studying to be an undertaker. Years later, in 1961, Epstein showed up at Ellison's apartment in Evanston, having changed his name to Don Forrester, gotten a nose job, and married a Protestant wife.

> The Don I'd known was lost. Gone somewhere; where the wry dynamite guys go when history and compassionless forces over which they have no control make them ashamed of their heritage, make them ashamed of what they look like and who they are. Forrester (as opposed to Epstein) was a nice-enough guy, I suppose. But in my sad eyes he was a loser. A sad, beaten guy who had fought as hard as he could . . . but had lost. (*Hornbook* 237)

The "compassionless forces" here—the "Forces That Crush," from the original title of the story "Are You Listening?"—return us to the great Ellisonian nemesis of assimilation and conformity, which may take the form of fascism (the Ticktockman) or of indifference (the dark urban god of "The Whimper of Whipped Dogs"). One of the shortest and most poignant prose pieces in *Mind Fields* is titled "The Silence," which accompanies a Yerka painting of a partly ruined cathedral, apparently being used as a barn, in which an abandoned pulpit stands on a floor of straw. "The silence at the pulpit," Ellison writes, "is the silence we heard when you did not answer cries for help" (40). Though the Holocaust as an historical setting is at best marginal to Ellison's work, some of the major themes that emerge from it—the brutalization of persecutor and victim, the illusion of safety through assimilation, the willful indifference of bystanders, the annihilation of the past, the human capacity for stunning heroism and sacrifice—have long been the focus of Ellison's strongest passions.

9 | MYTHS OF IDENTITY II

The Persistence of the Past

THROUGHOUT ELLISON'S CAREER, from his science fiction stories to his mythological fantasies and his explorations of his own identity as a writer and a Jew, one of the most consistently recurring themes is the notion that the past is never quite put to rest, that it not only shapes and influences the present but may erupt unexpectedly at any time: as a shower of jellybeans in "'Repent, Harlequin!'" a knife fight on New York streets in "Punky & the Yale Men," a Howdy Doody button in "Adrift, Just Off the Islets of Langerhans," the ghosts of dead Nazis in "Boulevard of Broken Dreams," or even the distinctive laugh of a favored aunt that survives for decades in TV laugh tracks in "Laugh Track" (1994; collected in *Angry Candy*). But the past is a different country for Ellison, one that abounds in contradictions. Ellison's view of childhood contains not only uncritical nostalgia for favored radio programs, movies, pulp magazines, and Clark Bars, but also fearful memories such as the schoolyard bullies and anti-Semites of "Final Shtick" and "One Life, Furnished in Early Poverty," the segregated world of "The Universe of Robert Blake," and the terrifying authority figures of "Free with This Box!" (1958), in which an eight-year-old boy is caught pilfering cereal boxes in search of comic-book-character premiums and taken to the police in order to teach him a lesson (the lesson he learns is distrust of police). Such incidents, many of them autobiographical, are the common clay of many Ellison characters, but as these characters enter middle age along with their creator, they begin to form more complicated pasts, to make choices which, like the incidents of childhood, threaten to re-emerge in some undetermined future. Increasingly, Ellison characters find themselves haunted by the ghosts of childhood and by the shadows of their own moral histories. Preserving the golden age of childhood may well be the underlying myth of a handful of stories like "Jeffty Is Five," but there is a darker side to Ellison's view of the past as well: stories of redress, in which "all the birds come home to roost"; stories of revenge and poetic justice; and stories in which the past is misused by simply remaining unused, which for Ellison is a far more serious sin than even the most ill-advised action.

"Jeffty Is Five": The Appropriation of Nostalgia

Of all the stories in *Shatterday,* the one that has most nearly attained the popularity and durability of Ellison's classic 1960s science fiction stories is "Jeffty Is Five" (1977), which has emerged, in retrospect, as one of the key stories in Ellison's career. Cited as one of his own favorite stories (*Shatterday* 9), it received both the Hugo Award from the World Science Fiction Convention and the Nebula Award from the Science Fiction Writers of America, appeared in two "year's best" annuals, and has been reprinted more often than any Ellison story except "'Repent, Harlequin!'" and "I Have No Mouth, and I Must Scream." Unlike those more pyrotechnic stories, however, "Jeffty" returns to the mine of autobiographical material that had informed such earlier stories as "One Life, Furnished in Early Poverty" and "Final Shtick," transforming that material into a fantasy of innocence lost that is one of Ellison's most poignant tales and one of the most important expressions of a theme that would come increasingly to haunt his work as he approached middle age: the past as both refuge and trap. In all of Ellison's collections from *Shatterday* on, we encounter a cast of characters who misused their past or—an even more serious crime in Ellison's universe—failed to use it all. But what may be most revealing about "Jeffty Is Five" is the manner in which these autobiographical materials effectively burn through the surface of the story, as evidenced by a relatively minor chronological flaw that escapes most readers. In his foreword to the story in *Shatterday,* Ellison alludes to the offstage action of the story's ending, which he says "somehow escapes the slovenly reader" (11). But while the ending does demand a degree of subtle inference on the part of the reader, it is the role of memory in the story that unpacks its meaning in ways that may have been unexpected even by the author.

Unlike "One Life, Furnished in Early Poverty" and other stories that draw on Ellison's childhood in Painesville, Ohio, "Jeffty" is notably free of references to anti-Semitism and names of real-life childhood bullies, as well as such deliberately autobiographical clues as the name of his school or street address. It is, in effect, a celebration of what was best about Ellison's childhood, divorced from the more unpleasant realities that he had so often dwelled on in earlier stories and memoirs. The narrator is Donny, an appliance salesman in an unidentified small town. When he was five years old, Donny's best friend was a five-year-old neighbor named Jeff Kinzer, or Jeffty. Sent away to live with his aunt for two years, Donny returns at the age of seven, not yet fully aware that Jeffty remains a five-year-old. At ten, Donny is sent away again, this time to military school, and when he returns at the age of fourteen, he finds Jeffty *still* only five—not retarded or stunted or developmentally disabled, but simply frozen at the age of five. When the twenty-two-year-old Donny returns from college to find Jeffty still unchanged, he begins to realize the withering effect this strange phenomenon is having on Jeffty's aging parents, who by now have been raising a bright, active five-year-old for seventeen years. Noticing that Jeffty owns a long-obsolete Captain Midnight decoder ring bearing the current year's date, Donny learns that there is an even more fantastic aspect to Jeffty's life: His radio still broadcasts new episodes of "Captain Midnight," "Tennessee Jed," "Hop Harrigan," "Terry and the Pirates," and other long-defunct programs. When Donny goes to the movies with Jeffty, the film the two of them see differs from what everyone else is watching, and is inevitably a new production starring actors like Humphrey Bogart and Spencer Tracy. When they go to the newsstand, Donny can magically purchase new issues of long-dead pulp magazines and comic books. In fact, when he is with Jeffty, Donny can recapture virtually all the pop-culture experiences and artifacts that defined his childhood, that are still the most profound icons of his desire, much like the Howdy Doody button in "Adrift, Just Off the Islets of Langerhans." Jeffty, on the other hand, is little more than a conduit between Donny and this lost past, barely characterized at all beyond the initial image of a bright, articulate five-year-old.

Unlike "One Life, Furnished in Early Poverty" or the various stories about writers discussed in the previous chapter, Ellison has here chosen a protagonist that seems to offer few parallels to himself, as if deliberately trying to distance himself from his narrator. Donny may treasure the parts of the past he has lost, but he is also an appliance salesman whose main product—television sets—represents the very technology that supplanted those old radio programs, pulp magazines, and comics. The key crisis he faces turns on what at first seems a minor oversight: Driving Jeffty to the movies, he stops briefly at his appliance store. For apparently the first time, Jeffty enters the store and is riveted by a display of TV sets that covers an entire wall. Alarmed at Jeffty's growing panic and terror—but faced with his own adult responsibility of managing an unexpected rush of customers at the store—Donny sends him ahead to the movie, where he is beaten by older kids whose radio he has borrowed and locked on to one of his broadcasts from the past. After rescuing Jeffty, Donny returns him to his home, where his mother takes him upstairs to bathe his wounds. She returns alone, and Donny hears the sound of rock music from the upstairs bathroom. A loud crackling noise is accompanied by the dimming of the living room lamp, and Donny rushes upstairs while Jeffty's parents sit motionless. The mother, Leona, we infer, had left the electric radio tuned to a rock station, knowing that Jeffty would reach for it from his bath to seek one of his programs from the past. Donny's last action, in the story's elegantly understated ending, involves not only trying to rescue his friend Jeffty but trying to save the fragments of his own past that Jeffty has come to represent. And it is here that the narrative distancing breaks down.

Is Donny's past his own, or is it Ellison's, or is it a codification of a kind of universal nostalgia that we are meant to accept as a convention abstractly representing the wonder of childhood, evoking a mythical Norman Rockwell America that everyone willingly appropriates, even when it matches nothing in their own experience—like those contemporary TV commercials in which a thirtysomething mother remembers her own childhood in images suggestive less of the 1980s, when she would actually have been a child, than of the 1950s. Much of the appeal of "Jeffty Is Five," however—even for younger readers—arises from the specificity of its nostalgia. Far from generic, these particular programs, movies, and magazines are clearly the treasured memories of a single individual. And that individual, given the story's logic, cannot be Donny.

Teasing out the chronology of the story is an interesting exercise. We know that its main action takes place not too long after Donny and Jeffty have reached the age of twenty-two—several of Jeffty's radio premiums bear "this year's" date—yet contemporary references to Goldie Hawn movies, Taco Bells, Clint Eastwood cop movies, 7-Eleven stores, and Tanzania place this action sometime around 1970. This is further supported by Donny's own references: he states that "*Captain Midnight* went off the air in 1950" (21) and later that "The Secret Squadron hadn't been on the air in twenty years" (22). But if this is the case, then both Donny and Jeffty were born in 1948, rendering absurd Donny's statement about the decoder ring, "I remember the one I had in 1945" (21) and virtually all his memories of popular culture from the 1930s and 1940s. Another time code, hinting that the story may actually have taken place sometime before 1970, is Donny's reference to his store's first promotion for the new Sony color television sets—the event that leads to Jeffty's terror-stricken confrontation with the wall of TVs. Sony introduced color televisions to the U.S. market in 1960, a date which would permit the two main characters to remember the 1940s, but that contradicts the post–1970 allusions in the tale. Finally, there is a *third* time code, again contradictory to the first two, which has to do with Donny's memories of his own childhood: At the age of seven, he recalls listening to "One Man's Family," "Information, Please," and other programs from the 1930s; at fourteen, his Saturday matinee entertainment included such films as *I Married a Witch* and *The Cat People,* both released in 1942. If he saw these films in the year of their release, Donny was born in 1928, which would make him a little old to be owning a Captain Midnight decoder ring in 1945 and fast approaching middle age by the time of the story.

This contradictory chronology has a simple explanation, of course: The memories, the passions, the tastes in movies and books attributed to Donny are all pure Ellison. Compare the story's cavalcade of pop culture with Ellison's account of his own childhood favorites:

> The world I made for myself was bounded on all four sides by fantasy. On the North, it was old-time radio programs—*Jack Armstrong; The Shadow;* Lux Presents Hollywood; *Quiet Please;* Fred Allen; *Land of the Lost*—on the South it was pulp magazines—*G-8 and His Battle Aces; The Avenger; Doc Savage; Blue Book; Argosy; Startling Stories*—on the East by comic books—*Airboy, Plastic Man;* The Spectre; Hawkman; The Pie-Faced Prince of Pretleberg; *Capt. Marvel*—and on the West by movies—Val Lewton's terror films; Wild Bill Elliott as Red Ryder with Robert Blake as Little Beaver; Laird Cregar as *The Lodger;* William Eythe and Veda Ann Borg and June Preisser and Don "Red" Barry and Lash LaRue . . . that whole crowd. (*Hornbook* 101–2)

Similarly, the "new" movies that Donnie and Jeffty see together are the movies Ellison would like to see: Humphrey Bogart in a John Huston adaptation of a Donald E. Westlake novel, Franchot Tone and Lionel Barrymore in a film of Alfred Bester's classic science fiction novel *The Demolished Man.* The authors featured in the miraculous pulp magazines they find include several science fiction and fantasy writers who died prematurely, as if to add to the litany of loss: Henry Kuttner (died 1958), Stanley G. Weinbaum (died 1935), Robert E. Howard (died 1936). Even the magazines Donny waxes nostalgic about disappeared far too early for him to have been familiar with them as a child: *Argosy All-Story Weekly* in 1948, *Doc Savage* in 1949, *Weird Tales* in 1954. And in speculating about how all this may be possible, Donny begins to sound like a suspiciously intellectual appliance salesman, invoking Hume and Borges and talking about "weakly violated" conservation of energy laws and "muon decay of the 'forbidden' kind: gamma decay that doesn't include the muon neutrino among its products" (27). This is gobbledygook, of course, but it is Ellison's gobbledygook, not Donny's: a mild bit of hand-waving to keep a faintly rationalistic science fiction edge to a tale of pure fantasy. And when Donny muses on the disappearance of the past, his voice virtually disappears into that of the author:

> Things are better in a lot of ways. People don't die from some of the old diseases any more. Cars go faster and get you there more quickly on better roads. Shirts are softer and silkier. We have paperback books even though they cost as much as a good hardcover used to. When I'm running short in the bank I can live off credit cards till things even out. But I still think we've lost a lot of good stuff. . . . Records don't feel right; they're not thick and solid like the old ones, they're thin and you can bend them . . . that doesn't seem right to me. Restaurants don't serve cream in pitchers any more, just that artificial glop in little plastic tubs, and one is never enough to get coffee the right color. You can make a dent in a car fender with only a sneaker. Everywhere you go, all the towns look the same with Burger Kings and McDonald's and 7-Elevens and Taco Bells and motels and shopping centers. Things may be better, but why do I keep thinking about the past? (14–15)

The question is never really answered in the narrative, for the simple reason that it cannot be. It's a question that takes us outside the narrative altogether, outside the world and mind of a youthful small-town salesman. By the end of the story, with the author appropriating larger and larger elements of memory, language, and sentiment, Donny has very nearly evaporated altogether, becoming as impossible and ghostly a figure as Jeffty himself. We are left, finally, with the bereft Donny facing a future far bleaker and less colorful than his past; with Jeffty's parents, haunted by their own lost years, and now by the role they have played in the death of a son; and with the wizard behind the curtain, Ellison himself, whose own desire is the engine that powers the story from the beginning. No one is really well served by the persistence of the past, seductive though it may be.

For all the affectionate nostalgia that characterizes "Jeffty Is Five," the past more often proves to be another of Ellison's traps, threatening either to immobilize characters and prevent them from meaningful action in the present (as almost happens to Donny, when he must choose between managing the chaos at his store or going ahead to the movie with Jeffty), or, more often, returning to haunt them for past crimes of indifference or irresponsibility. In "The Cheese Stands Alone" (1981; collected in *Stalking the Nightmare*), Alexander Cort is a dentist fleeing his unrewarding life who arrives in Monterey very early one morning, where the only open shop appears to be a fog-shrouded bookstore, inexplicably packed with customers standing almost motionless, each staring at the page of the book they are holding. An old woman motions him in and explains that "they found answers here" (205), either to almost trivial questions that had long haunted them, like where the first vampire came from (if vampires are created only by bites from other vampires), to more compelling mysteries, like that of a young man who had long felt a psychic link to an unknown other, despite being an only child. Sensing a trap—"I've seen places like this in television shows" (208)—Cort prepares to storm out, when the old woman asks him, "Wouldn't you like to know when you'll have the best moment of your entire life?" (208). Cort insists on learning the old woman's name before he agrees to open the book that contains his secret. Infuriated, since he is apparently the first to ask and she is apparently compelled to answer, she reveals that her name is Clotho and that she works with her sisters. (Clotho, of course, is one of the three Fates from Greek mythology, the sister responsible for spinning out the thread of life.)

Cort grows apprehensive about learning the best moment of his life. "What if it comes only a few years from now?" he asks. "What if I've only got a little while to achieve whatever it was I always wanted to achieve? How do I live with the rest of my life after that, knowing I'll never be any better, any happier, any richer or more secure; knowing I'll never top what

I did in that moment? What'll the rest of my life be worth?" (209). This *Our Town*–style question is at the heart of the story: How does one learn to recognize what is of value when it is at hand and to cope with the ordinariness of what follows? The knowledge Cort seeks, he suspects, will not only give him the rare privilege of knowing when it arrives that the moment is his best, but will condemn him to knowing that the rest of his life is downhill—a Faustian bargain at best and just as irresistible. When Cort finally looks at the book—which turns out to be a Big Little Book of the sort he had as a child—he learns that the peak moment of his life occurred when, at the age of ten, he miraculously caught a line drive during a sandlot baseball game. "He was the killer, the master of the world, the tallest thing on the face of the earth, big and bold and golden, adept beyond any telling, miraculous; a miracle, a walking miracle. It was the best moment of his life." And, he realizes, for as long as he lives, "nothing would match that moment" (213).

With tears in his eyes, Cort looks up at Clotho, who says, "You're lucky it wasn't one of my sisters. They react much worse to being screwed with" (213). His punishment, for an unspecified crime beyond simply being dissatisfied with his life, is to be trapped and immobilized by a single moment of his childhood, to be captured by the past. Unlike Clotho's other customers, however, Cort remains defiant, slamming the book shut and preparing to leave. "It's all futile," Clotho warns him. "You'll never know grandeur again. It's all dross, waste, emptiness. There's nothing as good if you live to be a thousand" (213). But he responds, "What's left may only be the tag-end of a shitty life . . . but it's *my* shitty life. And it's the only game in town, sweetie. The cheese stands alone" (214). Unlike Donny, Cort chooses to accept a less than perfect life rather than dwell on the perfection of the past, to take action even when he knows the limitations of any possible action in regard to his own happiness.

Unattainable—or unrecoverable—perfection is also the theme of another 1981 story, "Grail," a parody-quest tale which develops the conceit that True Love, the perfect romantic attachment, is manifested physically in the world, like the Holy Grail, and is attainable through dogged research, bribes, and Indiana Jones–style adventure. Christopher Caperton has experienced a series of unrequited passions for everyone from teachers to movie actresses to schoolmates, and he has read obsessively about the nature of love. By 1968, as an officer in Vietnam building a substantial fortune in black market drugs, he has fallen in love with his business partner, a Eurasian woman, who reveals to him while dying of a shrapnel wound that True Love not only exists but has had a wildly romantic provenance—hidden in Knossos in 2000 B.C. and excavated in 1900, passing through various hands throughout Europe before disappearing in 1946. She also provides him with a convenient spell to summon a demon who will help him locate the artifact but whose assistance can be treacherous. Over the next several years, Caperton follows a trail of smugglers, con men, and auction records until he arrives at the elaborately booby-trapped Manhattan apartment of a reclusive millionaire, where he again summons the demon for assistance and finally discovers True Love— which is "an enormous loving cup. It was as gaudy as a bowling trophy. . . . Engraved on the face were the words *True Love* in flowing script, embellished with curlicues" (*Stalking* 53). Inside it is a silver liquid that reveals to Caperton the faces of all the women he has loved, resolving into "the most unforgettable face he had ever seen" (54), a face that he does not recognize. In the end of the story, Ellison recounts the famous scene from *Citizen Kane* in which the aging Bernstein (played by Everett Sloane) recalls a young woman he once glimpsed on a ferry decades earlier and has never forgotten and a quotation from Japanese poet Tanaka Katsumi, which Caperton years later records in his journal: "I know that my true friend will appear after my death, and my sweetheart died before I was born" (54). Like Cort in "The Cheese Stands Alone," Caperton understands this to mean that his "curse" and "blessing" is "To reach the finest moment of one's life, and to *know* it was the finest moment, that there would never be a more golden more perfect, nobler or loftier or thrilling moment . . . and to continue to have to live a life that was all on the downhill side" (54).

THE MORAL UNIVERSE OF EC

The past, of course, comes increasingly to be made up not of the innocent choices of childhood or the memories of lost or unattainable loves but of the deliberate and often self-serving choices of adulthood—choices for which, in Ellison's fictive universe, we can never abrogate responsibility. As Stephen King has noted, in many of Ellison's tales which approach supernatural horror, "there is more than a whiff of those *Tales from the Crypt/Vault of Horror* ghastlies where the climax so often involves the evil-doer having his crimes revisited upon himself . . . only raised to the tenth power" (*Danse Macabre* 349). By invoking the classic EC horror comics of the early 1950s—the same comics, published by William Gaines, which led to a widespread censorship campaign, congressional hearings, and the eventual creation of the Comics Code—King identifies a key aspect of Ellisonian morality which is derived in great part from those very comics: namely, the notion of unagented retribution, of supernatural revenge meted out not by gods or demons but by a simple universal principle of balancing evil with evil, or at least gruesomeness with gruesomeness. In the EC stories to which King refers, a heinous crime is committed which goes unpunished or undetected in the natural world. King describes an example:

> The hero's wife and her boyfriend determine to do away with the hero so they can run away together and get married. . . . These two heels, who might have stepped whole and breathing from a James M. Cain novel, take the poor slop of a husband for a ride and the boyfriend puts a bullet between his eyes. They wire a cement block to the corpse's leg and toss him over a bridge into the river.
>
> Two or three weeks later, our hero, a living corpse, emerges from the river, rotted and eaten by the fish. He shambles after wifey and her friend. . . . One piece of dialogue from this story which I've never forgotten is "I am coming, Marie, but I have to come slowly . . . because little pieces of me keep falling off." (*Danse Macabre* 35)

It is characteristic of such tales that the reanimation is the work of no particular supernatural agency. "Divine retribution" is far too theological a concept for such resolutely secular tales, and the reader's own desire for poetic justice seems to be a sufficient cause to bring out the dead. Unagented retribution of one sort or another has long been a feature of Gothic novels and thrillers, but the EC comics virtually raised it to an aesthetic principle. One of Ellison's most direct and deliberate evocations of the EC moral universe is the 1994 story "Sensible City," in which a corrupt police lieutenant named W. R. Gropp and his thuggish accomplice, Mickey, are finally brought to trial for various heinous murders and dismemberments. They skip bail and promptly get lost in the getaway car. They approach a strange-looking town named Obedience, but Gropp, remembering the horror-story cliché of characters entering places that the audience clearly recognizes as "death places," orders Mickey to drive on. Not long after, however, the car begins to run out of gas, just as they are coasting into that very same town, somehow still ahead of them.

> In the rearview mirror Gropp saw the green fog rolling up thicker onto the roadway; and emerging over the berm, in a jostling slavering horde, clacking and drooling, dropping decayed body parts and leaving glistening trails of worm ooze as they dragged their deformed pulpy bodies across the blacktop, their snake-slit eyes gleaming green and yellow in the mist, the residents of Obedience clawed and slithered and crimped toward the car. (*Slippage* 208)

The scene couldn't have been more gruesomely colorful had it been the work of an acknowledged EC master like Graham Ingles, and its morality is just as arbitrary. The classic EC horror comics were disappearing just as Ellison was beginning his career—only one story of his, "Mealtime," was adapted in EC's *Weird Science Fantasy* in 1954—but their strangely grotesque vision of a universe in moral balance persists in his work, although usually in a far more restrained manner than that of "Sensible City," a story which is as much about our understanding of horror stories as a horror story itself.

As King points out, even when Ellison stories take place in a version of the EC moral universe, "the irony cuts with a keener blade in Ellison's work, and we have less feeling that rough justice has been meted out and the balance restored. In Ellison's stories, we have little sense of winners and losers. Sometimes there are survivors. Sometimes there are no survivors" (*Danse Macabre* 349). And sometimes the very question of what constitutes a survivor is ambiguous. In "Cold Friend" (1973; collected in *Approaching Oblivion*), the narrator, Eugene Harrison, begins by telling us that he "had died of cancer of the lymph glands" (37), but then he awakes in a deserted hospital and soon discovers that the entire universe has disappeared except for the few square blocks of Hanover, New Hampshire, where he lives, alone except for the occasional marauding Viking, Samurai warrior, German fighter plane, or various other threats—all of which he somehow dispatches with ease. Finally he meets a beautiful woman who introduces herself as Opal Sellers (her ice-cold skin gives the story its title). She eventually reveals that she is the cause of everything, having single-handedly wiped out the universe in order to be with him. She turns out to be a member of his high school graduating class whom he saved from embarrassment by lending her his mortarboard at the commencement ceremony and who has loved him ever since. As she reveals this, her illusory appearance drops away—in good EC fashion—revealing the real Opal Sellers, "one of the ugliest girls I'd ever seen" (49). Appropriately, this was one of the stories selected for adaptation in Ellison's own comic book, *Harlan Ellison's Dream Corridor*, in June 1995. The incident from his past that haunts Eugene Harrison is not a violent crime but a simple act of kindness which at worst was compounded into a crime of insensitivity as he remained unaware of Opal's love. But, as he notes in the end, "girls always got tired of me very quickly" (49), and Opal herself stalks off in anger, disappearing into the "glop" that surrounds his tiny world and leaving him absolutely alone—but having transferred her strange omnipotence to him. What is the source and the nature of the power that she so strangely obtains and unwillingly passes along to Eugene? In the irrationalist world of the EC tradition, not a clue is given, but we are again left with the suggestion that the universe is governed not so much by justice or morality as by simple balance, a morally charged version of the principle of complementarity, or of science fiction's cold equations.

"CROATOAN"

In one of Ellison's most controversial stories, and one that most clearly follows the EC horror-story formula, this notion of balance is linked, in characteristic Ellison fashion, with the theme of personal responsibility. The result is a story, powered in part by the same urban myths of alligators in the sewers that have informed such novels as Thomas Pynchon's *V.* (1961) and such movies as Lewis Teague's *Alligator* (1980), and which according to King accomplishes "the mind-numbing feat of simultaneously pissing off the right-to-lifers and the women's liberationists" (*Stalking* 11). The narrator, Gabe, is a cynical, manipulative lawyer who over a span of some eleven years has thoughtlessly impregnated a long series of girlfriends, including two who now run an abortion clinic and are regularly summoned to perform on-site procedures which result in the unwanted fetuses being flushed down the toilet. This time, however, the sound of the toilet flushing brings the mother, Carol, screaming into the bathroom, pleading for Gabe to "go find him." "I had never heard anyone sound that way, ever. Not ever. It frightened me. Riptides beneath the surface of her words created trembling images of shadow women drinking Drano, lying with their heads inside gas ovens, floating face up in thick, red bath water, their hair rippling out like jellyfish" (20). Gabe goes into the street, thinking to mark time pretending to search, but sees that she is watching him. Using a steel rod she has provided, he pries off a manhole cover and, somewhat to his own surprise, descends into the sewers. What he finds is a literal underworld, fetid, dank, and illuminated by a faint green fluorescence that reminds him of the fluoroscopes once used in children's shoe stores. "*My God,* I thought, *I must be out of my mind just to* be *here*. It had finally over-taken me; the years of casual liaison, careless lies, the guilt I suppose I'd *always* known would mount up till it could no longer be denied. And I was down here, where I belonged" (22).

The world of the sewers, with its odd smell "reminiscent of Florida mangrove swamps" (24) already seems to Gabe to be an outward projec-tion of his moral failings, but he hasn't yet even begun his underworld journey, which carries with it echoes of a long fantasy tradition of the underground as region of the outcasts, of the unwanted, of what Ellison called in a much earlier tale "the discarded." He passes a group of home-less men gathered around a small fire in an oil drum and feels vaguely threatened when one of the younger men appears to get up and follow him, but for the most part he is comfortable beneath the street, remember-ing an earlier spelunking expedition during which, instead of claustropho-bia, "I was—in some perverse way—wonderfully free" (23). The young bindlestiff finally confronts Gabe, asking him to leave: "You make it bad down here, mister" (28). Gabe refuses, but before he turns away, he tells the young man to take his hands out of his pockets, to show he has no weapons. "He had no hands. Chewed stumps, glowing faintly green like the walls where I had descended from the manhole" (28). This horror-movie scene has no apparent impact on Gabe at all, however, and he sim-ply turns and walks away, deeper into the tunnels. "Sometimes I cried, but I don't know why, or for what, or for whom. Certainly not for myself" (29). Yet he feels a growing willingness to accept a life underground "if I could not return" (28). He next encounters an alligator that has invaded a rat's nest and is "ripping the throats of baby rats" (29)—surely one of Ellison's more unlikely and unvisualizable images, gruesome though it may sound. He realizes what has happened to the young bindlestiff's hands, but instead of turning away in terror, he chooses to follow the beast, which has a leash around its neck. A brief interpolated memory, involving the five-year-old daughter of one of Gabe's many girlfriends, recapitulates the familiar folktale of how the alligators allegedly got into the sewers and bred.

Finally, Gabe follows the alligator to a fetid pool, which he willingly swims across to find an ancient iron door engraved with the letters CROATOAN, a word which he does not recognize but later remembers as the single clue left behind, carved into a tree, by Sir Walter Raleigh's lost Virginia colony of Roanoke. Surrounded by the sounds of approaching alligators, he panics, attempts to run, and falls. He is found by a child with fetal characteristics:

> Naked, deathly white, with eyes great and luminous, but covered with a transparent film as milky as a membrane, small, very young, hairless, its arms shorter than they should have been, purple and crimson veins crossing its bald skull like traceries of blood on a parchment, fine even features, nostrils dilating as it breathed shallowly, ears slightly tipped as though reminiscent of an elf, barefooted but with pads on the soles, this child stared at me, looked up at me, its little tongue visible as it opened its mouth filled with tiny teeth, trying to form sounds, saying nothing, watching me, a wonder in its world, watching me with the saucer eyes of a lemur, the light behind the membrane flickering and pulsing. This child. (32)

The child is only one of a huge and ancient community of children who, like the alligators which they have tamed (hence the leash), arrived in the underworld as the discarded—and among them, presumably, are all the unborn babies Gabe himself has been responsible for over the years. "I am the only adult here," he concludes. "They have been waiting for me. They call me father" (34).

"Croatoan" is not only one of Ellison's most powerful expressions of the retributive past. It is also one of his most haunting visionary tales, making virtually no attempt to rationalize its dream logic and drawing indiscriminately on popular folklore, archetypal mythic journeys, urban paranoia, and contemporary public and political debate. But it is the latter aspect of the story which in its original magazine publication, according to Ellison, "brought howls of outrage from male sexists, feminists, right-to-life advocates, pro-abortion supporters, and even a snotty note from someone in the

New York City department of drains and sewers" (*Strange Wine* 17–18). While it seems unlikely that the *Magazine of Fantasy and Science Fiction* has ever had quite such a colorful readership, it's easy to see how the story might be read as an anti-abortion tract built around the conceit that virtually all fetuses are viable people who, if only given a chance, would learn to train alligators. "The sin is not so easily gotten rid of," Stephen King writes in his discussion of this story in *Danse Macabre*. "[The fetuses] are the embodiment of such Old Testament maxims as 'Sin never dies' and 'Be sure your sin will find you out'" (350). King also notes the EC-comic moral structure of the tale, with the protagonist doomed to live out his life in a world created largely by the products of his own irresponsible past actions, but adds:

> Most of all, we sense outrage and anger—as with the best Ellison stories, we sense personal involvement, and have a feeling that Ellison is not so much telling the tale as jabbing it viciously out of its hiding place. It is the feeling that we are walking over a lot of jagged glass in thin shoes, or running across a minefield in the company of a lunatic. Accompanying these feelings is the feeling that Ellison is preaching to us . . . not in any lackluster, ho-hum way, but in a large, bellowing voice that may make us think of Jonathan Edwards's "Sinners in the Hands of an Angry God." (350–51)

There is indeed a sense that Ellison is preaching loudly at us, but exactly what is he preaching? Midway through the story, when Gabe is remembering his relationship with Carol, he comments, "Why didn't I take precautions? Again, there's no logic to it. I thought she was; and for a while, she was. Then she stopped. She told me she had stopped, something internal, the gynecologist had suggested she go off the pill for a while. She suggested vasectomy to me. I chose to ignore the suggestion. But chose not to stop sleeping with her" (26).

The key issue, as it almost always is for Ellison, is not public policy but personal choice. Gabe has chosen to ignore the suggestion of a vasectomy, chosen to continue sleeping with Carol, chosen to abrogate all responsibility for precautions, and apparently has consistently made these choices with a series of girlfriends for more than a decade. His abortionist friends regard him as a "public menace" and "a thoughtless cocksucker" (27), but still, after all those years, they continue to bail him out. And Carol chooses to continue her relationship with someone she knows to be irresponsible. The fetuslike underground children are no more than manifestations of all these collective choices, of the irresponsibility of adults, just as the alligators they ride are folk manifestations of the impulsiveness and irresponsibility of children. Gabe's fate may be poetic justice, but it is not at all clear that it is a punishment: His final words express not horror but wonder, and his arrival in the underground world may well be as much redemption as payment for past sins.

"All the Birds Come Home to Roost"

Michael Kirxby, the lawyer protagonist of "All the Birds Come Home to Roost" (1978; collected in *Shatterday*), has a similarly exploitative history of womanizing, only in his case it's not the fetuses of the children he has fathered but the women themselves who begin reappearing in his life, in reverse order from his most recent relationships. Again, there is no particular crime Kirxby has committed—only a long accumulation of unsuccessful relationships and practiced seductions—and again there is no identifiable agency to bring about his fate. After describing to his latest conquest, Martha, bits and pieces of his history—particularly his disastrous first marriage to Cindy, who has been institutionalized for more than seventeen years—Kirxby finds himself revealing details of the marriage that are not usually part of his bedroom script, including an incident when he beat her because she mumbled while he was trying to study. We learn that Martha, too, has broken up with Kirxby and that she only ran into him by accident earlier in the evening. Soon Jerri, the woman he had left for Martha, shows up in his office with no other explanation than "I felt an urgent need to see you again" (271). Within days, the woman he dated before Jerri appears, and within a month "in reverse order of having known them, every female with whom he had had a liaison magically reappeared in his life" (272). The key word, of course, is "magically," since neither the narrator or Kirxby pauses for a moment to consider any possible reason for what seems less and less like a string of coincidences. A pattern is being established which, Kirxby realizes, will inevitably return him to the scene of his crime—his first wife, Cindy, who he says "very nearly took me with her to the madhouse" (270). He flees to Vermont and then to the Bahamas, but continues to meet the women from his past even in such unlikely locations. He tries hiding out in his apartment, but the next in line shows up at the exact moment that he opens the door for a pizza delivery. Kirxby realizes that the next to appear will be Marcie, and finally Cindy, the insane first wife. He flees into the street in a panic, only to collide with Marcie as the story ends.

Kirxby's abject terror of Cindy is the element of horror on which the story hangs, and while she is nothing as spectacular as a rotting corpse returning from the grave in an EC comic or an aborted fetus riding a sewer alligator, she becomes the symbol of the moral balance that must be restored in Kirxby's world. More important, she is a figure not of super-natural terror but of a failed marriage, and what we know about her is dis-torted through the self-aggrandizing viewpoint of Kirxby, who has come to use her and her madness as a means of gaining maternal sympathy from his later conquests, "the sort of thing they loved to hear" (266). Kirxby's attitude toward mental illness proves to be no more enlightened than his attitude toward women, and is in fact consistent with the unfortunate stereotyping of madness that characterized the horror comics and folktales in which madmen or madwomen are invariably predatory and vengeful, if not uncontrollably violent. But the actual details of the relationship are ambiguous at best. We are told, for example, that Cindy's father was abu-sive toward her mother, that Cindy herself "secretly wanted to ball the old man," and that "she flipped and went off the deep end" upon learning that he was dying from a brain tumor (266). Kirxby's response to this family trauma is simply to abandon Cindy—"I got out just in time"—who is then committed to an asylum by her mother. Her other "crimes" include suicide attempts, belittling remarks, one tryst with a lover, and "the time she took off and sold the furniture and cleaned out the savings account" (267). The key incident, however, is the mumbling, "making remarks you just *knew* were crummy, but she'd do it under her breath, just at the threshold of audibility" (267). This is what finally led to him punching her in the face and beating her with a bedroom slipper. In relating the incident to Martha, Kirxby claims, "It was the first time I'd ever hit a woman" and that when he realized what he was doing he crawled across the room and sat "like a scared animal, my hand over my eyes . . . crying . . . scared to death" (268). Adroitly, in his own narration, Kirxby takes an incident in which he viciously beats a woman whom he believes to be mentally ill and manages to portray himself as the cowering, weeping victim. Given the portrayal of this key incident, it's a bit difficult not to suspect that narrator reliability is an issue in the story as a whole.

And yet there is still the shadow of Ellison, whom one has to believe is neither as narcissistic nor as violent as Kirxby; in fact, he makes a particular point of stating in his introduction, "I am not the Michael Kirxby of this story" (*Shatterday* 262). But he also mentions the emotional disorders of his own first wife, Charlotte, and describes how *Playboy* editor Victoria Haider, by simply asking him what was so awful about the marriage, forced Ellison to confront the "horrible memories" that presumably, in the story, are transmuted into the incident of the mumbling. Apparently these memories provide the template for a kind of primal crime in what is essentially and structurally a horror story, but by placing similar memories into the mealy mouth of Michael Kirxby, he diminishes the authority of their authenticity. Ellison may very well have felt himself victimized by a mentally disturbed wife, but Kirxby is easily as much victimizer as victim, and the story is structured in the classic horror-tale mode of W. W. Jacobs's "Monkey's Paw," in which the gruesome conclusion is left to the reader's inference. Dramatic as this ending may be, one can't help but suspect there may be a second reason for it—simply that what might happen between Cindy and Kirxby could unravel his entire questionable narrative. With "All the Birds Come Home to Roost," Ellison is still knocking about in the vengeful moral universe of EC, but by now his topic and his characters have grown a little too complex for such easy denouements.

REVENGE

Almost inevitably, Ellison's fiction in this mode would address the topic of revenge, which is one of only a handful of narratively useful human motivations in the moral world of EC, along with greed, lust, and pathological devotion. Revenge has in fact become a significant part of the Ellison myth, thanks in part to various exploits reported in fannish folklore and on occasion by Ellison himself, as in the 1983 essay "Driving in the Spikes: An Essay on Anger and Revenge by a Master of the Form" (reprinted in *The Essential Ellison*), which recounts a number of episodes ranging from Ellison's childhood loss of his dog to his contretemps with publishers and even offers, advice-column style (the piece was originally published in *Los Angeles* magazine), ten rules for "the effective implementation of your anger and barbaric need for vengeance" (1006). Revenge has also been a common motif in Ellison's fiction since the very earliest stories. "Rat Hater" (1956), for example, describes a former mobster tied to a chair and left to be eaten by rats for having killed the narrator's sister eighteen years earlier. Even "I Have No Mouth, and I Must Scream" is driven mainly by the vengefulness of the computer I AM. "I don't believe there is such a thing as 'divine retribution,'" Ellison has written. "The universe is neither malign nor benign. It's *just there,* and it's too busy keeping itself together to balance the scales when some feep has jerked you around. I am a strong adherent of the philosophy that one must seek retribution oneself" (*Shatterday* 95). But in the most significant revenge tales in *Shatterday,* the protagonists are again caught up in forces not quite in their control, as though retribution were something approaching a universal principle or an aspect of the brutal system of checks and balances that seems to be at the heart of the EC moral universe. Once again, the question of agency is left ambiguous: The offenders are dramatically punished for their crimes, but the putative revengers are not quite fully responsible for the nature and extent of the punishment.

In "In the Fourth Year of the War" (1979), for example, the narrator claims that his mind is inhabited by a "despicable personage" named Jerry Olander, who compels him to commit a series of murders as revenge for offenses dating back to his childhood—all of which turn out to be thinly disguised versions of episodes from Ellison's own past, much as the memories in "Jeffty Is Five" turn out to be Ellison's memories. The first victim is the narrator's Uncle Carl, now in his late sixties, whom the narrator holds at least partially responsible for his father's death. His father, he tells us, "had managed Carl's jewelry store during the war, when Carl had gone off to the Navy" (233), on the understanding that when Carl returned, he would make him a partner. The father postponed his dreams of opening his own store, working "twelve, fifteen, eighteen hours a day building up the clientele" for the jewelry shop, but "when the war was over, and Carl came home, and my father finally summoned up the courage to call in the promise, Carl had him thrown out of the store." The narrator continues:

> I never knew why, really. I was a child. Children are never told the whys of family disasters. They just happen. You wouldn't understand, children are told; and then, in the next breath, they are told, You mustn't hate your Uncle Carl for this, he has his reasons.
>
> But my father had to start all over again. At the age of fifty. He rented a small apartment on the second floor in a business district close to the Loop, and he opened a jewelry shop. It was two long flights up, one steep

set of stairs, a landing, and a switchback flight half as long but just as steep. . . .

One year. He lasted one year, almost to the week of opening the new store. And on a Sunday morning, sitting in his big chair by the old Philco radio, he had a sudden smash of a coronary thrombosis and he died. (233-34)

In his 1972 essay "My Father" (collected in *The Essential Ellison*), Ellison describes the actual incident as follows:

After that, my Dad went to work for my uncles in Painesville, in their jewelry store. I was a little kid at the time, and knew none of what had gone down.

Years went by, and my Dad thought he owned a piece of the store—Hughes Jewelry on the corner of State & Main in Painesville. I was too busy fighting for my life to pay much attention, and I was always running away, but then in 1947, after my Uncle Morrie had come back from the War, it turned out my father *didn't* own anything. He had been the manager of the store, had built up the clientele and won friends all through town—he was the only Jew ever taken into the Moose Lodge in Painesville, a town famed for its anti-Semitism—but when the crunch came down, my old man was out on his ass. . . . So at close to the age of fifty, my father had to open his own store.

He couldn't get ground floor space on Main Street, so he took an upstairs suite, and sold from there. . . . It was a grueling existence. The fucking climb up those stairs alone was murder. That staircase went almost straight up, and he had to make that climb twenty times a day.

Well, it killed him a year later. (495–96)

Except for transplanting the jewelry store from Painesville to Chicago, Ellison has left the original incident virtually unchanged, suggesting that "Jerry Olander" is not only a psycho alternate personality for the tale's narrator, but a fantasy revenge figure for Ellison himself. He is a means of transplanting injustices from the real world into the comic-book moral universe so that they may be redressed by the same forces of balance that come to haunt his less sympathetic characters.

After suffocating his uncle with a pillow, Ellison's narrator, again under the control of Jerry Olander, proceeds to seek out another figure from his childhood, a "woman I wasn't even certain was still alive. She had had my dog gassed, *put to sleep* as they tell it to children, one summer when I was away at camp. Her name was Mrs. Corley, and she had lived down at the end of our street in Evanston" (236). Ellison makes clear the autobiographical referent in his introduction to the story in *Shatterday,* but he describes the incident in greater detail in his essay "Driving in the Spikes." Upon returning from a miserable experience at summer camp, the young Ellison is distraught to learn that his beloved dog is dead.

> He learns that the old woman who lives up the street, who has lived here all the years the little boy and his dog and his family have lived on that street, found the pup in her yard and called the dog catcher, and before the father knew about it, the dog had been gassed. The little boy is told the animal was "put to sleep," but he knows his friend was gassed, was killed. (1004)

Remarkably, in the story, Mrs. Corley turns out to be still alive, still at the same address, and the narrator kills her by tying her up in front of her gas stove and turning on the jets. Five additional murders are committed, and finally Jerry commands the narrator to seek out his ex-wife Nancy, from whom he had parted on friendly terms—but who left scars that Jerry insists must be revenged. Throughout, the narrator insists that "Jerry Olander never came from within me. He was from outside, a rejected thing. And he inhabited me without my consent" (238). But Jerry is more than a psychological symptom or a hysterical construct occupying the narrator in the manner of Norman Bates, and to read the story as a simple tale of madness is to diminish its complexity and ignore its significant autobiographical content. Olander is, in effect, an agent of unrealized revenge, a fantasy figure from another moral universe intruding on the narrator's world and mind, turning the real world into a gruesome but somehow satisfying horror comic.

This dynamic is extended even further in "The Man Who Was Heavily into Revenge" (1978), in which the mysterious forces at work are identified as an "emotional gestalt," a buildup of universal rage "surging down the line seeking a focus" until it finds, almost at random, a point of discharge (98–99). This time, the culprit is not a figure from the distant past but an unethical contractor named William Weisel, whose shoddy work, substandard materials, and inflated prices have left his client, Fred Tolliver, with a disastrously leaky and unusable guest bathroom. Despite repeated requests, Weisel arrogantly refuses to implement repairs, and because "building inspectors had been greased and the job had been signed off" (97–98), he cannot be sued. Tolliver swears to get even, but he is clearly powerless to do so—until strange things begin to happen to Weisel. A service station attendant refuses to sell him gas because "Fred Tolliver doesn't want me to" (99); his Rolls runs out of gas in heavy traffic, he rips his cashmere jacket getting out to push it, and suffers a hernia trying to wrestle it to the curb; traffic zooms by ignoring his pleas for help and almost killing him (he hears one woman shout, "Tolliver!"); he can't catch an elevator after he walks to his office and slips and falls on the stairs; he finds a note from his wife telling him she has left him and cleaned out the bank account; he begins to develop a migraine for the first time in his life. "He had been given more than sufficient evidence that something malevolent and purely anti-Weisel was floating across the land" (102) and that Tolliver is somehow responsible. Disaster follows upon disaster, until Weisel is reduced to a homeless, alcoholic wreck, unable even to reach Tolliver to apologize and promise the needed repairs. Finally, arrested and thrown in the drunk tank, he hangs himself.

Tolliver, meanwhile, is unaware of his epic-scale revenge. He is increasingly depressed and consumed by the thought of having been cheated. He begins to neglect his own business of violin repair and fails to complete work on an expensive instrument, forcing a musician to miss a recital and subsequently to swear revenge in terms that are almost an exact echo of Tolliver's own. "The emotions sang, the electrons danced, the focus shifted, and the symphony of frustration went on" (110). Tolliver, it seems, may become the next focus of an endless chain of retribution, even though his intentions aren't nearly as venal, his crimes not nearly as long-standing, as Weisel's. As in the classic Western gunslinger tale, as in Ellison's own tale of revenge on the freeways, "Along the Scenic Route," the ostensible victor not only fails to enjoy the fruits of his victory but immediately becomes the next target. "The Man Who Was Heavily into Revenge" may lack the colorful tastelessness of the old horror comics, but its vision of vengeance as a kind of energy built from the collective will, and of hapless individuals who unknowingly becomes solenoids for that energy, is fully in keeping with the cosmology of getting even that characterized them.

"Shadows of Lives Unlived"

If the personal past seems at times to be Ellison's version of a Dantesque inferno, with Jeffty's parents trapped in his endless childhood, Michael Kirxby of "All the Birds Come Home to Roost" fated to live his love life in reverse, and Weisel and Tolliver caught up in a cosmic cycle of revenge, Ellison has reserved a special circle of this hell for those individuals whose only real sin is inaction or invisibility, of failing to live their lives meaningfully, if at all. In "Jane Doe #112" (1990; collected in *Slippage*), he refers to such characters as "shadows of lives unlived" (112). Such figures are not necessarily slothful or mean-spirited, and often they are no more than victims of "the forces that crush"—middle-class conformity, corporate values, urban indifference, family pressures. While anonymity itself is not a sin in Ellison's universe—some of his favorite wish-fulfillment figures are "secret masters" who disguise their godlike powers by living unnoticed— the passivity of those who allow themselves to be made anonymous is something he repeatedly condemns. These are characters who, to use one of Ellison's favorite but least attractive words, permit their individualism to be "leached" out of them by the external world, and who compromise rather than fight back—like the defeated customers standing motionless in the bookstore of the Fates in "The Cheese Stands Alone."

One of the earliest examples of such a figure is Albert Winsocki of "Are You Listening?" (1956; discussed in chapter 2), whose life grows so anonymous and undistinguished that he literally disappears from the world. "Shatterday" (1975) might almost be viewed as a late companion piece to that early story, only in this case the uninvolved protagonist, rather than simply fading away, is challenged to defend his existence by a doppelgänger figure who first appears when Peter Novins, trying to find out why his date is late at the restaurant, absentmindedly dials his own phone number instead of hers. Another Peter Novins answers the phone, and the two enter into increasingly hostile banter, which in further conversations over the next week becomes a struggle for survival to determine which of them will continue to be Peter Novins. Although the tastes, interests, and memories of the two are identical, the original Peter Novins, a public relations agent, appears to have been conflicted or ambivalent about a number of key issues in his life, and to have literally split in two along the lines of these issues. The version of Peter who calls himself Jay (an unused middle name of the original—as in Harlan Jay Ellison) is furious at the original's treatment of his ailing mother in Florida, for example. A month earlier, Novins had stayed at his mother's apartment during a business trip, but he grew so frustrated that he pretended to cut the trip short and checked into a hotel instead. When his mother discovered the ruse, she called Novins's apartment. Jay—the aspect of Novins who feels a strong sense of filial responsibility—answered the phone and wound up inviting her to live with him in New York. Peter, learning of this, is outraged: "How the hell am I going to take care of that old woman in New York? I've got work to do, places I have to go, I have a life to lead." But Jay responds, "You just lost your mother. Chew on *that* one, you creep" (327). In the battle for continued existence, Jay has cornered a significant symbol of authenticity.

The next day, Jay cancels a profitable account with a huge corporation whose environmental depredations were disguised by the public relations campaign Novins, with some misgivings, had designed. Peter, isolated in a hotel room because Jay has changed the locks on the apartment, grows increasingly achy and nauseous, which he takes as signs that he is losing the battle. Jay continues his program of reparations, contacting women Novins had mistreated and pursuing a genuine commitment with one of them. In the end, he visits Peter in the hotel room in what turns out to be their first and last face-to-face encounter. "I don't know what the trigger was that broke us apart," Jay says, "but it happened and I can't be too sorry about it. If it hadn't happened I'd have been you till I died. It would have been a lousy life and a miserable death" (331). When he departs, Peter begins literally to fade away—"The last remaining daylight shone through him" (332)—and the bill for his hotel room is later paid by "Peter Jay Novins," a version of the name meant to suggest not the victory of one aspect of Novins over the other but rather a reintegration and reordering of his original personality, and in particular a reassertion of his defining values, which had been repeatedly compromised by the earlier Novins.

Despite his various compromises and inadequacies, Novins is not such a repeat offender—like Gabe in "Croatoan" or Kirxby in "All the Birds Come Home to Roost"—that moral balance must be restored by external agencies; it is in fact Novins himself (or his other self) who chooses to make up for lost time with his mother, to finally stand on principle in his professional life, to repair relationships with women. The Novins who grows transparent and fades away at the end is only one of a succession of such figures in Ellison, neither particularly bad nor good, whose anonymity is often imaged as literal transparency or translucency. In "Jane Doe #112," Ben Laborde finds himself haunted by a group of such ghostlike figures (even though the narrator tells us they are not ghosts), as well as by memories that he knows he is too young to have (shades of "Jeffty Is Five").

He flees New Orleans for Chicago and eventually his boyhood home of Hudson, Iowa, where he finally receives an explanation from two of his ghosts, a pale middle-aged woman and a very old man. Laborde, it seems, has for centuries been "using" the lives of other, less passionate individuals. Invoking such "people who live life more fully than others" such as Hemingway, Fitzgerald, Churchill, and Amelia Earhart, the woman explains: "You were one of the passionate ones. You lived at a hotter level. And every now and then, every once in a while, you just leached off someone's life who wasn't up to the living of it. You're a magpie. You came by, whenever it was, 1492, 1756, 1889, 1943 . . . we don't know how far back you go . . . but you passed by, and someone was wearing a life so loosely, so unused, that it just came off; and you wore it away, and added it on, and you just kept going, which way it didn't matter, without looking back, not even knowing" (239–40).

But Laborde is hardly a heroic figure, and he is not even really who the story is about. "We don't blame you," the woman continues. "It was our own damned fault. We just weren't up to the doing of it, the living of our own lives" (240), and now she and her companion are reduced to shadows, waiting to pass on. When they finally do, Laborde returns to New Orleans, "by way of cheap restitution," to pay back a small portion of what he has borrowed by exhuming the anonymously buried body of a young woman, yet another failed life, and reburying her in her home in West Texas.

In "Count the Clock That Tells the Time" (1978; collected in *Shatterday*), Ellison introduces another such figure, Ian Ross, who "had come to realize he had not, in any remotely valuable manner, *lived* his life. He had wasted it" (211). Ross travels to Scotland in an effort to live out at least one of his fading dreams, but once there he realizes he is completely "out of phase with all around him . . . an alien object. A beer can thrown into the grass" (212). But then the landscape begins to shift around him. The sun disappears, and shadows of myriad things and events appear around him: cities, mountains, great sea creatures, what appears to be the Children's Crusade, epic battles, natural disasters, a superfast futuristic freeway, an amusement park. He finds himself able to remember every detail of his life since childhood, and he comes to focus on a single painful episode when none of the invited guests showed up for his eleventh birthday party, a moment when Ross became convinced of his own invisibility and uselessness, establishing the pattern he would later follow. In the strange netherworld he now inhabits, he comes across a succession of figures who offer him clues to what has happened. A crippled old woman explains that the swirl of phantom events may be "bits and pieces of the past, going through on its way somewhere" (217). A crazed alchemist tells him:

> "[W]e are victims of the law of conservation of time. Precisely and exactly linked to the law of the conservation of matter; matter, which can neither be created nor destroyed. Time exists without end. But there is an ineluctable entropic balance, absolutely necessary to maintain order in the universe. Keeps events discrete, you see. As matter approaches universal distribution, there is a counterbalancing, how shall I put it, a counterbalancing `leaching out' of time. Unused time is not wasted in places where nothing happens. *It goes somewhere.* It goes here, to be precise. In measurable units (which I've decided after considerable thought, to call 'chronons')." (219)

This pseudoscientific doubletalk masks what turns out to be one of the clues to understanding what Ellison is really attempting in this story: dramatizing, without resorting to the moral value system of EC horror comics, the idea of "balance" as a kind of universal principle ordering the relationship of the individual with the universe. The notion of "unused time," of course, is a notion fraught with moral implications, but the story as a whole refrains from the summary judgments entered against characters in tales like "Croatoan" or "Sensible City." The alchemist's explanation of how Ross ended up in this world has a kind of Alice-in-Wonderland logic to it: "'You wasted your life,'" he says. "Wasted time. All around you, throughout your life, unused chronons were being leached out, drawn away from the contiguous universe, until their pull on you was irresistible" (220). With nothing solid to anchor him in his own reality, Ross is doomed to an eternity in this metaphysical limbo of unused time. He meets a woman named Catherine Molnar, who has similarly wasted her life, and they fall in love—though each remains aware that the other seems nearly transparent ("she could see mist through the flesh of his hands"), that their existence is fragile at best. As they begin to enjoy their time together, to truly live for the first time, they are unable to continue their existence in limbo, and they begin to disappear, growing fully transparent and dissolving into "invisible motes" that are "sent where needed to maintain balance" (226). Their late-blooming love may offer them a kind of moral redemption in the end, but it comes too late to save them from their own wasted lives.

THE THANATOS MOUTH

As is probably evident by now, Ellison's view of the past is inseparable from the theme of loss, and the theme of loss in Ellison's fiction is almost inseparable from the changing preoccupations of the author—the loss of childhood and of the surviving aspects of the world of childhood, like radio program and Clark Bars; the loss of identity through failure to act or to live; the loss of missed opportunities and failed rebellions. By the 1980s and 1990s, his stories began more overtly to reflect such personal anxieties as his apparent failure to find lasting romantic attachments, the loss of his parents, and the increasingly frequent deaths of his friends and colleagues. The romanticized past of "Jeffty Is Five" or "The Cheese Stands Alone," the lost opportunities of "Grail" or "All the Birds Come Home to Roost," began to give way to more personal tales of suffering and loss, and this eventually became the major organizing theme of Ellison's 1989 collection, *Angry Candy*. Death became such an obsessive preoccupation at the time of this collection that the introduction, titled "The Wind Took Your Answer Away," turns into an almost morbidly sentimental litany of friends' deaths that occurred between 1985 and 1987, with names arrayed down the margins of the page like tombstones. "And so I went a little more than a little bit mad about all the deaths," Ellison wrote. "And the stories started reflecting it. 'Paladin of the Lost Hour' and 'Eidolons' and 'The Avenger of Death' and 'Laugh Track' and I saw the thread, and one day actually had the strange dream that opens 'The Function of Dream Sleep' and I knew that I had to write that story to make some sense of all this misery and loneliness and aching" (*Angry Candy* xxvi).

More than almost any other Ellison story, "The Function of Dream Sleep" (1988) reads like a work of personal exorcism. The protagonist, McGrath, grieving over the recent death of friends, awakes suddenly one night to find "a huge mouth filled with small, sharp teeth closing in his side" (*Angry Candy* 301). It then disappears, leaving the sensation that something has escaped from his body. His ex-wife gets him a referral to a dream therapy group, the REM Group, led by a woman named Anna

Picket, who detains him after the session and, by merely touching his head, is nearly sent into spasms by the force of his grief. She invites him to the *real* REM group, a group which meets in a remote house and whose members seem all maimed or disabled. Upon McGrath's arrival, they urge him to fall asleep, but upon awakening he realizes that something during his sleep has wreaked havoc on the group, killing some members and further injuring others. Anna Picket explains the true nature of the group: "We absorb," she says. "We take illness. We've always been with you. As far back as we can know. We have always had that capacity, to assume the illness. There aren't many of us, but we're everywhere" (317). But the intensity of McGrath's loss was far more powerful than the group expected, and when the mouth opened in his side, similar mouths opened in each of them, creating vast destructive energy. Pickett mentions that the only one who might be able to help McGrath is a reclusive, feared physician named Le Braz. Arriving at Le Braz's estate, McGrath is greeted at the door by a horribly burned figure, who ushers him into the library to meet Le Braz, who explains, "You are a remarkable person. Not one living person in a million has ever seen the Thanatos mouth. Not one in a hundred million has felt the passage of the soul. Not one in the memory of the human race has been so tormented that he thought it was real, and not a dream" (322). The burned figure then explains Le Braz's own story, of having suffered so after his wife's death that he found a means of bringing her back, only to have her suffer the horrible half-life of a burn victim. The function of dream sleep, she explains, is to permit sorrows and memories of loved ones to depart the body at night, and the Thanatos mouth is the means of their departing; without such release, life would be unbearable, and the souls of the departed would be incomplete. Sometime later, McGrath's dreams turn pleasant, and the Thanatos mouth opens to release his agony, this time as it should, without his knowledge.

Despite its similarities to "Adrift Just off the Islets of Langerhans"—a figure suffering under a debilitating curse and unbearable loss seeks help from a kindly Frankenstein-like figure, who helps him find the resolution in his own body—"The Function of Dream Sleep" is very much a product of a particular moment in Ellison's life, when mortality seemed all too imminent. With hyperbole that verges on the grandiose, McGrath is revealed not merely as a sensitive soul suffering the deaths of friends but as virtually the only human in history to experience, witness, and believe in the Thanatos mouth, Ellison's surreal image of purgation. Despite the essentially trite message of its ending—that one has to let go—the story strives to be an epic of grief and suffering, with McGrath a stand-in for Ellison's own feelings of loss. The main problem is twofold. In the first place, the bizarre image of the mouth serves as an image not of McGrath's pain and loss but of his refusal or inability to process mature grief—a refusal or inability that results in the injury or death of several people. In the second place, the structure of the story seems inappropriate for a tale of suffering. McGrath is presented not as an individual of extraordinary sensitivity nor even as a Job-like figure but rather as a figure of power. His progression follows that of any number of science fiction wish-fulfillment fantasies involving secret masters, from A. E. Van Vogt's Jommy Cross to Frank Herbert's Paul Atreides, who realize that something is different about themselves, seek assistance, and find themselves working their way through increasingly secret tiers of power until they arrive at the final stronghold of secret masterdom. McGrath's first encounter is with a doctor who does not understand his condition, then with a REM group whose capabilities do not begin to address his needs, then with a healer who finds his energy so powerful that she must refer him to the *real* REM group, characteristically hidden in a wealthy redoubt, and when even that group is almost literally blown away by his unprecedented power, he finds his way to the Magus himself, where the secret is finally revealed. It is not at all dramatically convincing that McGrath's grotesque encounter with Le Braz's tortured, disfigured wife should somehow release him from his grief, but it *is* consistent with the science fiction hero whose final prize is self-knowledge. Grief alone does not earn heroic status, however.

And yet, during this period of loss, Ellison persistently tried to make it so. "The Avenger of Death" (1987), published the year before "The Function of Dream Sleep" and also collected in *Angry Candy,* takes another unprepossessing figure, a meek bookstore owner, and transforms him into the antideath crusader of the title, wandering the city killing "takers," or agents of death (personified here as Bill, or the Dustman), as a kind of revenge, not for personal friends lost, but for losses to the culture at large. Famous names pepper the story like a litany of Ellisonian cultural icons (Bert Lahr, Groucho Marx, Huey Long, Ernie Pyle, John Lennon, Brendan Behan, Frank Herbert, Aleister Crowley, Helen Keller, etc.). The bookseller, Pen Robinson, stumbles into this line of work after finding a recent check from a man named Chatley somehow buried in the pages of an old book unopened for many years. His attempt to track down the owner of the check leads to a mysterious interrogation by shadowy figures he takes to be intelligence agents. Finding another card in the book, he locates Chatley, hidden in the stairwell of a building and being consumed by a strange, boiling blue light. Chatley reveals that he is one of the Takers and that he is being punished for not having "taken" Robinson at his appointed time. He also reveals the secret of identifying other agents of death, and Robinson begins his quest—until one day he is interrupted by the Dustman himself—none other than Robinson's own father, who had died in a mill accident when the young Robinson was fourteen years old.

"The Avenger of Death" is weak on internal narrative logic, and it's unclear what sort of moral balance is supposed to be restored by Robinson's various assassinations of figures who are, after all, functionaries, but the central conceit is powerful. The appearance of Robinson's father at the end, to welcome him into the "family business," is more expedient than revelatory, but it reflects what may have been for Ellison the key to the story's emotional tenor: Ellison was almost fifteen when his own father died, and the quest for the lost father shows up more than once in his fiction. Nearly a decade after "The Avenger of Death," Ellison published another dream-scenario of a reunion with a father—this time a man who had died when his son was only ten months old—called "Midnight in the Sunken Cathedral" (collected in *Slippage*). Again, the logic of the story gives way to the depth of emotion that underlies it. While exploring the ocean floor in the Bahamas, Dennis Lanfear thinks of his father, "whom he had loved and admired more than he had ever been able to say, ever been able to tell the man" (292)—but since we later learn that Lanfear was only ten months old when his father was smashed in a hydraulic punch press in an auto plant in 1952, the notion of failed opportunities loses much of its resonance. While the imagery of the story, with its vast underwater waterfalls and precipitous cliffs, is far richer than in "The Avenger of Death," the morality of the story isn't much different, and the mythology is even more dreamlike. Lanfear's father reveals to him that the great underwater civilization of Atlantis was relocated wholesale to Mars and that the Atlanteans, as absolute masters of space and time, can bring people back from the past, enabling Lanfear, after forty-one years, to enjoy long conversations with his father—though in the end, we catch a glimpse of the corporeal Lanfear's body floating face-down in the Atlantic. The magic of the story turns out to be, as in so many such tales, the simple magic of desperation.

10 | THE SELF ON TRIAL

Fragmentation and Magic Realism

FOR ALL HIS STYLISTIC and conceptual innovation, especially by the standards of the commercial fiction arenas of science fiction, fantasy, and horror, Ellison had never really been known as an structural experimentalist. Even when he incorporated typographical or visual effects in such stories as "Pretty Maggie Moneyeyes" (1967) or "The Region Between" (1970), these resulted as much from a 1960s passion for design as from any radical reinterpretation of form, and the stories themselves remain driven by fairly straightforward narrative arcs and character relationships. Much the same might be said of Ellison's most famous science fiction classics, "I Have No Mouth, and I Must Scream" and "'Repent, Harlequin!' Said the Ticktockman," which, for all their intense imagery and bravura manipulation of narrative voice, are fundamentally tales of rebellion and revenge, even though the latter was notably innovative for its time in its use of non-linear chronology. Among writers trained in commercial storytelling venues, there has always been a vague mistrust of the "literary" short story, whether it be John Cheever in the 1950s, Ann Beatty in the 1970s, or T. Coraghesson Boyle in the 1990s, and this mistrust is even greater when it comes to avant-garde modes of fiction such as stream of consciousness, objectivism, the deliberately fragmented "cut-up" method of William Burroughs, or the French *nouveau roman*—all movements whose influence on genre fiction in the 1950s and 1960s proved to be short-lived. Ellison, too, has occasionally joined in the genre writer's criticism of stories in which nothing seems to happen or in which events seem unconnected by clear causality or are left deliberately unresolved, and when he speaks of story construction he often speaks in terms drawn from commercial fiction artisanship, such as the narrative "hook," the importance of clearly defined conflict, and the "payoff."

At the same time, he has often shown impatience with readers who demand unambiguous resolutions and explicit narrative exposition. "I've found more and more frequently these days that even fairly intelligent people reading good books come to the end of a story with a quizzical expression on their faces," he writes in *Strange Wine*. "Unless they have been told with nailed-down precision that John dies in the fire and Joan marries Bernice and the secret message in the codex was that we are all alien property, many readers have no idea what the point of the story may have been" (231). In his introduction to "Jeffty Is Five" in *Shatterday,* Ellison again complains that "the ending of the story somehow escapes the slovenly reader" (11). Although some readers have found such remarks gratuitous and even offensive—feeling that a story's subtleties ought not to be advertised by the author—the fact is that such comments are less an attack on readers than an expression of the frustrations of an author growing increasingly impatient with reader expectations engendered by the conventional protocols of popular narrative tradition. On occasion, this has led Ellison to mistake narrative subtlety or indirection for a kind of affected obtuseness, as when he concludes "The Boulevard of Broken Dreams" with an allusion that he clearly expects many of his readers to miss. In other cases, such as "The Deathbird," it is clear that the linear plotting of traditional popular fiction cannot sustain the kind of mythic resonance he wants to achieve.

We have already seen how, at key points in his career, Ellison almost fortuitously discovered ways of overcoming those frustrations by moving into new and more open markets: The men's magazines provided liberation from the tight formulas of the digest genre magazines; the atmosphere of experimentation during the period of the New Wave actively engendered narrative and stylistic innovation (such as J. G. Ballard's "condensed novels" and fragmented narratives); Ellison's own growing reputation and gradual escape from the restrictive label of science fiction writer offered even more freedom from genre expectations. Only in the mature phase of his career, though, has Ellison consistently and consciously begun to move beyond traditional means of structuring stories and to explore techniques of reinventing the short story by recombining its core elements in distinctly postmodern ways, fracturing and multiplying narratives and narrative units, exploring the intersections of the narrative and visual arts (and even, to a limited degree, computer gaming), and revisiting genre materials in new and more authoritative ways. Like a handful of other writers in the science fiction, fantasy, horror, and mystery fields, Ellison transformed himself from a writer whose works could be said to inhabit genre into a writer whose works were inhabited *by* genre: a writer whose authority finally exceeded that of his milieux.

COMPOSITE STORIES AND VIGNETTES

One such technique, which Ellison has refined for more than two decades, involves constructing a fiction from a series of smaller, semi-independent narrative units—sometimes vignettes or anecdotes, sometimes prose poems, sometimes interpolated comments or memoirs, sometimes complete short-short stories—which may be related only thematically or even stylistically. The episodic novel, of course, is a tradition of its own, with examples in American literature ranging from Melville's *The Confidence-Man* (1857) to Jerzy Kosinski's *Steps* (1968), but it is less common for a short story writer to use such a technique within a single story. In Ellison's case, this may well be a technique that initially evolved out of expedience, as a way of stringing together fragments or short pieces that might otherwise seem simply undeveloped ideas. As early as 1959, Ellison's "May We Also Speak?" in *Rogue* was subtitled "Four Statements from the Not-So-Beat Generation" and consisted of four brief sketches or vignettes intended to capture the tone of what Ellison later called the "hung-up generation." In 1962, also in *Rogue,* he gathered three of his more effective, if understated, character studies, "Robert Blake's Universe" (later retitled "The Universe of Robert Blake"), "Mona at Her Windows," and "G.B.K.—A Many-Flavored Bird" under the collective title "Trio"; perhaps because the stories themselves were more substantial, the grouping achieves a sense of diffuse early-1960s alienation that none of the stories individually could likely have achieved. But in both of these cases, the stories seem to have been written independently of one another and assembled for magazine publication more as samplers than as thematic wholes.

In 1973, the same year in which he interpolated an autobiographical fragment in "The Deathbird," Ellison wrote a "Harlan Ellison Hornbook" column titled "The Day I Died," moving a step further toward the composite narrative by imagining different scenarios of his own death and writing brief dramatic anecdotes about each one: being knifed in New

York in 1973, dying of pneumonia in a Scottish farmhouse while working on his magnum opus, losing a battle to stomach cancer in 1986, etc. None of the anecdotes in this "essay-fiction" last more than a paragraph, but the idea was clearly appealing, since Ellison would return to this approach again. "The Pale Silver Dollar of the Moon Pays Its Way and Makes Change" (1994; collected in *Slippage*) mixes real and fictional episodes of the narrator's life with historical events in key years from 1934 to 1992. In "Where I Shall Dwell in the Next World" (1992; collected in *Slippage*), Ellison uses the technique to address that annoying and incessant reader question regarding sources of ideas and inspiration. Here the conceit is that stories come from misheard remarks, and as illustration he offers short fantasy scenarios spun from simple misunderstandings: "Necro Waiters" (from Necco wafers), "Trees Rabelais" (from something his wife said that began with "Please"), etc. (Ellison has also commented that the title of "Jeffty Is Five" partly originated from mishearing a snatch of conversation at a party.)

Another factor that may have contributed to the evolution of the composite story was Ellison's occasional stunt of "performance writing," committing to write so many stories or pieces under tight circumstances, such as in the window of a bookstore, which tended to produce shorter and more fragmented work. The most famous of these stunts, attempting to write a story a week in the window of the Change of Hobbit bookstore in Los Angeles in 1976, resulted in a piece called "From A to Z, in the Chocolate Alphabet," made up of twenty-six short-short stories, pastiches, or one-liners in the tradition made popular in science fiction by Fredric Brown, whose pungent short-short stories, often turning on a bad pun, were popular in the 1950s. (The piece is included in *Strange Wine* and was adapted as a comic book in 1978, illustrated by Larry Todd.) Most of these are simply provocative but undeveloped ideas, such as the notion (under "E") that five hundred elevators in the United States are equipped with special relays to take them below the basement level into a frightening netherworld whose denizens are the anonymous, zombielike riders so often seen in elevators. There is almost no deliberate attempt to maintain any sort of thematic or dramatic unity among the twenty-six parts of the "story," but patterns do seem to emerge: hidden or lost communities (Atlanteans, elevator people, mind readers, intelligent seals, troglodytes who live in city dumps and consume garbage), monsters of folklore and myth (vampires, golems, zombies, demons, rocs, werewolves, poltergeists), and allusions to favorite writers (Lewis Carroll, Philip K. Dick).

The first of Ellison's composite stories to seriously strive for some sort of cumulative aesthetic effect, "Eidolons" (1988; collected in *Angry Candy*), began in a manner similar to that of "The Chocolate Alphabet." "'Eidolons,'" wrote Ellison, "came from the assemblage of a congeries of misheard remarks, altered to form brief allegories or tone-poems. I did one each week as introduction to my stint as the host of a radio show" (*Slippage* 173). The story (whose title simply refers to an image or a phantom) consists of thirteen numbered but untitled sections wrapped in a frame story narrated by a Melmoth-like figure named Vizinczey, who introduces himself as an international pariah for reasons not made clear. In Australia, Vizinczey comes upon one of Ellison's ubiquitous mysterious little shops, this one selling miniature soldiers of astonishing detail and authenticity, which he gradually realizes are not models at all but actual soldiers snatched from the battlefields of history and somehow miniaturized and frozen in place. When the shop owner dies, apparently killed by a crossbow quarrel from one of his tiny prisoners, he passes on to the narrator an ancient scroll containing various secrets of life.

The segments that make up the bulk of the story are supposedly fragments from that scroll, though Ellison makes no real effort to present the episodes as consistent with any ancient European culture or even as consistent with the chronology of the scroll as outlined in the frame—there are, for example, quotations from Camus, allusions to Tinker Bell, the Hindenburg, and *The Sun Also Rises,* a brief memoir about growing up after the Great Depression. The segments begin with dreamlike meditations on friendship and responsibility, all set in the kind of spiritual twilight that Ellison calls "the hour that stretches" (or *djam karet,* an Indonesian phrase that Ellison has returned to repeatedly): a message from a dead friend is formed in dust motes on a forgotten book, winds from the top of the world unite separated lovers with "memories of those who have gone before," an anonymous authoritative voice announces a suspension "for the next few weeks" of irrational or hateful thinking (*Angry Candy* 205). An allegorical battle is joined between the forces of art and the forces of commerce, and a deformed singer becomes an image of the mystery and inaccessibility of art. Gradually, the segments begin to gain a more particularized focus, with brief character sketches of women who might once have been the narrator's lovers, an account of an apparent nightmare in which the narrator is threatened by "a billowing web" found in his kitchen at night, and finally a childhood memory in which a usually generous father refused a handout to a bum, leaving the adult narrator haunted by the mysteries of compassion. In the end, the frame narrator Vizinczy alludes to six more selections from the scroll, not included, which reveal such secrets as "the power to bend others to your will, or the ability to travel at will in an instant to any place in the world, or the facility for reading the future in mirrors" (212). The irony, of course, is that no such supernatural gifts are revealed in the thirteen segments which are included, unless we realize—as Ellison apparently wants us to—that what magic is available in the world is only the magic of memory, observation, art, and compassion.

For all its cumulative power, "Eidolons" never quite hangs together either as a unified narrative (which it makes only token attempts to achieve) or as an internally consistent suite of prose poems and memoirs (which is closer to its apparent goal). The frame narrative, in which Vizinczy learns from his experience with the scroll to become a secret doer of good deeds rather than a compulsive criminal, is a fairly clunky device which fails to add significantly to the power of the individual episodes, even though it makes for a characteristic Ellison redemption-fable on its own terms. A much more unified tale, "Scartaris, June 28" (1990; collected in *Slippage*), organizes its episodes by means of a central godlike character who first appears as the victim of an Alabama lynch mob, calmly releasing himself from the noose two hours after his own hanging. Later, he shows up in Wisconsin to persuade a young man to attend the funeral of a bully who used to beat him, and then on an airliner where he challenges a fundamentalist minister's beliefs and, sympathizing with the aging and tired parents of a retarded woman, creates a fatal aneurysm in the woman's brain. He appears on the shore of the Aegean in Greece, murmuring the word *levendis* (a Greek term for one who enjoys life), and explaining to a local resident that his true home is far out in the sea and was mentioned by Plato. (This allusion to Atlantis is one of several in Ellison's recent work in which the legendary continent becomes a kind of magical Valhalla for lost gods or departed souls; see also "Midnight in the Sunken Cathedral" and "From A to Z, in the Chocolate Alphabet"). After a brief episode with a young woman in Zurich, the protagonist travels to Iceland, where, by following the clues of the characters in Jules Verne's *Journey to the Center of the Earth,* he prepares to depart the world by descending into the volcano described in that novel, to visit the Earth's hollow interior. Though any of these episodes might provide the basis for a separate story, the central role played by the protagonist, in his shifting guises, unites the various episodes into a cumulative thematic whole.

Easily Ellison's most successful experiment with the composite story is "The Man Who Rowed Christopher Columbus Ashore" (1991), which aggressively advertises its fluid nature not only by shifting its godlike main character freely through time and space but by changing titles four times in midstream—the text is periodically interrupted with announcements beginning "This is a story titled" followed by the new title: "The Route of Odysseus," "The Daffodils That Entertain," "At Least One Good Deed a Day, Every Single Day," and, at the very end, "Shagging Fungoes." As with "The Chocolate Alphabet," some of the thirty-five sections are no more than cynical one-liners, while others constitute short-short stories unto themselves. But more than with any of his other experiments with this form, Ellison now strives to find formal means of unifying a text whose narrative is deliberately fragmented. Each section, for example, begins by restating the name of the protagonist—"Levendis," the same Greek word as in "Scartaris, June 28"—in boldface, then giving the date (the segments take place daily from October 1 through "the 35th of October"—a deliberate clue that the tale is moving from representation into myth), then almost always establishing where the action takes place and what Levendis's particular disguise is on this particular date. The effect is that of a catalog or chronicle whose entries occasionally erupt into partial narratives but which finally depends upon the cumulative effect of the various details that go to make up the episodes. Levendis is an enigmatic figure who sometimes seems no more than a bystander to history and at other times displays godlike powers by raising or lowering everyone's IQ, creating a cure for bone marrow cancer, or isolating Tibet with snowstorms. He is, in effect, a secret master, a kind of composite god whose function parallels the composite nature of the story, a god who is partly a figure of omnipotent will and partly an expression of the collective power of those anonymous individuals who transform history in profound but unrecognized ways—like the man who rowed Christopher Columbus ashore.

The story, which was the first of Ellison's to be selected for *The Best American Short Stories* annual (in 1993, with Louise Erdrich as editor), is essentially a series of moral-fantasy vignettes that initially seem almost random, until we realize that the central figure in each—Levendis—is a kind of renegade time traveler, a cosmic version of Ellison's more famous Harlequin. As he explains to a young boy in the ruins of a Greek theater in

Turkey, "I am an unlimited person living in a limited world" (*Slippage* 8). Like the Harlequin, his actions are sometimes comically absurd, such as assuming the form of a Boy Scout to help an old woman across a street— against her will—and he is eventually caught and removed from his position by the faceless "Front Office" and something ominously called the "Master Parameter" (15). But his role is far more ambiguous than that of Harlequin. Sometimes his actions are simply cruel, like killing a cat; at other times they are bitterly ironic, such as sending a basket of fruit to parents who have given their son a gun as a present, even though it's the same gun that his older brother had used to kill himself. As if to underline the randomness of the forces that Levendis represents, Ellison has him silently watch skinheads savagely beat an interracial couple in Chicago, taking no action, but the very next day, in an almost identical incident in Pennsylvania (in one of the few cases where successive episodes are linked), he intervenes and murders each of the skinheads. In a thematically related later episode, Levendis spectacularly murders a former KKK leader running for office in Louisiana, but—with the irony typical of such acts in Ellison's universe—thus leaves the electoral field open to one of Joseph Mengele's former assistants, a child mutilator, and an "illiterate swamp cabbage farmer" (*Slippage* 15). Levendis, in fact, proves to be a fairly murderous character. He also kills a truck driver (for dumping toxic waste) and a group of surviving POWs in Cambodia (he spares one, who later becomes his own daughter's lover). On the other hand, he takes pity on a welfare mother who tries to save her children from rats, saves the life of a prostitute in New York in 1892 by providing her with penicillin (thus ensuring the birth of her child, who will grow up to save millions of lives), restores the Dalai Lama to the throne in Tibet, is present at the liberation of Buchenwald in 1945, and serves as attorney for a woman athlete in a lawsuit in which she seeks to be admitted to professional baseball.

While many of these episodes reflect Ellison's characteristic themes and preoccupations—racism, economic injustice, secret history (Levendis presents evidence that Marilyn Monroe actually murdered JFK, but destroys all remaining evidence that would reveal what happened to Jimmy Hoffa, Amelia Earhart, and Ambrose Bierce), one intervention that recurs in several venues involves proselytizing for quality in the arts, and in these episodes—which almost inevitably appear self-referential on Ellison's part—we gain perhaps the strongest clues to the story's governing rhetoric.

Speaking before a "convention of readers of cheap fantasy novels," he says, "We invent our lives (and other people's) as we live them; what we call 'life' is itself a fiction. Therefore, we must constantly strive to produce only good art, absolutely entertaining fiction" (15). But, as if to underline the futility Ellison himself must have felt from time to time speaking before such groups, not a word of what Levendis says is understood, since he delivers his speech in Etruscan. He delivers a similar message to a group "representing the country & western music industry," arguing that the "one real evil in the world is mediocrity" (3). In Utah, he takes a group of "art-ignorant" Mormon schoolchildren to view Robert Smithson's famous environmental sculpture *Spiral Jetty,* and quotes Smithson's words: "Establish enigmas, not explanations" (9; the same quotation is later invoked in Ellison's *Mind Fields,* where it seems acutely apt for the surreal paintings of Jacek Yerka that accompany Ellison's words).

While such comments and quotations resonate with our own attempts to discern meanings in the very story we are reading, the most telling single literary allusion in the tale occurs on day twenty, when Levendis drives a rented van with a loudspeaker through the streets of Raleigh and Durham, North Carolina, advising the residents that "perhaps they should ignore their bibles today, and go back and reread Shirley Jackson's short story, 'One Ordinary Day, with Peanuts'" (10). This 1954 story, in which an enigmatic figure named Mr. Johnson moves through his day helping strangers with seemingly random acts of kindness: helping a mother and son prepare to move, bringing a young couple together and paying for their lost wages if they take the day off on a date, sending another couple seeking an apartment to the one just vacated by the mother and son, paying for a veal cutlet lunch for a beggar, offering a racing tip to a cabdriver. At the end of the day, we learn that *Mrs.* Johnson has spent her day creating unhappiness and havoc that balances Mr. Johnson's kindnesses: accusing a woman of shoplifting, sending dogs to the pound, filing a complaint that may have gotten a bus driver fired. The two agree to change roles on the following day, and then they sit down happily to dinner. Mr. and Mrs. Johnson are Levendis's direct literary ancestors, wry personifications of the vicissitudes of daily fortune.

Jackson, a rare fantasist of her time whose work graced both the pages of the *New Yorker* and the *Magazine of Fantasy and Science Fiction* (where this tale originally appeared), might well be regarded as one of Ellison's literary godmothers, though the understated, elliptical fantasy of her short fiction (as opposed to her more traditionally Gothic ghost-novels) would not become a regular feature of Ellison's repertoire until fairly late in his career. One episode in particular of "The Man Who Rowed Christopher Columbus Ashore" could almost be a segment from the Jackson story, complete with its middle-class domestic mise-en-scène: Levendis, in a supermarket in Wisconsin, deliberately sets up a collision between the shopping carts of a lonely, aging homosexual and an equally lonely legal secretary, then causes them to become allies as he screams rudely at them. Outside, he lets the air out of the woman's tires, knowing that she will need a lift to the gas station and that a friendship will begin to blossom. Like most of the best segments of "The Man Who Rowed Christopher Columbus Ashore," this brief but touching vignette is the seed of its own unwritten tale, a small kindness that serves as an emblem of the randomness of life and of the fractal nature of the larger tale, with its fragments and anecdotes suggesting stories within stories within stories. In a strange way, "Columbus," with its rich catalog of unwritten story ideas, carries among its undertones an Ellisonian version of the sort of anxiety that a much younger Keats articulated in "When I Have Fears." Edging past middle age, his inventiveness showing no signs of flagging, Ellison has found in the composite tale not only a new form of discontinuous narrative structure but a kind of reservoir for unwritten tales, a hedge against silence, against the end of tales.

MIND FIELDS

Apart from "The Man Who Rowed Christopher Columbus Ashore," Ellison's most intriguing use of the very short fiction/prose poem/meditation in the 1990s came via an unusual after-the-fact collaboration with Polish artist Jacek Yerka in a book titled *Mind Fields* (1994), which consists of thirty-four paintings by the surrealist artist, each accompanied by a brief story or prose piece by Ellison. Originally asked to write an introduction to a collection of Yerka's work, Ellison found the paintings—all acrylic on canvas, and all painted between 1981 and 1993—so compelling that, instead of the introduction, he offered to write original short fictions to accompany each one. The idea of writing stories to fit paintings wasn't entirely new to Ellison. He was, after all, one of those who suffered the indignities of trying to write stories to match prepurchased magazine cover illustrations back in the 1950s. But Yerka, whose imagination seems in its way as unpredictable as Ellison's own, provided considerably more fertile ground for Ellison's inventions, which have always had a strong visual aspect.

Throughout *Mind Fields,* Ellison seems to begin with a general emotional tenor suggested by his response to the painting, then imagines a scenario of his own that reflects this tenor, and finally (in most but not all cases) returns to the painting to find points of congruity with Yerka's images. It works more often than one might expect, especially given the strikingly different cultural sensibilities of the two artists. Most of Yerka's images derive from the fields and cottages of his native rural Poland, upon which he works delightful surrealist transformations showing the clear influence of the fantasy paintings of Bosch, Brueghel, and others: the wall of a stone cottage metamorphoses into a cave wall, which in turn becomes waves of water; a thatched-roof barn soars above the countryside on dragonfly wings; fields of grain hide whole villages or collections of strange objects; an apparent erupting volcano proves on closer inspection to be a vast cityscape at night. Ellison, on the other hand, has been accused of many things in his fiction, but pastoralism isn't one of them. Much of the fascination in the collection derives from the question of how Ellison's sharp-edged American urban imagination can interact with Yerka's ominous but essentially gentle dreamscapes. A painting called *The Agitators,* for example, shows five aging men standing or kneeling before a tiny forest church, which seems to transmute into an even tinier cathedral at its rear. Ellison's inventive conceit is that the church had indeed once been a cathedral, and the worshipers had numbered more than three hundred, but as the congregation shrank so did the size of the church. So far, the tale seems consistent with the kind of religious allegory that seems apparent in the painting, except for an odd reference to Erroll Garner–style music, heard when the church shrinks. But the five men in Ellison's story are not congregants but complainants, and their complaints are decidedly secular and American: Too much power to stop traffic is given to road construction flagmen in "those offensive Day-Glo orange vests," trading cards are a cheat with no bubble gum included in the package, Victor Mature was a completely talentless actor (46). Even in such cases as this, in which Ellison incorporates the exact scene of the painting into his fiction, he jarringly shifts the context and the characters from Yerka's world into his own.

But for the most part, the counterpoint works startlingly well. A painting called "Fever" (all the titles are Yerka's except two pieces called "Susan" and "Ellison Wonderland") shows a bedridden figure, only hands showing, cowering under menacing clouds. Ellison turns this into a Borgesian parable of an Icarus who survived the fall but suffered amnesia and still lives as a minor accountant in Switzerland who dreams each night about the sky. A crowded cupboard with hands peeking out of a drawer becomes an image of the afterlife of a Holocaust resistance fighter (discussed in chapter 8). Two of Ellison's strongest pieces have virtually no direct narrative relationship to the accompanying painting except for the title. "Base" is a bleak but sardonic anecdote in which the narrator is awakened in the middle of the night by police asking him to come downtown and identify a body. He provides them with all the positive identification they request, but then reveals to the reader that he has no idea who the body was, and that the police probably called a wrong number. The Yerka image is of two vaguely human-shaped mattresses resting under an outdoor canopy made up of junk. "Attack at Dawn" completely abandons any attempt to explain why a Volkswagen which is also half-lizard is being attacked by what appear to be biomechanical planes; instead, Ellison spins a tale of a daughter's well-planned righteous rebellion against her father in a corporate setting. Both the image and the tale touch upon themes of transformation and confrontation, but share little else in common.

In a few cases, Ellison turns to the resources of science fiction to find narrative analogues of the paintings. For Yerka's image of a printing press in a ramshackle shed, *Shed of Rebellion,* he evokes a nightmare postliterate future, suggestive both of Ray Bradbury's *Fahrenheit 451* and C. M. Kornbluth's "The Marching Morons," in which a thuggish and semiliterate video journalist boasts of using the latest technology to cover violent government reprisals against an underground movement called the "Resistance Readership Alliance." Yerka's two visions of fantasy-cities, "Eruption" and "Ammonite," become tales of the lost or hidden civilizations that might have built such structures, each of which reflects the recurring Atlantis theme in Ellison's later work. "Under the Landscape"— the only piece to accompany two paintings, each depicting a small village hidden beneath fields of grass or wheat that serve as the villages' rooftops—returns to the composite narrative form, telling the stories of a half-dozen children brutalized in various ways in 1993, followed by three versions of what happens to them as adults, and how the world splits into two alternate possibilities in 2009, when a behavior control device called the Passion Inhibitor is either embraced or rejected by the medical and legal communities (in the world in which it is rejected, all the former abused children become great successes, but if the Passion Inhibitor is used, they are turned into anonymous drudges).

Other pieces, like episodes of "The Man Who Rowed Christopher Columbus Ashore," touch upon aspects of art or writing. "Metropolis II"—the painting shows a village street lined with old appliances and furniture instead of buildings—is narrated by a world-famous author lionized in a way even more excessive than that of Crowstairs of "All the Lies That Are My Life"; here even the names of the adulators are mentioned, and it is a litany of intellectual trendiness: Barzun, Kristeva, Paglia, Deran, Clute, Hardwick, Sontag, Gilder, Chomsky. But this brief vignette parallels that much longer story in another key way. The narrator reveals that all the elaborate stories he has told about his background over the years are complete fictions and that his real past is much closer to the seedy world depicted in the painting, "the shantytown that gave me birth" (16). Fearful that word of his inauspicious beginnings and various betrayals on his way to success might damage his reputation ("Somehow, I do not think the Literary Establishment would subsidize posters"), the narrator informs his listener that the two of them must duel to the death once this story has been told. Although few of the details of the narrator's real or imagined backgrounds suggest actual autobiographical elements, the notion of an invented past is more clearly delineated here than almost anywhere else in Ellison's fiction. In another tale, "Truancy at the Pond" (the image is of a crystal-clear pond beneath which can be seen an elaborate network of pipes, which may also be tree roots), Michelangelo invites art critics to view his latest masterpiece, a topiary garden with a clear pond at its center. At first, the critics are astonished: "'Perfection,' they said. And, 'Flawless'" (48). But they soon begin finding minute imperfections in the work, and Michelangelo promptly shoves them into the pond, where they sink without a trace.

Most of Ellison's fictions in *Mind Fields* can stand on their own and don't need the paintings to make sense. But in a few cases, a genuine synergy sets in, and the painting-plus-text becomes something entirely apart from either work individually. Of the three most personal pieces in the book, two are those for which Ellison himself chose the titles. "Ellison Wonderland" is vintage Ellison paranoia, made oddly appropriate to Yerka's desolate Antonio Gaudi–like buildings rising from muddy waters. In the story, the narrator reveals that he has at last unmasked the lifelong conspiracy that has kept his sense of being-in-the-world off-balance, and that the moment of revelation occurred when, at a Minneapolis airport, he read the departure time of his flight as 1:45 and his wife corrected him, saying it was 1:54. Looking again, he noted that the board did indeed say 1:54, but rather than assume a slight misreading on his part, he takes this as evidence of the conspiracy that controls his life by causing him to question his own judgment. He escapes from the world—and "the woman they had programmed to be my wife" (64)—and flees to the mysterious city of Yerka's painting. "Susan" is a sensitive and understated little romance of mortality—Ellison describes it as a valentine to his wife Susan—which, in its story of a husband who seeks to protect his new wife from his nightmares, which he says not only "come to life" but "killed and ate my first four wives" (26), resonates perfectly with Yerka's equally understated image of a bed and lamp in a wooded landscape. The final piece in the book, "Please Don't Slam the Door," may be the most affecting of all. It's not really Yerka's most original painting—by now we've grown accustomed to his floating landscapes, rural cottages, and volcanic structures—and it's not Ellison's strongest prose, verging on cloying sentimentality in its description of a beautiful child who sends dreams back into the world from his magical treehouse. But image and text combined work far more effectively than either alone, and they become a moving elegy to the young son Yerka lost during the preparation of the book, and to the child's sense of wonder.

REVISIONING GENRE

At the same time that Ellison was experimenting with fragmented, discontinuous, or miniature narratives, he was also increasingly engaged in revisiting many of the genre materials that he had worked with throughout his career, but with a new eye toward recombining these materials in increasingly complex ways. His 1997 collection *Slippage* included not only "The Man Who Rowed Christopher Columbus Ashore" and "Scartaris, June 28," but tales of angry demons, vengeful gods, brutal killers, cannibals, psychic vampires, dryads, dragons, and other mythical beasts. "She's a Young Thing and Cannot Leave Her Mother" is a gruesome horror tale based on the legend of Sawney Beane; by taking its time to develop a character relationship it becomes far more effective than "Sensible City" (discussed in chapter 9), whose plot is, as noted, about as sensible as that of an EC horror comic. Ellison's preoccupation with mythology is again evident in "Chatting with Anubis," "Darkness upon the Face of the Deep," and "The Lingering Scent of Woodsmoke." But in "Darkness upon the Face of the Deep," the Hittite god is little more than a Lovecraftian monster-in-a-vault (the story works better when it focuses on the testy relationship of the two old but slightly distrustful friends who unleash the beast), and "The Lingering Scent of Woodsmoke" is a slight tale involving dryads gaining a new kind of vengeance on Nazi war criminals. "The Dreams a Nightmare Dreams," about the extinction of the dinosaurs, and "Keyboard," about a vampire computer, are little more than underdeveloped one-joke tales, the latter of which might have fit seamlessly into *Mind Fields* had there been an appropriate dinosaur painting. One tale even harks back to the very early years of Ellison's career: "The Few, the Proud" is a science fiction story in the Kyben war sequence that dates back to the 1950s (see chapter 2) and is narrated in the same 1950s style of cocky dramatic monologue that now seems dated, but at its center is an act of passion and protest that is pure Ellison, and it reminds us that science fiction hadn't seen much of this until he came along. But the longest and most important story in the book is also the one that most clearly demonstrates Ellison's interest in transforming the genre materials of his past into denser, more complex, and more resonant narratives.

"Mefisto in Onyx"

"Mefisto in Onyx" (1993) is a rare Ellison story sustained principally by the ingenuity of its plotting, which in turn depends upon a careful manipulation of point of view. The tale is narrated by Rudy Pairis, a young black drifter and former Rhodes scholar who since childhood has possessed the gift of being able to enter the minds or "landscapes" of others, a skill which he calls "jaunting" (in an apparent homage to science fiction writer Alfred Bester, who in his classic 1956 novel *The Stars My Destination* used the term to refer to teleportation). Pairis uses the skill sparingly, however, because he finds the contents of most people's minds distressing. "If Aquinas had had my ability," comments Pairis, "he'd have very quickly gone off to be a hermit, only occasionally visiting the mind of a sheep or a hedgehog" (*Slippage* 127). Pairis's longtime friend and onetime lover, Allison Roche, a district attorney who has recently won multiple convictions against a famous serial killer named Henry Lake Spanning, now contacts him with an unusual request. She wants him to determine Spanning's guilt by "jaunting" into his mindscape, even though Spanning is already on Death Row and has been convicted on the basis of overwhelming evidence, including eyewitnesses. Roche, it seems, is not only now convinced of the innocence of the man she convicted but has fallen in love with him.

Despite considerable misgivings, Pairis eventually agrees and meets Spanning in prison, finding him good-looking ("even for a white guy") and extraordinarily ingratiating. When he "jaunts" into Spanning's mind, he is shocked to discover that the convicted man is innocent of all the crimes of which he has been accused and that the mutilated old woman with whom he was caught in a dumpster was simply a victim he had been trying to rescue and who died in his arms. Even more startling, perhaps prompted by reliving the death of the old woman, Pairis suddenly realizes that he *himself* is the murderer and that his memory of the crimes has been sealed off in what amounts to a separate personality. "The other Rudy Pairis had come home at last" (159). Pairis confesses, providing detailed accounts not only of the crimes of which Spanning had been accused but of more than a dozen other unsolved murders, and is himself sentenced to the electric chair. On the day of his execution, the now free Spanning shows up in the visitors' gallery together with Roche, and when Pairis attempts again to jaunt into his mind, he finds it blocked—an experience he had never before encountered. Then Spanning appears in *his* mind, and he realizes that Spanning, too, possesses the ability to jaunt. Spanning explains that he was in fact the murderer all along and that Pairis's apparent memories of committing the crimes were nothing more than elaborate constructions planted in his mind during the few minutes that he visited Spanning on Death Row.

Spanning, in fact, claims that not only is he able to enter other people's minds but he can transfer his entire consciousness into other bodies (an act which he calls "shriking"), and that he has survived for centuries by doing this, like a demon possessing a succession of victims. His various incarnations are a litany of such famous murderers, including Gilles de Rais, Vlad Tepes (the model for Dracula), Jack the Ripper, the Boston Strangler, Ed Gein (the model for Robert Bloch's novel *Psycho*), Charles Manson, and John Wayne Gacy. Now, inside Pairis's mind, he taunts him with racial slurs and with plans of butchering Allison Roche. But in a final reversal, Spanning finds that he cannot escape from Pairis's mind. During *his* time on Death Row, Pairis was able to deduce what had happened to him and to develop a strategy to trick Spanning in return. He berates Spanning for his naive egotism, accuses him of exaggerating or inventing most of his history, of failing the moral responsibilities of his talent, most of all of failing to learn. Pairis then transfers his mind into Spanning's body, leaving Spanning trapped just as the warden throws the switch of the electric chair. Pairis, now in the body of a white man, feels free to pursue his love of Roche, realizing that his lifelong failures have been due neither to his strange gift nor to his skin color, but because "I have always been one of those miserable guys who *couldn't get out of his own way*" (168).

When "Mefisto in Onyx" appeared in the October 1993 issue of *Omni* magazine, it was heralded as "Harlan Ellison's First Novella in 15 Years" and the longest piece of fiction *Omni* had ever published. It appeared as a separate specialty press book that same year, was quickly optioned for film adaptation (though the film plans later became stalled), and was generally well received by reviewers, with Eric P. Nash in the *New York Times,* for example, viewing it as "a reminder that Ellison has not lost has capacity to convey stark, staring psychosis." It received the Bram Stoker Award from the Horror Writers of America, the Locus reader's poll award from *Locus: The Newspaper of the Science Fiction Field,* and a nomination for the World Fantasy Award. No doubt part of the reason for the novella's popularity is the relative familiarity of its form, its twin climactic plot twists, and its use of recognizable genre materials, even though these materials are transformed somewhat by Ellison's ambitious use of a black narrator and his efforts to broaden the thematic base of the narrative to include questions of racism and personal responsibility.

One commentator, Darren Harris-Fain, wrote that the story "reads like a cross between Alfred Bester's science fiction classic *The Demolished Man* and Thomas Harris's *The Silence of the Lambs*" (Barron 369). Neither comparison is inappropriate: As we've already noted, Bester's novel gave Ellison the term *jaunting,* and *The Demolished Man* (1953), widely recognized as one of the few successful science fiction/mystery hybrids, concerns a murderer in a future society in which the police force includes trained "espers," or mind readers. Thomas Harris's famous 1988 novel, on the other hand, is entirely lacking in overtly fantastic elements, and (together with its 1981 predecessor *Red Dragon* and its 1990 film adaptation) is credited by some critics with having shifted the focus of much horror fiction during the 1990s away from supernatural figures and toward the gruesome but all-too-recognizable figure of the serial killer. Harris's plot, in which a young and somewhat innocent figure with unresolved issues from the past is brought into a prison to aid investigators by establishing a kind of psychic link with a famously inhuman serial murderer, bears obvious parallels with "Mefisto in Onyx," although much of Harris's novel focuses on the procedural aspects of the ongoing criminal investigation, while in Ellison's case the pursuit and capture of Spanning is barely mentioned at all.

Essentially, then, the genre building blocks of "Mefisto" come from both science fiction, with its long catalog of telepaths (including many who seem as alienated and lonely as Pairis) and contemporary crime/horror fiction. But Ellison seeks to develop a more complex, character-based story as well: Why has Pairis been unable to profit, or even attain moderate happiness, from his extraordinary gift? And why is he unable to act on his abiding feelings for Allison Roche until he shifts into the body of a handsome blue-eyed white man? By the end of the tale—in an unexpected thematic reversal that comes on top of the climactic plot twists—we are told that it was neither telepathy nor racism that limited Pairis but his own inability to act without getting in his own way. By much the same token, Pairis suggests, Spanning's questionable career as a master criminal is less the result of grandiose evil than of simple mediocrity and lack of imagination. Spanning's tragedy is not merely that he is a psycho killer but that he can't think of much else to do. These major themes are introduced not as an integral part of the unfolding action but by means of tour de force narrative riffs and speeches by Pairis, who sometimes nearly even lapses into dialect in delivering them. "You so goddam stuck on yourself, Spankyhead," he says to Spanning just before leaving the killer to die in the electric chair, "you never give it the barest that someone else is a faster draw than you. . . . Know what your trouble is, Captain? You're old, you're *real* old, maybe hundreds of years who gives a damn old. That don't count for shit, old man. You're old, but you never got smart. You're just mediocre at what you do" (166).

For all its ambition of fusing familiar genre materials with broad themes of racial tension and the construction of identity, "Mefisto in Onyx" is not without its flaws. In order for the plot twists to work, Ellison has to concoct some fairly tenuous motives for Spanning to allow himself to be caught in the first place and then for waiting in prison three years before executing his plan to trap Pairis. Pairis, on the other hand, turns out to be an only semireliable narrator. Here Ellison faces the famous dilemma that Agatha Christie raised in her 1926 *The Murder of Roger Ackroyd* in which the narrator must carefully measure out what information is given to the reader since he himself, in the closing pages, will be unmasked as the murderer. Pairis must avoid telling us about the new psychic skills he learned while in prison, in order to spring them on us at the last minute, always an awkward moment in a first-person narrative. It is also unclear how Pairis knows that Spanning will be in the visitors' gallery at his scheduled execution. Finally, the evocative title of the tale is explained in a rather murky scene, unrelated to the main action, that seems to cast Pairis as both Faust and Mefisto in his relationship to Roche, and that tends to flatten the implicit Faustian theme involving Spanning. But as a whole, "Mefisto in Onyx" is the most successful of Ellison's mythical crime tales since "The Whimper of Whipped Dogs." An earlier crime story, "Soft Monkey" (1988), also featured a black protagonist, a homeless woman who becomes a hunted murder witness. It won an Edgar Award in short fiction from the Mystery Writers of America. But it's a far less substantial piece than either "Whimper" or "Mefisto." It develops a less ingenious plot and makes far less inventive use of genre materials, despite some scenes of extraordinarily dramatic realism.

After *Slippage*

At the end of the millennium, Ellison's fiction continued its evolving dialogue between the idioms of genre fiction and the possibilities of postmodern techniques, and he continued to inhabit an aesthetic and moral ground largely of his own making. The stylistic and narrative traditions that go to make up his fiction are traditions that are today found almost nowhere else. Echoes of the witty fantasy that John Collier or Shirley Jackson or Roald Dahl mix with the hard-boiled narrative economy of a Henry Slesar or Stanley Ellin, the mordant wit of Robert Bloch or Gerald Kersh (whom Ellison cites as his favorite writer), and occasional tonalities from Fritz Leiber, H. P. Lovecraft, and Alfred Bester (who may be Ellison's most immediate predecessor among science fiction writers, and who is paid subtle homage in "Mefisto in Onyx"). This is the region of the vernacular grotesque, a world in which (to take further examples from *Slippage*) an uneducated small-time hood can describe his demon pursuer as "a creature of stygian darkness" (in "Crazy as a Soup Sandwich") or a distinguished academic scholar of myths can narrate a whole story in a voice that sounds like Andy Griffith ("The Museum on Cyclops Avenue"). In each of these cases, the tale's basic premise is familiar—a deal with the demon and a variation on the disappearing-shop motif (which Ellison has used often)—but Ellison's characters and dialogue give each a distinctive, off-balance spin, and in almost every case the tale leads in unpredictable directions.

The questions that continue to haunt Ellison haven't changed that much over the years: How we choose to inhabit our lives, what our best and worst and most symbolic moments are and what they mean. In "Anywhere but Here, with Anybody but You," a husband whose wife has fled realizes he has defined himself only in terms of "my life till now," and he sets out in search of a desolate freedom. Another character recovers lost moments with a father he never really knew (in Atlantis, of all places) in "Midnight in the Sunken Cathedral." In "Pulling Hard Time," murderers are forced to relive, in infinite loops, the absolutely worst moments of their lives (this is a kind of counterpoint to Ellison's "The Cheese Stands Alone," in which characters could not escape the best moments of their lives). The best of Ellison's late fiction is fascinating because of its very liminality, its unmistakable provenance, its voice. If some readers find Ellison's frequent mythifying pretentious, and others view his genre work as too populist, it may be because he occupies a part of the literary landscape that is all but deserted except for him: a region where small-time hoods coexist with Anubis, pulp narrative hooks lead to postmodern fragmentation, high passion flows from tough technique.

In late 1999 and early 2000, only a few months separated the publication of two "historic" collectors' issues of leading science fiction magazines, each of which had featured many Ellison stories over the years: the six hundredth issue of the world's oldest science fiction magazine, *Amazing Stories,* founded in 1926, and the fiftieth anniversary issue of the *Magazine of Fantasy and Science Fiction.* In many ways, these two magazines symbolize two ends of the spectrum of Ellison's fiction. *Amazing Stories,* which had begun life as the original science fiction pulp only to see its role as the leading magazine in the field usurped by the more intellectual *Astounding Science Fiction* after 1937, had fallen on hard times with stunning regularity in the years since, and by the 1950s had become one of the secondary markets for young science fiction writers like Ellison; among the Ellison stories that first appeared there are such early hackwork titles as "Escape Route" (1957), "Gnomebody" (1956), "The Plague Bearers" (1957), and "The Vengeance of Galaxy 5" (1958). The *Magazine of Fantasy and Science Fiction,* in contrast, has generally been viewed as the most sophisticated of the digest magazines that supplanted the pulps in the 1950s, and it became one of the major outlets for Ellison's more ambitious or experimental stories, such as "Jeffty Is Five" (1977), "Adrift, Just off the Islets of Langerhans" (1974), "The Deathbird" (1973), and "All the Lies That Are My

Life" (1980). It seems fitting, then, that for the celebratory anniversary issues of these two very different magazines, Ellison should contribute stories that reflect these contrasting aspects of his career. The story that appeared in the six hundredth issue of *Amazing Stories,* written as a tribute to Ellison's pulp ancestors, is titled "The Toad Prince; or, Sex Queen of the Martian Pleasure-Domes," and was originally written in 1991 for a small press called Pulphouse, edited by Kristin Kathryn Rusch and Dean Wesley Smith. The *Magazine of Fantasy and Science Fiction* story, on the other hand, titled "Objects of Desire in the Mirror Are Closer than They Appear," begins with the genre materials of the crime story but quickly evolves into an oblique narrative unlike almost anything Ellison had written before.

"The Toad Prince," accompanied in its original magazine appearance by a wonderfully lurid pulp illustration by Don Ivan Punchatz, is a lark, but a weighty lark, recasting the familiar fairy tale of the Frog Prince into a tale of an Earthborn prostitute named Sarna whose successful career on the Martian frontier—serving both human settlers and the oppressed Martians—is interrupted when a "yellow" (a half-breed Martian descended from Martian women raped by Earth settlers) is murdered in her room, leaving behind a mysterious toadlike creature called only "one of the Six" (23). Forced to flee for her life when a long overdue Martian revolution threatens to kill all the human settlers, she learns that the toad-thing can communicate with her telepathically, offering to help save her and all the other humans on Mars, if she will help it reunite with its five siblings, from whom it has been separated for something like a million years. Skeptical but desperate, she agrees, and most of the story involves the quest to find each of the siblings—a glowing ball, a globule of water, a handsome, gray-haired man, and a "cloud of syrupy, milky effluvium" (31). Each adds a different function to the gestalt that is the Six—eyes, knowledge, legs, nerves, muscles—and as the being approaches wholeness, Sarna begins to realize that it is an insane ancient god, long ago banished into multiplicity, and that its reunification threatens the very survival of humans on Earth as well as on Mars. They (it?) give Sarna a glimpse of what the Earth will look like in a century, reduced to a fetid swamp full of strange beasts. To her astonishment, the five assembled segments inform her that she herself is the sixth and final component, and "suddenly the barriers shattered in her mind and a flood of memories poured back. . . . A million years of memories" (32). The human part of Sarna that remains, however, wills the entire entity to plunge into the sun, sacrificing herself but saving the universe—and, presumably, leaving Mars to the control of the native Martian revolution.

At its pulp-narrative level, this fast-moving tale of a plucky Earth girl who saves the universe from a senile, malevolent, Lovecraftian god is no more than a good-natured tribute to the magazines of Ellison's childhood, the magazines that died out only a few short years before his own professional career began. But it is not a parody or burlesque, and except for its initial situation, it is not particularly comic in execution. In its major subtext, it offers a sardonic critique of the sexist, capitalist, and imperialist values that were implicit in so many of the space operas of the 1930s and 1940s. Like Ray Bradbury's 1950 *Martian Chronicles,* it portrays an ancient race of golden-skinned Martians, whose survival is threatened by crass settlers from Earth. In Bradbury, the Martians eventually are killed off entirely by Earthborn diseases, in a manner that clearly seeks to evoke the genocide of native American populations in the United States. In "The Toad Prince," Ellison's Martians are compared to Pacific islanders: "Golden, as the Samoans, the Melanesian, had been . . . long ago on Earth. And as with the ancient peoples, the reavers had taken more than just the innocence of the alien culture: they had raped and dominated, savaged and strip-mined both Mars and its Golden people" (20). Instead of the military commanders and explorers who served as pulp heroes, Ellison chooses a prostitute who is herself a victim of the exploitation of what is only briefly referred to as the "New System" of commerce on Earth and Mars. And when the violent Martian revolt threatens to butcher the entire human colony, Sarna's reaction is to realize that she has been brainwashed by imperialist values as surely as her true godlike nature has been hidden from her. "How I let myself be led by emotion into believing it was Terran property; by what right does Earth rule the planet Mars . . . ? By what right does any race enslave another?" (33). The story of an obscure individual who secretly saves the universe may have been a favorite plot of pulp science fiction writers, but the story of a hero reconstituted as a god who then *refuses* to save human colonists from aliens is far more unusual. Even as Ellison mimics the style and pacing of the old *Amazing Stories,* he critiques and revises the genre that gave him his earliest successes.

The much shorter and more poignant tale "Objects of Desire in the Mirror Are Closer than They Appear," with its title which evokes Luis Buñuel's 1977 film *That Obscure Object of Desire,* begins on nearly as familiar a note, but—like Buñuel's films—quickly shifts into a dream-world where time is fluid and obsessions become real. While working on the case of a serial killer of prostitutes, homicide detective Francine Jacobs is called in to investigate a bizarre murder scene: three famous supermodels wailing hysterically over the corpse of an old man nearly decapitated in an alley next to a mission house. The only apparent witness, an alcoholic former aerospace worker, claims that he first heard the three girls laughing and singing, followed by the flash of a bright green light and "some kinda music" (26), and then the sound of the girls screaming. The witness admits to having returned later and stolen the old man's shoes and socks, as well as the murder weapon, a machete.

The case grows still stranger: The coroner estimates the age of the victim, who had appeared to be about sixty, at a hundred and two, and further reports that the body contains fully functional organs for two separate bodies—one male and one female—and that the female body was about three months pregnant. The three supermodels, too distraught to be useful witnesses, all claim that they loved the victim so deeply that they can't live without him. Shortly thereafter, they disappear from custody in another flash of green light. That night Francine, already distraught and withdrawn over an unspecified recent event involving someone named Andy, dreams that "the one real love of my life came to me" in the form of a woman appearing in a green light and offering to release Francine from "a life that was barely worth living" (30). The supermodels, she learns, have told this figure of Francine's beauty, and she makes love to Francine before taking her away "to a place where the winds were cinnamon-scented." In the story's conclusion, Francine says, "I am very old now," having lived long in the cinnamon-scented place and grown tolerant of her lover's moving back and forth in time, shifting sexual identities, but her discovery that the figure is now transferring her/his affections to an unborn child becomes unbearable. Equipped with the machete, Francine vows that "from this dream neither he nor she will ever rise. I am in the green light now, with the machete. It may rain, but I won't be there to see it" (30). In other words, Francine plots to commit the crime with which the story began, completing a cycle that shifts from reality through dream and back to reality.

Like "The Toad Prince," "Objects of Desire" was originally written for another venue than the magazine which first published it. It was, in fact, one of Ellison's performance stories, written in a window to match the unlikely premise of a hundred-year-old pregnant corpse, which had been supplied to Ellison on the spot. Unlike "The Toad Prince," however, the tale manipulates its genre materials and personal Ellisonian themes in thoroughly unexpected ways. The initial setting echoes the seedy, ominous urban backstreets of "Soft Monkey" and "The Whimper of Whipped Dogs" as well as of a generation of hard-boiled police procedurals. The key fantastic element, a sexually dimorphic time traveler, will be familiar to science fiction readers from Robert A. Heinlein's famous 1959 story "All You Zombies," which constructs an elaborate scenario in which the male protagonist, originally born with both male and female reproductive organs, manages through time travel to both impregnate him/herself and give birth to himself, making him literally the only member of his entire family. The romantic notion of True Love made manifest, of course, echoes Ellison's own more sardonic "Grail" (discussed in chapter 9). And the character of Francine, a lonely and embittered figure descended from a long line of Ellison's women-victims, from Mona at Her Windows and Jenny to Maggie Moneyeyes, offers some hints that the story may be in part another psychological portrait of a disturbed mind: She is unable to resume her life after Andy, she is envious of the supermodels, she believes—even though she herself is in her forties—that her boss is "twice, maybe three or four times, my age" (29), and at the end she becomes as vengeful as a Greek goddess.

What is most significant about the story in the context of Ellison's work, however, is its virtually complete interpenetration of dream and reality. Read purely as a mystery, it leaves major questions unanswered even though the initial murder is finally explained; read as science fiction, the time-loop remains unresolved because no rationale is offered to account for either the origins of the mysterious old man or the manner in which the dream world is made to fold back on the real world. In other words, the story does not permit, and does not reward, a one-dimensional reading. It is, like much of Ellison's more provocative work, radically uneven in tone, profoundly irrationalist at its core, and yet both psychologically and spiritually apt: Francine Jacobs, like almost all of Ellison's more memorable characters, is liberated from the entrapment of her life only to find herself in another trap, this one of her own making.

ENVOI
Ellisioniad

THERE IS, PERHAPS, an Ellison monomyth. It involves a hero, unsettled and alienated, who, possibly through the agency of a little phantom shop tucked away in the mysterious streets of a crumbling city, discovers himself to be a Secret Master, or a displaced alien, or a lost god from Atlantis. He does not quite belong in the realm of the ordinary, and he does not live in ordinary time. He lives in the hour that stretches. He performs numerous generous deeds in secret. He finds that he has a magical capacity for well-plotted revenge against those who have done him ill, even in the distant past, but he is also the victim of a vengeful universe, perhaps in thrall to a mad god, which will not let him escape his past or return to it. He seeks True Love. He seeks his father. He seeks his lost friends. He seeks the boy he once was. He learns that the clues he needs to complete his quest are hidden within his body, or in his dreams, or buried in the backyard of his childhood home.

Or he is a writer who, despite his legendary achievements both in literature and in film, his unprecedented success as both best-selling author and *litterateur,* his worldwide fame, his endless parade of honors, his glamorous celebrity friends, has never escaped entirely from the dusty playground of Lathrop Grade School. Apart from his personal accomplishments, his heroism has been earned through acts of intellectual knight-errantry. He seeks to vanquish the mediocre, the formulaic, the elitist, the sycophantic, the dishonest, the conformist. He smashes the walls of the literary ghetto that trapped and sometimes destroyed his most beloved and illustrious predecessors. He manically disrupts the Literary Establishment—an actual place with actual members—like the Marx Brothers at the opera. He wins the battle with posterity: His books will be read for decades, centuries. He inspires awe. He earns the respect of his oldest friend.

He learns the world has been stripped of hope, and he sees those around him immobilized, vacant, their spirits leached out by the forces that crush. With only the resources of mind and body, with no clear guidance or hope of success, with no precedents, with no certainty of what action is appropriate or even possible, he nevertheless takes action. He can only be defined by the actions he takes or has taken or will take. He is trapped, bound, alone. There is nothing he can do.

He acts.

Appendix

Stories and Screenplays by Harlan Ellison Discussed in the Text, and Major Collections in Which They Appear

This checklist is intended as a supplement to the "Works Consulted" listing and as a convenience to aid the reader in locating specific Ellison titles in generally available collections. It lists only those titles discussed at some length in the text and is in no sense an attempt at a complete bibliography or a complete indexing of story collections.

Key to Book Titles

AA   *Alone against Tomorrow*
AC   *Angry Candy*
AO   *Approaching Oblivion*
BL   *The Beast That Shouted Love at the Heart of the World*
DS   *The Deadly Streets*
DB   *Deathbird Stories*
EE   *The Essential Ellison: A 50-Year Retrospective*
EW   *Ellison Wonderland*
FL   *From the Land of Fear*
GJ   *Gentleman Junkie and Other Tales of the Hung-Up Generation*
IH   *I Have No Mouth, and I Must Scream*
LA   *Love Ain't Nothing but Sex Misspelled*
MF   *Mind Fields*
ND   *No Doors, No Windows*
PG   *Paingod and Other Delusions*
SH   *Shatterday*
SL   *Slippage*
SN   *Stalking the Nightmare*
SW   *Strange Wine*
TI   *A Touch of Infinity*

"Adrift, Just off the Islets of Langerhans: Latitude 38°54'N, Longitude 77°00'13"W." *Magazine of Fantasy and Science Fiction,* October 1974. DB, EE

"All the Birds Come Home to Roost." *Playboy,* March 1979. EE, SH

"All the Lies That Are My Life." *Magazine of Fantasy and Science Fiction,* November 1980 (abridged). SH

"Along the Scenic Route." *Adam,* August 1969 (as "Dogfight on 101"). BL, DB, EE

"Are You Listening?" *Amazing Stories,* December 1958. AA, EW, BL

"The Avenger of Death." *Omni,* January 1988. AC

"Basilisk." *Magazine of Fantasy and Science Fiction,* August 1972. DB

"Battlefield." *Space Travel,* November 1958 (as "His First Day at War"). EW

"The Beast That Shouted Love at the Heart of the World." *Galaxy Science Fiction,* June 1968. BL

"Boulevard of Broken Dreams." *Los Angeles Review #1,* ed. Stephanie Berstein and Carla Harryman, 1975. SW

"A Boy and His Dog." *New Worlds,* April 1969. BL, EE

"The Cheese Stands Alone." *Amazing Stories,* March 1982. SN

"Count the Clock That Tells the Time." *Omni, December* 1978. SH

"The Crackpots." *If,* June 1956. PG

"Croatoan." *Magazine of Fantasy and Science Fiction,* May 1975. SW

"Daniel White for the Greater Good." *Rogue,* March 1961. GJ, LA, EE

"The Dead Shot." *Trapped,* April 1957. DS

"The Deathbird." *Magazine of Fantasy and Science Fiction,* March 1973. DB, EE

"Demon with a Glass Hand." TV script. *The Outer Limits,* production no. SF#42, shooting final, August 19, 1964.

"Eidolons." *Magazine of Fantasy and Science Fiction,* July 1988. AC

"Final Shtick." *Rogue,* August 1960. EE, GJ, LA

"The Function of Dream Sleep." *Midnight Graffiti,* June 1988. AC, EE

"GBK—A Many-Flavored Bird." *Rogue,* June 1962. LA

"Glowworm." *Infinity Science Fiction,* February 1956. EE

"Gnomebody." *Amazing Stories,* October 1956. EW

"Go toward the Light." *Magazine of Fantasy and Science Fiction*, January 1996. SL

"Grail." *Twilight Zone,* April 1981. EE, SN

"Hadj." *New York Post Weekend Magazine,* October 1956. EW

"Harlan Ellison's Movie." Script. Los Angeles Free Press, 1973.

"Have Coolth." *Rogue,* June 1959. GJ

"I Have No Mouth, and I Must Scream." *If,* March 1967. AA, EE, IH

I, Robot: The Illustrated Screenplay (with Isaac Asimov). New York: Warner Aspect, 1994.

"I'm Looking for Kadak." *Wandering Stars.,* edited by Jack Dann. New York: Harper and Row, 1974. AO

"In the Fourth Year of the War." *Midnight Sun #5,* 1979. SH

"Invulnerable." *Super-Science Fiction,* April 1957

"Jane Doe #112." *Ellery Queen's Mystery Magazine,* December 1990. SL

"Jeffty Is Five." *Magazine of Fantasy and Science Fiction,* July 1977. EE, SH

"Johnny Slice's Stoolie." *Guilty,* July 1956 (as "I Never Squealed"). DS

"Kid Killer." *Guilty,* March 1957. DS

"Knife in the Darkness." *Cimarron Strip* #1260-0704, final draft, May 4, 1967.

"Life Hutch." *If,* April 1956. AA, EE, TI, FL

"Look Me in the Eye, Boy!" *Guilty,* May 1957. DS

"Made in Heaven." *Trapped,* August 1956 (as "The Big Rumble"). DS

"The Man Who Rowed Christopher Columbus Ashore." *World Fantasy Convention Program Book,* 1991; *Omni,* July 1992. SL, EE

"The Man Who Was Heavily into Revenge." *Analog,* August 1978. EE, SH

"Mealtime." *Space Travel,* September 1958. EW

"Mefisto in Onyx." *Omni,* October 1993. SL, EE

"Mom." *Silver Foxes,* August 1976. EE, SW

"Nedra at f:5.6." *The Gent,* February 1957 (as "The Hungry One"). ND

"Neither Your Jenny nor Mine." *Knight,* April 1964. EE, LA

"The New York Review of Bird." *Weird Heroes,* vol. 2, edited by Byron Preiss. New York: Pyramid, 1975. SW

"The Night of Delicate Terrors." *The Paper: A Chicago Weekly,* April 8, 1961. EE, FL, GJ, LA

"Night of Thanks but No Thanks." *Detective Comics,* #567, October 1986

"Now You're in the Box." *Rogue,* November 1958. GJ

"Objects of Desire in the Mirror Are Closer than They Appear." *World Horror Convention Program Book,* 2000. EE

"One Life, Furnished in Early Poverty." *Orbit 8,* edited by Damon Knight. New York: Putnam, 1970. EE, AO

"Paingod." *Fantastic,* June 1964. DB, PG

"Paladin of the Lost Hour." *Universe 15,* edited by Terry Carr. New York: Doubleday, 1985. AC, EE

"A Path through the Darkness." *Fling,* January 1963. LA

"A Prayer for No One's Enemy." *Cad,* March 1966. EE, LA

"Pretty Maggie Moneyeyes." *Knight,* May 1967. DB, EE, IH, LA

"Punky and the Yale Men." *Knight,* January 1966. EE, LA

"Rain, Rain, Go Away." *Science-Fantasy,* December 1956. EW

"'Repent, Harlequin!' Said the Ticktockman." *Galaxy Science Fiction*, December 1965.

"The Resurgence of Miss Ankle-Strap Wedgie." EE, LA

"Run for the Stars." *Science Fiction Adventures,* June 1957. BL, TI

"Scartaris, June 28." *Borderlands*, edited by Thomas Monteleone. New York: Avon Books, 1990. SL

"Sensible City." *Magazine of Fantasy and Science Fiction,* October/November 1994. SL

"Shatterday." *Gallery,* September 1975. SH

"Shattered like a Glass Goblin." *Orbit 4,* edited by Damon Knight. New York: Putnam, 1968. BL, DB, EE

"Silent in Gehenna." *The Many Worlds of Science Fiction*, edited by Ben Bova. New York: Dutton, 1971. AO

"The Silver Corridor." *Infinity,* October 1956. AA, EW

"The Sky Is Burning." *If,* August 1958. EE, EW, FL, TI

"Soldier." *Fantastic Universe,* October 1957 (as "Soldier from the Future"). EE, FL

"There's One on Every Campus." *Rogue,* November 1959. GJ

"This Is Jackie Spinning." *Rogue,* August 1959. GJ

"The Toad Prince, or Sex Queen of the Martian Pleasure Domes." *Amazing Stories* 71, no. 5 (2000): 18–33.

"Trojan Hearse." *Infinity,* August 1956.

"The Truth." *Rogue,* September 1959. GJ

"Twilight in the Cupboard." MF

"The Universe of Robert Blake." *Rogue,* June 1962 (as "Robert Blake's Universe"). LA

"The Untouchable Adolescents." *Super Science Fiction,* February 1957.

"Valerie." *Los Angeles Free Press,* November 3–24, 1972. EE, LA

"The Whimper of Whipped Dogs." *Bad Moon Rising.*, edited by Thomas M. Disch. New York: Harper and Row, 1973. DB, EE, ND

"The Wind beyond the Mountains." *Amazing Stories,* January 1957 (as "Savage Wind"). EW

"World of the Myth." *Knight,* August 1964. IH

NOTES

Chapter 1

1. One of the more amazing documents in the history of science fiction as a subculture is longtime fan Sam Moskowitz's overheated history of the early days of science fiction fandom, with its petulant adolescent debates among the handful of East Coast fans who organized the first "Worldcons." The book is unselfconsciously titled *The Immortal Storm* (1954).

2. Ironically, Ellison's would-be collaborator, David Ish (who at the time was only fifteen), would go on to use the Worldcon as the setting for a mainstream short story, "The Fantasy People," which he sold to the extremely prestigious *New World Writing* series of paperback literary anthologies in 1956. Ish's story appears in *New World Writing: Ninth Mentor Selection* (New York: New American Library, 1956) and is apparently the only work of fiction Ish published. An account of Ish's later life and career is included in Ellison's introduction to the story "Wonderbird" in the second edition of *Partners in Wonder* (New York: Pyramid, 1975) 279–83.

Chapter 2

1. As collectors are all too aware, Ellison has long had a habit of recombining stories in different collections and changing the contents of a collection from one edition to the next. The 1974 reprint of *Ellison Wonderland,* for example, replaced the story "The Forces That Crush" with "Back to the Drawing Boards," added an introductory essay, and revised some of the story introductions. ("The Forces That Crush," under its original magazine title, "Are You Listening?" had appeared in Ellison's 1969 collection *The Beast That Shouted Love at the Heart of the World*.) A 1984 "preferred text" edition retained the contents of the 1974 version, but restored the original copy and rewrote portions where Ellison felt the text had

been corrupted by inept editors. The page numbers in the remainder of this chapter refer to this edition.

2. "Mealtime" was actually one of Ellison's earliest short stories, written while he was a student at Ohio State and published in that university's humor magazine, *The Sundial*. Retitled "Upheaval," it became his first tale to be adapted to comic books, in issue #24 of *Weird Science Fantasy* in 1954. It was again retitled as "A Case of Ptomaine" for its appearance in the September 1958 issue of *Space Travel* and restored to its original title for this collection.

CHAPTER 5

1. The three laws, quoted in the opening of Ellison's screenplay, are as follows: "1. A robot may not injure a human being, or, through inaction, allow a human being to come to harm; 2. A robot must obey the orders given it by human beings except where such orders would conflict with the first law; 3. A robot must protect its own existence as long as such protection does not conflict with the first or second laws" (*I, Robot* 4–5).

WORKS CONSULTED

WORKS BY HARLAN ELLISON

Alone against Tomorrow: Stories of Alienation in Speculative Fiction. New York: Macmillan, 1971.

Angry Candy. New York: New American Library, 1989.

Approaching Oblivion: Road Signs on the Treadmill toward Tomorrow. New York: Walker, 1974.

The Beast That Shouted Love at the Heart of the World. New York: Avon, 1969.

The City on the Edge of Forever: The Original Teleplay That Became the Classic Star Trek Episode. Clarkston, Ga.: White Wolf, 1996.

"Commuter's Problem." *Fantastic Universe,* June 1957.

"The Deadly Nackles Affair." *Rod Serling's The Twilight Zone Magazine,* February 1987, 22–31.

The Deadly Streets. 1958. New York: Ace, 1983.

Deathbird Stories. New York: Bluejay Books, 1983.

"Demon with a Glass Hand." *The Outer Limits* production no. SF#42, shooting final, August 19, 1964.

An Edge in My Voice. Norfolk: Donning, 1985.

"Eggsucker." *The Savoy Book*, edited by David Britton and Michael Butterworth, 128–44. Manchester: Savoy Books, 1978.

Ellison Wonderland. 1962. New York: Bluejay Books, 1984.

The Essential Ellison: A Thirty-five-Year Retrospective, edited by Terry Dowling, with Richard Delap and Gil Lamont. Omaha: Nemo Press, 1987. Revised and expanded as *The Essential Ellison: A 50-Year Retrospective*. Beverly Hills: Morpheus International, 2001. (Page citations in text are to the first edition.)

From the Land of Fear. New York: Belmont, 1973.

Gentleman Junkie and Other Stories of the Hung-Up Generation. New York: Ace, 1983.

The Glass Teat: Essays of Opinion on the Subject of Television. New York: Ace, 1973.

The Harlan Ellison Hornbook. New York: Penzler Books, 1990.

"Harlan Ellison's Movie." *Edgeworks,* vol. 3: *The Collected Ellison.* Clarkston, Ga.: White Wolf, 1997.

Harlan Ellison's Watching. Los Angeles: Underwood Miller, 1989.

I Have No Mouth, and I Must Scream. New York: Ace, 1983.

Keynote address, International Conference on the Fantastic in the Arts, Fort Lauderdale, Fla., 1988.

"Knife in the Darkness." *Cimarron Strip* #1260-0704, final draft, May 4, 1967.

Love Ain't Nothing but Sex Misspelled. New York: Ace, 1983.

"Loving Reminiscences of the Dying Gasp of the Pulp Era." *An Hour with Harlan Ellison* (audiotape). Harlan Ellison Record Collection, 1983.

"Memoir: I Have No Mouth, and I Must Scream." *Starship* 17 (summer 1980): 6–13.

Memos from Purgatory. 1961. New York: Pyramid, 1975.

Mind Fields: The Art of Jacek Yerka/The Fiction of Harlan Ellison. Beverly Hills, Calif.: Morpheus International, 1994.

"Nackles." *Rod Serling's The Twilight Zone Magazine,* February 1987, 31–33, 89–94.

"The Night of Thanks but No Thanks." *Detective Comics,* #567, October 1986, 1–15.

No Doors, No Windows. New York: Ace, 1983.

"Objects of Desire in the Mirror Are Closer Than They Appear." *World Horror Convention Program Book,* 23–30. Denver: World Horror Literary Society, 2000.

The Other Glass Teat: Further Essays of Opinion on Television. New York: Ace, 1983.

Paingod and Other Delusions. New York: Pyramid, 1965.

Partners in Wonder. 2d ed. New York: Pyramid, 1975.

Shatterday. Boston: Houghton Mifflin, 1980.

Sleepless Nights in the Procrustean Bed. San Bernardino, Calif.: Borgo Press, 1984.

Slippage. New York: Houghton Mifflin, 1997.

Spider Kiss. New York: Ace, 1982.

Stalking the Nightmare. Huntington Woods, Mich.: Phantasia Press, 1982.

Strange Wine. New York: Harper and Row, 1978.

"A Time for Daring." *The Book of Ellison,* edited by Andrew Porter, 101–16. New York: Algol Press, 1978.

"The Toad Prince; or, Sex Queen of the Martian Pleasure Domes." *Amazing Stories* 71, no. 5 (2000): 18–33.

A Touch of Infinity/The Man with Nine Lives. New York: Ace, 1960.

Web of the City. New York: Ace, 1983.

"The Whore with a Heart of Iron Pyrites; or, Where Does a Writer Go to Find a Maggie?" *The Book of Ellison,* edited by Andrew Porter, 141–54. New York: Algol Press, 1978.

With Isaac Asimov. *I, Robot: The Illustrated Screenplay.* New York: Warner Aspect, 1994.

With Richard Corben. *Vic and Blood: The Chronicles of a Boy and His Dog.* New York: St. Martin's Press, 1989.

With Ken Steacy. *Night and the Enemy.* Norristown, Pa.: Comico, 1987.

Works Edited by Harlan Ellison

Dangerous Visions. New York: Doubleday, 1967.
Again, Dangerous Visions. New York: Doubleday, 1972.

Other Sources

Adams, Stephen. "The Heroic and Mock-Heroic in Harlan Ellison's 'Harlequin.'" *Extrapolation* 26 (winter 1985): 285–89.

Aldiss, Brian W., and David Wingrove. *Trillion Year Spree: The History of Science Fiction.* New York: Atheneum, 1986.

Asimov, Isaac. *In Memory Yet Green: The Autobiography of Isaac Asimov, 1920-1954.* New York: Avon, 1980.

Barron, Neil, ed. *Fantasy and Horror: A Critical and Historical Guide to Literature, Illustration, Film, TV, Radio, and the Internet.* Lanham, Md.: Scarecrow Press, 1999.

Bonn, Thomas L. *Under Cover: An Illustrated History of American Mass Market Paperbacks.* New York: Penguin, 1982.

Booth, Wayne C. *The Rhetoric of Fiction.* Chicago: University of Chicago Press, 1961.

Boucher, Anthony. "The Publishing of Science Fiction." *Modern Science Fiction: Its Meaning and Future,* edited by Reginald Bretnor, 23–42. New York: Coward McCann, 1953.

Brady, Charles J. "The Computer as a Symbol of God: Ellison's Macabre Exodus." *Journal of General Education* 28 (1976): 55–62.

Brians, Paul. *Nuclear Holocausts: Atomic War in Fiction, 1895–1984.* Kent, Ohio: Kent State University Press, 1987.

Clareson, Thomas. *Robert Silverberg: A Primary and Secondary Bibliography.* Boston: G. K. Hall, 1983.

Clute, John, and Peter Nicholls, eds. *The Encyclopedia of Science Fiction.* New York: St. Martin's Press, 1993.

Cobb, Joann P. "Medium and Message in Ellison's 'I Have No Mouth, and I Must Scream." *The Intersection of Science Fiction and Philosophy: Critical Studies.* Westport, Conn.: Greenwood Press, 1983.

Crider, Allen Billy, ed. *Mass Market Publishing in America.* Boston: G. K. Hall, 1982.

Crow, John, and Richard Erlich. "Mythic Patterns in Ellison's *A Boy and His Dog.*" *Extrapolation* 18 (May 1977): 162–66.

Dann, Jack, ed. *Wandering Stars: An Anthology of Jewish Science Fiction and Fantasy.* New York: Harper and Row, 1974.

Davis, Kenneth C. *Two-Bit Culture: The Paperbacking of America.* New York: Houghton Mifflin, 1984.

Delap, Richard. "Harlan Ellison: The Healing Art of Razorblade Fiction." *Magazine of Fantasy and Science Fiction,* July 1977, 71–79.

De Los Santos, Oscar. "Clogging Up the (In)Human Works: Harlan Ellison's Apocalyptic Postmodern Visions." *Extrapolation* 40 (spring 1999): 5–20.

Dillingham, Thomas F. "Harlan Ellison." *Dictionary of Literary Biography,* vol. 8: *Twentieth-Century American Science Fiction Writer,* edited by David Cowart and Thomas Wyme, Pt. 1, 161–69. Detroit: Gale Research, 1981.

Dowling, Terry. Introduction to *Deathbird Stories,* by Harlan Ellison. Norwalk, Conn.: Easton Press, 1990.

———. "Introduction: Sublime Rebel." *The Essential Ellison: A Thirty-five-Year Retrospective,* edited by Terry Dowling, with Richard Delap and Gil Lamont. Omaha: Nemo Press, 1987.

Eliade, Mircea. *Myth and Reality,* translated by Willard R. Trask. New York: Harper, 1968.

Farmer, Philip José. *Doc Savage: His Apocalyptic Life.* Rev. ed. New York: Bantam, 1975.

Francavilla, Joseph. "The Concept of the Divided Self and Harlan Ellison's 'I Have No Mouth, and I Must Scream' and 'Shatterday.'" *Journal of the Fantastic in the Arts* 6, nos. 2–3 (1994): 107–25.

———. "Mythic Hells in Harlan Ellison's Science Fiction." *Phoenix from the Ashes: The Literature of the Remade World,* edited by Carl B. Yoke, 157–64. Westport, Conn.: Greenwood, 1987.

Franklin, H. Bruce. "*Star Trek* in the Vietnam Era." *Science-Fiction Studies* 21 (March 1994): 24–34.

———. *War Stars: The Superweapon and the American Imagination.* New York: Oxford University Press, 1988.

Greene, Grahame. "The Lost Childhood." *The Lost Childhood and Other Essays.* New York: Viking, 1951.

Greenland, Colin. *The Entropy Exhibition: Michael Moorcock and the British 'New Wave' in Science Fiction.* London: Routledge and Kegan Paul, 1983.

Gruber, Frank. "The Life and Times of the Pulp Story." Foreword to *Brass Knuckles: The Oliver Quayde Human Encyclopedia Stories.* Los Angeles: Sherburne Press, 1966.

Harris-Fain, Darren. "Created in the Image of God: The Narrator and the Computer in Harlan Ellison's 'I Have No Mouth, and I Must Scream.'" *Extrapolation* 32 (summer 1991): 143–55.

Hart, Sue. "Theater as Informer to the Future in the Works of Harlan Ellison." *The Dark Fantastic: Selected Essays from the Ninth International Conference on the Fantastic in the Arts,* edited by C. W. Sullivan III, 121–27. Westport, Conn.: Greenwood Press, 1997.

Heinlein, Robert A. "Coventry." *Six Great Short Novels of Science Fiction,* edited by Groff Conklin, 65–118. New York: Dell, 1954.

Kael, Pauline. *5001 Nights at the Movies.* New York: Holt, Rinehart and Winston, 1985.

King, Stephen. *Danse Macabre.* New York: Berkley, 1982.

———. Foreword to *Stalking the Nightmare,* by Harlan Ellison. Huntington Woods, Mich.: Phantasia Press, 1982.

Letson, Russell. "Locus Looks at Books: Reviews by Russell Letson." *Locus* 27, no. 1 (July 1991): 19, 50–51.

McNelly, Willis E. Foreword to "I Have No Mouth, and I Must Scream." *The Mirror of Infinity: A Critic's Anthology of Science Fiction,* edited by Robert Silverberg, 246–50. New York: Harper and Row, 1973.

Malekin, Peter. "The Fractured Whole: The Fictional World of Harlan Ellison." *Journal of the Fantastic in the Arts* 1, no. 3 (1988): 21–26.

Malzberg, Barry. *The Engines of the Night: Science Fiction in the Eighties.* New York: Doubleday, 1982.

Marcus, Greil. *Mystery Train: Images of America in Rock 'n' Roll Music.* 4th ed. New York: Plume, 1997.

Merril, Judith, ed. *England Swings SF: Stories of Speculative Fiction.* New York: Ace, 1968.

Moorcock, Michael. Foreword to *The Fantasies of Harlan Ellison.* Boston: Gregg Press, 1979.

Nash, Eric P. Review of "Slippage." *New York Times,* September 21, 1997, sec. 7, p. 25.

Nicholls, Phil. "On the Edge of Forever: The TV SF of Harlan Ellison." *Vector: The Critical Review of Science Fiction,* 135 (December 1986/January 1987).

Nye, Russell. *The Unembarrassed Muse: The Popular Arts in America.* New York: Dial, 1970.

O'Brien, Geoffrey. *Hard-boiled America: The Lurid Years of Paperbacks.* New York: Van Nostrand, 1981.

Patrouch, Joe. "Harlan Ellison's Use of the Narrator's Voice." *Patterns of the Fantastic,* edited by Donald M. Hassle, 63–66. Mercer Island, Wash.: Starmont House, 1983.

————. "Symbolic Settings in Science Fiction: H. G. Wells, Ray Bradbury, and Harlan Ellison." *Journal of the Fantastic in the Arts* 1, no. 3 (1988): 37–45.

Platt, Charles. *Dream Makers: The Uncommon People Who Write Science Fiction.* New York: Berkley, 1980.

Poirier, Richard. *The Performing Self: Compositions and Decompositions in the Languages of Contemporary Life.* New York: Oxford University Press, 1971.

Porter, Andrew, ed. *The Book of Ellison.* New York: Algol Press, 1978.

Priest, Christopher. "The Last Deadloss Visions." London: Christopher Priest, 1987.

Roberts, Thomas J. *An Aesthetics of Junk Fiction.* Athens: University of Georgia Press, 1990.

"Rogue Notes." *Rogue,* August 1960, 2.

Rubens, Philip M. "Descents into Private Hells: Harlan Ellison's 'Psy-Fi.'" *Extrapolation* 20 (winter 1979): 378–85.

Russ, Joanna. *To Write like a Woman: Essays in Feminism and Science Fiction.* Bloomington: Indiana University Press, 1995.

Silverberg, Robert. "Harlan." *Magazine of Fantasy and Science Fiction,* July 1977, 63–70. Reprinted in Robert Silverberg, *Reflections and Refractions: Thoughts on Science-Fiction, Science, and Other Matters,* 299–306. Grass Valley, Calif.: Underwood Books, 1997.

————. "The Jet-Propelled Birdbath." *The Book of Ellison,* edited by Andrew Porter. New York: Algol Press, 1978.

————. "Sounding Brass, Tinkling Cymbal." *Foundation* 7–8 (1975): 6–37.

Slusser, George E. *Harlan Ellison: Unrepentant Harlequin.* San Bernardino, Calif.: Borgo Press, 1977.

Spinrad, Norman. *Science Fiction in the Real World.* Carbondale: Southern Illinois University Press, 1990.

————, ed. *Modern Science Fiction.* Garden City, N.Y.: Anchor Doubleday, 1974.

Stevens, Carol D. "The Short Fiction of Harlan Ellison." *Survey of Science Fiction Literature,* edited by Frank D. Magill, 3:1978–88. Englewood Cliffs, N.J.: Salem Press, 1979.

Sturgeon, Theodore. Introduction to *I Have No Mouth, and I Must Scream,* by Harlan Ellison, ix-xiii. New York: Ace, 1983.

Talese, Gay. "Frank Sinatra Has a Cold." *The Frank Sinatra Reader,* edited by Steven Petkov and Leonard Mustazza, 99–129. New York: Oxford University Press, 1995. Originally published in *Esquire,* April 1966, 89-98+. Reprinted in Talese, *Fame and Obscurity,*173–208. New York: Dell, 1981.

"The Talk of the Town: Evolution and Ideation." *New Yorker,* September 16, 1967.

Thurston, Robert. Afterword to *The Fantasies of Harlan Ellison,* 301–16. Boston: Gregg Press, 1979.

Todorov, Tszvetan. *The Fantastic: A Structural Approach to a Literary Genre,* translated by Richard Howard. Ithaca: Cornell University Press, 1975.

Watson, Christine. "The Short Fiction of Ellison." *Survey of Modern Fantasy Literature,* edited by Frank D. Magill, 3:1516–19. Englewood Cliffs, N.J.: Salem Press, 1983.

Weil, Ellen R. "The Ellison Personae: Author, Storyteller, Narrator." *Journal of the Fantastic in the Arts,* 1, no. 3 (1988): 27–36.

Wendell, Carolyn. "The Alien Species: A Study of Women Characters in the Nebula Award Winners, 1965–1973." *Extrapolation* 20 (winter 1979): 343–54.

Westfahl, Gary. *Cosmic Engineers: A Study of Hard Science Fiction.* Westport, Conn.: Greenwood Press, 1996.

White, Michael D. "Ellison's Harlequin: Irrational Moral Action in Static Time." *Science-Fiction Studies* 4 (July 1977): 161–65.

Williamson, Jack. "Science Fiction, Teaching, and Criticism." *Science Fiction Today and Tomorrow,* edited by Reginal Bretno, 309–30. New York: Harper and Row, 1974.

Wolfe, Gary K. Interview with Harlan Ellison, July 28, 1987, and subsequent dates.

Yolen, Jane. *Briar Rose.* New York: Tor, 1992.

Web Resources

Newsgroup: alt.fan.harlan-ellison

Day, Chris. "The Sequential Ellison" (comic book bibliography). http://www.enteract.com/~chrisday/Ellison

WyattRick. "Ellison Webderland." http://www.harlanellison.com

Zuzel, Michael. "Islets of Langerhans." http://www.teleport.com/~mzuzel/islets.html

INDEX